NEW
DIRECTIONS IN
PRIMARY
EDUCATION

NEW DIRECTIONS IN PRIMARY EDUCATION

Edited and Introduced by
Colin Richards
(University of
Leicester)

 The Falmer Press

(A member of the Taylor & Francis Group)

First published 1982

Reprinted 1985 and 1986

ISBN limp   0 905273 26 5
        cased 0 905273 27 3

Jacket design by Leonard Williams

Printed and bound by Taylor & Francis (Printers) Ltd
Basingstoke

The Falmer Press
(*A member of the Taylor & Francis Group*)
Falmer House
Barcombe, Lewes
Sussex BN8 5DL
England

Contents

Acknowledgements

The Publishers are grateful to the following for permission to reproduce copyright material:

The Controller of Her Majesty's Stationery Office for extracts from *A View of the Curriculum* (1980) and *Primary Education in England: A Survey by HM Inspectors of Schools* (1978).

The Editor and Publishers of *Education 3–13* for:

MACDONALD, B. (1976) Who's afraid of evaluation? 4(2), 1976.

BRIAULT, E. (1979) The politics of primary contraction 7(1), 1979.

ELLIOTT, J. (1979) Accountability, progressive education and school-based evaluation 7(1), 1979.

BLYTH, J. (1979) Teaching young children about the past 7(2), 1979.

WHITE, J. (1979) The primary teacher as servant of the state 7(2), 1979.

KERR, J. and ENGEL, E. (1980) Should science be taught in primary schools? 8(1), 1980.

Adam and Charles Black for HARLEN, W. (1980) Matching from RICHARDS, C. (Ed) *Issues for the Eighties*, A.C. Black (Publishers) Ltd.

The Editor and Publishers of *Journal of Curriculum Studies* for KING, R. (1978) Multiple realities and their reproduction in infant classrooms 10(2), 1978, Taylor & Francis Ltd.

The Editor and Publishers of the *British Educational Research Journal* for GALTON, M. (1979) Stategies and tactics in junior school classrooms 5(2), 1979, Carfax Publishing Company.

Kogan Page Limited for STONIER, T. (1979) Changes in western society: educational implications from SCHULLER, T. and MEGERRY, J. (Eds) *Recurrent Education and Lifelong Learning*, World Year Book of Education, Kogan Page.

General Editor's Preface

What is primary education becoming? How is it poised to set about its task today? And is that task changed from yesterday? How does the future of teaching in the primary school appear in the light of changed social, political and economic circumstances, and as importantly, in the light of a quarter of a century of increasingly sophisticated study of purpose and practice in primary schools?

It is to these and other questions that this volume is addressed. It is a timely collection, edited and introduced by Colin Richards, ordered and organized to enable the major issues in primary education to be isolated and studied.

Like most significant contributions to our understanding of primary education, this Reader focuses not only on ends but also on beginnings, and on practices; and does not ignore 'theory', but what the Reader does, and successfully, is to hold theory close to practice and to the contemporary issues in primary schooling.

Philip H. Taylor
Birmingham
June 1981

NEW DIRECTIONS IN PRIMARY EDUCATION

Editor's preface to the second impression

It is very encouraging for an editor to be asked to write a preface to the second impression of his reader only three years after its initial publication. It is even more encouraging when the reader is concerned with the advanced study of primary education, an area which until comparatively recently had been neglected by academics in favour of the apparently more contentious and complex areas of secondary and higher education. Perhaps the second impression helps mark the coming of age of primary education in academic terms!

As editor I would like to feel that the new impression is needed for two main reasons. Firstly, the reader hopefully meets the needs of tutors and students on advanced or honours level courses in primary education for a text which opens up issues, reveals complexities, avoids dogmatism and 'right-answerism' and encourages speculation regarding future developments in this important area of practical endeavour and academic study. Secondly, the reader has hopefully identified issues which are still in currency and which are felt by professionals to be making a significant impact, for good or ill, on primary education as it moves into the mid- and late-eighties. As an observer and analyst of the educational scene, I believe my second point has considerable validity, though I cannot comment with any authority or personal knowledge on the validity of my first contention.

Those of us involved in, and concerned for, primary education need to be continually dissatisfied, not with the performance of particular children in our schools, but with our own activities and our understanding of them. Professional dissatisfaction needs to be informed by flexible professional intelligence if the former is to be constructive rather than negative, and responsive rather than dismissive, as the circumstances of primary education change. This second impression hopefully makes a small contribution to encouraging and sustaining appropriate professional dissatisfaction and intelligence.

Colin Richards
Richmond
North Yorkshire
June 1985

Foreword

The problem of 'standards' in education is a perennial one to which no definitive answer can be given. Whatever can or cannot be said about standards of children's attainment in primary schools, there can be little doubt that the standard of professional writing *about* primary education is rising. The banality and over-simplification which characterized so much discussion and comment a decade or so ago are being replaced by a professional literature which does greater justice to the complexities, imponderables and value issues inherent in the enterprise of providing a primary education. The contributions to this book have been chosen or commissioned partly to illustrate the increase in quality, sophistication and acuity of recent writing in the primary field.

But as the title of the book suggests, the papers have also been chosen with other criteria in mind. Each discusses one or more developments which I as editor have identified as new directions for primary education. There is, of course, an ambiguity about 'new directions'. These could be trends which I as editor would *like* to see established during the eighties; they could be trends which I believe are *going* to be established during the eighties. The contributions relate to developments of the latter kind; they embody or examine issues which are rapidly gaining in currency and seem *likely*, for good or ill, to have a significant impact on primary education. I am aware of the dangers of prediction. The Plowden Report of 1967 claimed to recognize a number of 'quickening trends' leading to more 'progressive' approaches; the report proved to be mistaken. The trends identified here may meet a similar fate, though I believe them to be more firmly rooted in the realities, rather than the mythologies, of primary education and its politico-social context.

The book is intended for serious students of primary education, not for laymen, interested or otherwise. It is designed as a source book for teachers on advanced diploma and degree courses as well as for under-graduate students studying primary education to honours level. With this audience in mind it attempts to open up emerging issues for further scrutiny rather than to summarize established positions or foreclose discussion. It seeks to inform and, primarily, to provoke its readers to deepen their professional understanding and to sharpen their judgement; it does not seek to persuade them that any one course of action or ideological position is the right one. The stance which informs the book and which, hopefully, will inform its use in lectures and seminars in the advanced study of primary education is summed up in a passage from Elliot Eisner's book, *The Educational Imagination* (Macmillan 1979):

> The hunt for recipes, rules, formulas, and other nostrums to solve educational problems is a hopeless one. Contexts change and the configurations of schooling within those contexts also change. Sophisticated educational planning needs to consider both and to anticipate that 'final' solutions will always be temporary at best. To say this is not to argue for slipshod thinking, bootstrap judgements, or seat-of-pants analyses. I am not arguing for in- nocence on the part of educational scholars or professionals. I am arguing against unrealistic aspirations, pseudo science, and the host of other bandwagons, bad analogies, and panaceas that emerge in the field each year. We need, I believe, to recognize the contingent character of educational practice, to savor its complexity, and to be not afraid to use whatever artistry we can muster to deal with its problems. For the curriculum planner this means a life of continual uncertainty: the contingent is inherent in educational planning; yet these emerging contingencies need not provide a sense of discomfort but an array of opportunities to exercise one's imagination, to cope with new problems, to make qualitative judgements as well as theoretical ones. What one uses to deal with these contingencies are not pat procedures, but ideas, concepts, frames of reference. One must work with such tools as means guided by a flexible form of intelligence.   (p. 33)

New Directions in Primary Education seeks to provide ideas, concepts and frames of reference and to contribute to the further development of flexible forms of professional intelligence.

Colin Richards
Leicester
March 1981

1
Introduction:
The End of
A Golden Age?

Primary Education: 1974–80

Colin Richards
University of Leicester

Starting Point

Normally within the state system a child's primary education lasts for a minimum of six years. Except for those now in middle schools, children who entered reception classes as five-year-olds in 1974 emerged as primary leavers in 1980. During that six-year period the children themselves are unlikely to have been conscious of many changes (except in their own capabilities), though in fact the pressure on their playground and hall space may have eased, the number of new teachers per year may have fallen and the number of 'dinner ladies' and 'helpers' in their school may have been reduced. Class teachers during that same period are more likely to have noticed a marked increase, followed by a decline, in the purchasing power of their salaries, a reduction in available resources and support services, an increase in union activity, a reduction in promotion prospects and a general increase in dissatisfaction and unease. Heads are very likely to have become aware of changes in their schools' economic and 'political' circumstances: in particular, a marked reduction in resources which could be purchased through capitation allowances and an increase in parental concern about the achievements of pupils. All such changes have not affected every school and every teacher, but many have had an effect. They are illustrative of more general tendencies which have made the period 1974–80 very different from the corresponding period in the previous decade.

Providing an overview of such general developments is not easy when there are some 20,000 English primary schools and some 200,000 teachers and especially when 'there is a sense in which there is not a system in Britain, but rather a legal framework within which many independent bodies operate' (Peston, 1979, p. 11). However, without some such overview it is difficult to relate one development to another or to relate particular instances to more general tendencies. What follows is a tentative attempt to provide a backcloth against which some new directions in English primary education can be identified. With its mixture of facts and impressions the account tries to indicate ideas in currency and issues in context; it does not claim to be based on what was actually happening in *all* 200,000 classrooms!

The choice of 1974 as the starting point for this analysis is a deliberate one. In the decade prior to 1974 primary education began to shed something of its 'Cinderella' status. Between 1960 and 1974 capital expenditure on primary schools increased tenfold in money terms and doubled its share of total capital expenditure on education; total expenditure on primary education increased in real terms by 54 per cent between 1964 and 1974; real current expenditure per pupil increased 15 per cent in the period 1970–74; primary pupil-teacher ratios in England and Wales improved from 1:28.3 in 1965 to 1:24.7 in 1974 (according to Peston, 1979). Primary education was the subject of three-year inquiries by the Central Advisory Councils for Education whose reports published in 1967 endorsed the curricular and pedagogic trends they detected and brought the sector into the political limelight. Building programmes, action research projects, the expansion of nursery education and of teacher training and the provision of extra allowances and resources in EPA areas all acknowledged the new priority being accorded the sector both by the Wilson administrations of 1964–70 and the succeeding Heath government whose White Paper, *A Framework for Expansion* (1972) promised 'to bring about a shift of resources within the education budget in favour of primary schools'. Characterized by post-Plowden euphoria, primary education was witnessing 'a golden age', even though in 1972 there was a disquietening report on reading standards (Start and Wells, 1972) and in December 1973 government expenditure cuts were announced by Antony Barber following a tremendous increase in world oil prices.

Though there were no startling educational events in 1974, a number of developments can be traced back to that year. It was the year when the Barber cuts began to have an impact, when local government was reorganized, when an announcement was made about the setting up of the Assessment of Performance Unit, when the feasibility study for the HMI primary survey was undertaken and when the Houghton report on teachers' pay was issued. In January 1974 Terry Ellis took up his headship at William Tyndale Junior School; in September the Bullock Report, recommending a system of monitoring, was submitted to the Secretary of State; and, in December, Burstall reported that following a large-scale evaluation study there was 'on balance' no case for the further extension of primary French (Burstall *et al*, 1974). It was also in 1974 when the number of primary children in England and Wales first fell from a peak the previous year and when the Permanent Secretary at the Department of Education and Science 'wondered aloud' to an OECD examining panel 'whether the Government could continue to debar itself from what had been termed "the secret garden of the curriculum"'.

The period since 1974 could be presented in a variety of ways, each with its advantages and disadvantages. Instead of presenting a chronology of significant events or characterizing the period in terms of the activities of particular individuals, this chapter analyzes developments in *primary* education in terms of four general topics – contraction, curriculum, pedagogy and evaluation. In relation to each topic, particular issues are identified, and selected events and persons in turn related briefly to these.

Contraction

In contrast to the expansion and optimism noted above, 'the educational story of the last few years is one of a retreat from optimism and a decline not only in the value placed upon education but also in the scale of the enterprise' (Bernbaum, 1979, pp. 1–2). Contraction provides the backdrop against which other educational developments have occurred. The long-term impact of contraction is impossible to determine but already it has had important repercussions for the education service in general and for primary education in particular. Even so its significance has, arguably, not fully penetrated the consciousness of many practitioners whose frames of reference are still embedded in the expansive context of that 'golden age' before 1974. Contraction has taken, and continues to take, a variety of forms: *demographic, economic* and, more elusively, a contraction in *expectations*.

In terms of demography the primary school population in England and Wales reached a peak in 1973 when there were about $5\frac{1}{4}$ million children in maintained nursery and primary schools; by 1979 numbers had fallen by about half a million (Collings, 1980). During the period 1974–79 the total number of qualified teachers in English nursery and primary schools fell by almost 3,000 to 194,000, though the pupil-teacher ratio improved from $1:24.9$ to $1:23.1$, thus sustaining the improvement from 1965 already noted (DES, 1979b). This drop of half a million pupils coupled with central government and local authority policies has had a decimating effect on primary teacher training (Hencke, 1978); has resulted in considerable staff redeployment; and has caused the closure or amalgamation of a very considerable number of schools. Falling rolls have contributed to the disappearance of remedial teaching and other part-time provision in some schools; to a greater incidence of mixed-age classes; to a lessening of teacher mobility across local authority boundaries; and to problems in covering an appropriate range of work in the curriculum (Thomas, 1980). Such difficulties are likely to be exacerbated in the next five years since a further fall of one million primary-aged pupils will occur in England and Wales by 1986. Of the 30 per cent decline in primary population between 1974 and 1986 only just over a third had affected schools by the beginning of 1980. Whereas policy-makers in the fifties and sixties were preoccupied by the problems of teacher supply and school building for a rapidly expanding population, those of the eighties will be preoccupied with the still more difficult task of managing a contracting service (as discussed by Eric Briault in his article). Any changes in curriculum, pedagogy, evaluation, organization development or educational research suggested later in this book will take place against this backcloth.

The demographic turndown occurred at the same time as the rate of growth of most western economies declined sharply. The mid- and late-seventies were years of economic recession with a relative decline in world trade, large increases in rates of unemployment and, in the United Kingdom, an unusually high rate of domestic inflation. In Britain, big spending services such as education 'ground to a crawl as the hare of public expenditure was harnessed to the tortoise of economic growth' (MacDonald, 1979, p. 28). Pressures for greater cost-effectiveness grew stronger; politicians such as James Callaghan in his 1976 Ruskin College speech wondered whether the education service was giving value for money. In view of demographic trends and developing political disillusionment with education (referred to below) education budgets were tempting targets, especially in crisis years such as 1976 when a package of £6000 million public expenditure cuts was announced. It is, however, important to note that, comparing 1974/75 with 1978/79, central government's total current and capital expenditure on state schools fell less than is commonly supposed: there was a fall of £406 million in capital expenditure partly compensated by a rise of £319 million on current expenditure at 1979 survey prices (White Paper Cmnd. 7841, 1980). There were some major casualties: for example, capital expenditure for nursery education peaked at £46 million in 1975/76 and fell to less than £15 million in succeeding years. What did contract during this period was *planned* expenditure for the expansion of the education service. However, the four years from 1980 onwards certainly threaten more substantial 'real' cuts in government expenditure. Attention here has been focused on central government, but throughout the latter half of the seventies local authorities, too, were instituting economies in the education service, partly because of pressure on their locally-generated resources – as witnessed by successive cuts in capitation allowances in 'real' terms, cut-backs in-service provision of various kinds and drastic reductions in ancillary services.

Less easy to characterize and to document is a third aspect of contraction – contraction in political, public and professional expectations of schooling. The following extract from an editorial written towards the end of 1974 provides the background to this disillusionment and illustrates the emergence of professional awareness of it:

In retrospect the period 1960–70 may well appear as a golden age for education. During that decade educational institutions were regarded as very important indeed, even vital to our future well-being as a nation. Expenditure on education rose rapidly; expansion was the order of the day; public interest grew greater and more informed. Education was claimed as a most important factor in promoting social equality, racial harmony, technological advance, economic prosperity, individual mental health. On both sides of the Atlantic public funds were grasped eagerly in attempts to bring these claims to reality. Yet this reality has remained elusive; education has not produced startling changes in the wider society. With recent cut-backs in expenditure, reaction to ROSLA, fall-off in university applications and retrenchment in teacher education, could we be witnessing the beginnings of governmental and public disillusionment with educational institutions? If so, then part of the blame lies with those in education who have claimed too much, who have promised goods they couldn't possibly deliver, unaided by major social and economic changes in society.   (Richards, 1975, p. 3)

By the mid-seventies politicians had become highly sceptical about the relationship of educational investment to economic growth and about the socially equalizing effects of such investment. The grandiose claims of the 'sixties were replaced in Callaghan's Ruskin College speech by more sober, pragmatic purposes: 'to equip children to the best of their ability for a lively, constructive place in society and also to fit them to do a job of work' (Callaghan, 1976). From viewing education as a social panacea, and primary education in particular as a major weapon against poverty, politicians became much more circumspect in their statements about education: a suspicion, even resentment, of being misled by educationists could be detected. It is less easy to document public and professional reactions: how far the former shared politicians' bold aspirations and consequent disillusionment is not clear, though there were certainly worries about educational standards, which are discussed later. How far professionals shared the decline in expectations is not easy to discover. Undoubtedly, some were disillusioned that the education service had not fulfilled the social democratic ideals of the 'sixties. All were caught up in the general unease and disillusion of a nation (and education system) in crisis and contraction. At national level the unbridled assertions of the previous decade were far less in evidence – both during the 'Great Debate' of 1977 and its aftermath. The heady idealism of Plowden gave way to the more circumspect, measured aspirations of the 1978 HMI primary survey and, in part, of this present book. However, it has to be acknowledged that what some may applaud as realistic aspirations, others may regard as the colourless, sombre products of pragmatism and retrenchment.

C. Richards

Curriculum

For our purposes the curriculum can be regarded as comprising those patterns of educational experience or courses of study provided by teachers in primary schools. In the period 1974–80 the primary curriculum was an area of ideological conflict and a number of issues in particular became the centre of attention: *range, structure, appropriateness, consistency* and *continuity*. Such conflict was inevitable in a democratic society. The curriculum is a vehicle for introducing children to *valued* skills, predispositions, interests, concepts, attitudes and substantive knowledge. 'Valued' is a most significant adjective: within our society and its teaching profession there is disagreement over what is 'valuable' and the curriculum inevitably reflects that conflict. As Alan Blyth remarked, 'Everybody agrees that curriculum matters. That is probably the extent of agreement about curriculum' (Blyth, 1978, p. 25). Throughout the 'seventies the primary curriculum and primary pedagogy were the *foci* of ideological conflict. At least four major ideologies could be identified (Richards, 1979):

(a) *'liberal romanticism'* – celebrating the supremacy of the child in the teaching-learning situation and regarding the curriculum as the sum total of learning experiences both offered to them and created by them as they interact with their surroundings (see Rowland's article for the beginnings of a reformulation).

(b) *'educational conservatism'* – stressing the importance of continuity with the past and the curriculum as the repository of worthwhile cultural elements which need transmitting from one generation to another.

(c) *'liberal pragmatism'* – holding an increasingly influential middle ground position, viewing the curriculum as a set of learning experiences largely but not entirely structured by the teacher, but respecting to some degree both the individuality of the child and the importance of cultural transmission.

(d) *'social democracy'* – viewing the curriculum as a means towards realizing social justice and focused around the social experience of pupils.

Discussion as to the purposes of the primary curriculum continued throughout the 'seventies – stimulated by empirical data from the Aims of Primary Education project (Ashton *et al*, 1975), given sharper, more urgent focus by Auld's castigation of the ILEA for having no policy 'as to the aims and objectives of the primary curriculum being provided in its schools' (Auld, 1976) and carried further by DES publications since the 'Great Debate'. In particular, from 1976, Her Majesty's Inspectorate took a public lead on curriculum matters based on developing and clarifying a

12

professional consensus. How far such a consensus is possible among conflicting ideological interest groups is a question which may be answered in the 'eighties.

The *range* of the primary curriculum was a continuing issue from 1974 onwards. There were some moves towards its narrowing. Alarmingly readable, simplistic Black Paper writings (for example, Boyson, 1975; Cox and Boyson, 1975, 1977) reasserted the need for concentration on the 'basics' (usually interpreted as reading, writing and ciphering), albeit sometimes with concessions to a minimum body of scientific, historical, geographical and religious knowledge. There was a growing consensus that primary French was best excluded unless capable staff, adequate resources and a substantial degree of curriculum continuity could be assured. On the other hand, there was increasing advocacy of the place of science – as witnessed by the HMI primary survey and Schools Council initiatives. The former argued that, with the inclusion of science, 'the curriculum is probably wide enough to serve current educational needs' (DES, 1978, p. 126). Hard evidence, publically available, about the range of the curriculum was almost non-existent. The primary survey did provide evidence as to the extent to which certain curriculum items appeared in the classes inspected, but no overall analysis of the range of the primary curriculum was published. Lack of comprehensive information remains a major shortcoming in professional and public discussion of curriculum range.

Between 1974 and 1980 there was major concern over the issue of *structure* in the primary curriculum, though compared with complaints about its absence there were far fewer attempts to spell out what this 'structure' might be. In this connection Bennett was an important opinion-former. Following his attempted evaluation of the relationship between teaching styles and pupil progress he suggested that 'careful and clear structuring of activities together with a curriculum which emphasizes cognitive content are the keys to enhanced academic progress' (Bennett *et al*, 1976, p. 160) but provided no analysis of what that structuring entailed. Lack of structure was a prominent slogan in the war-cries of Black Paper critics. Only occasionally did such critics argue their case through: one such was Bantock who criticized the approach of the modern British primary school 'in its more progressive guise' for failing 'to convey the structures of knowledge in a coherent fashion' thereby fostering 'a magpie curriculum of bits and pieces, unrelated and ephemeral' (Bantock, 1980, p. 44). This concern over possible fragmentation and trivialization of the curriculum was echoed, in part at least, by HMI criticisms of the topic approach where they noted a danger of both fragmentation and repetition unless teachers were very clear of the ideas, skills and techniques that children might learn as they progressed through primary school (Thomas, 1980). Unlike Bantock and the Inspectorate, too many people equated 'structure' with organized instruction in the 'basics'. Recent work on primary science (for example, Harlen, 1978, 1980b), the social subjects (Blyth *et al*, 1976) and mathematics (DES, 1979 and see also the second article in section two) has gone some way to spelling out skills, concepts, principles and generalizations, in this way providing tentative structures to various areas of knowledge in relation to which schools might plan and sequence the learning experiences offered to pupils. In this book the papers by Blyth, Oliver, Alexander and Kerr and Engel provide illustrations of work with similar concerns.

The *appropriateness* of the curriculum is a perennial question, though professional discussion of the form of its supposed inappropriateness tended to shift from the early to the late seventies. Throughout the period 'child-centred' educationists argued that the curriculum experienced by many children was inappropriate to their 'needs' and 'interests'. In the early 'seventies 'needs' and 'interests' were also invoked by community-centred advocates such as Midwinter (1972) who accused most urban schools of failing to provide a curriculum which connected with the local community-context and which helped children respond creatively to the challenge of living in disadvantaged areas. Both such views were less publicly in evidence by the end of the decade when a different form of inappropriateness was being highlighted. According to the primary survey 197 there was considerable mismatch between the capacities of the children and the work they were being given, this mismatch being particularly marked in the case of abler compared with average and below average pupils and older compared with younger pupils (see the immediately following paper and the paper by Harlen). Discussion of this ability-linked inappropriateness was accompanied by an increasing concern for suitably providing for the 'gifted': much effort went into identifying such children, less into providing suitable material and teaching strategies. One other recent development needs noting, though it has yet to develop a substantial public or professional voice. It is being argued that current suggestions for rendering the primary curriculum more appropriate have completely failed to take cognizance of the 'information and knowledge revolution' that is already upon us. Tom Stonier's paper in this book provides a view of the future that might be used to substantiate this charge.

Lastly, *consistency* and *continuity* are two related concepts referring to issues of increasing importance in curricular discussion. Curriculum consistency is a 'horizontal' concept referring to the extent to which all pupils at a particular stage, whether in the same class or different classes, are introduced to a similar set of curricular elements. References to a core curriculum (as in the Yellow Book prepared for the Prime Minister by the DES in 1976), to a 'protected part of the curriculum' (in the 1977 Green Paper) and to 'a framework for the school curriculum' (DES, 1980) involved consideration of the degree of curriculum consistency believed appropriate for English and Welsh schools, primary as well as secondary. Recent government thinking is crystallized in a statement from *A Frame-*

Start of the NC?

work for the School Curriculum: 'The Secretaries of State consider that the diversity of practice that has emerged in recent years, as shown particularly by HM Inspectors' national surveys of primary and secondary schools, makes it timely to prepare guidance on the place which certain key elements in the curriculum should have in the experience of every pupil during the compulsory period of education' (p. 5). Curriculum consistency is examined in more detail later in an article of that title where an attempt is made to draw out a number of distinctions, to discuss recent developments and to suggest implications for policy-makers.

Curriculum continuity is a 'vertical' concept referring to the extent to which curricular experiences offered pupils relate to, and build on, those offered previously. Continuity can refer to the transition pupils experience between primary and secondary stages, to intra-school transition as children move from class to class, and to continuity of experience within any one class during the course of a school year. The key question here was posed by Shiela Browne: 'How far and in what ways is continuity essential to a valid curriculum?' (1977, p. 37). After the 1944 Act establishing primary and secondary stages of education, lip-service was paid to the notion of inter-stage continuity, but it was only in the 'seventies with the widespread incidence of comprehensive secondary education (and three-tier systems in particular) that the problem of continuity was highlighted. The primary survey commented that 'the importance of continuity in the curriculum of the (contributory and receiving) schools was largely overlooked' (p. 39); the wider adoption of primary French was discouraged partly for the same reason; and many curriculum projects cutting across stages (for example, Science 5–13) did not make much impact in overcoming the divide at eleven. Intra-school continuity is becoming increasingly recognized as a major problem: local authority guidelines, curriculum review documents and renewed attention to record-keeping are all illustrative of a growing concern for the continuity of children's experience within schools. Harlen's paper in this book reveals a parallel concern for providing continuity of experience within the same class over a school year. Both curriculum consistency and continuity, however, raise a number of difficult professional issues concerned with teacher autonomy, curriculum planning and implementation, school policy-making (see Garland's article) and local and national responsibilities for curriculum decision-making – all issues raised in the Government's revised framework document *The School Curriculum* discussed later in the article on curriculum consistency.

1981

Pedagogy

By pedagogy is meant that complex of teaching approaches, skills, strategies tactics and forms of organization through which the curriculum is transacted by teachers and pupils. Like the primary curriculum, pedagogy was the subject of considerable controversy but, compared with the curriculum, a smaller number of developments could be discerned.

The most obvious of these, both to the teaching profession and the general public, was the virulent criticism of so-called 'informal', 'modern' or 'progressive' methods which gathered force from 1969 onwards. There is little doubt that the Plowden report of 1967 marked the acceptance of 'child-centred' ideology as the orthodoxy of primary education, at least as perceived by many policy-makers, commentators and educationists. That it was ever so regarded by the majority of teachers is much more questionable. Plowden gave a general endorsement to methods of teaching which were less directive than those presumed to have characterized elementary education and its post-1944 counterpart. Plowden found it impossible to characterize these less directive methods succinctly or unambiguously; others since, except the most extreme critics, have found it equally difficult (see Bennett *et al*, 1976, Galton *et al*, 1980). But within eight years of Plowden's publication criticisms of these methods were widely publicized in the media – fuelled initially by Black Paper polemicists who, alone, had no difficulty in characterizing them – as based on the belief that 'children should not be told anything but must find out for themselves' (Cox and Dyson, 1969).

Criticism reached a peak in 1976 with the publication of Bennett's *Teaching Styles and Pupil Progress*; the Auld Inquiry into the William Tyndale Junior School (where, it appeared, 'progressive methods' had been taken to an extreme); and the leaked observations of the Inspectorate about the use of 'the child-centred approach' (not adequately defined) in the hands of less able or inexperienced teachers. 1976 was a particularly significant date in the pedagogic debate of the 'seventies. It is important to note that prior to that time no detailed characterization of teaching methods ('modern' or otherwise) in English primary schools had been put forward; there had been very little evidence as to the incidence of different methods and, with the exception of a study by Gardner (1966), no large-scale, reasonably comprehensive assessment of their effectiveness in terms of pupil performance had been attempted. From 1976 onwards *attempts* were made to place pedagogic debate on a sounder conceptual and empirical base.

The word 'attempts' needs stressing, since the phenomena under investigation are very complex (whether considered theoretically or practically) and the systematic study of primary pedagogy is in its early infancy (see the later articles by Galton and Rowland). Bennett himself attempted to capture something of this complexity by deriving twelve inadequately characterized 'teaching styles' from a cluster analysis of junior teachers' questionnaire responses. A similarly inadequate categorization was employed in the primary survey which postulated two broad approaches to teaching: 'mainly didactic' and 'mainly exploratory'. Recently (as later discussed in Galton's article), the ORACLE project attempted a more rigorous analysis, distinguishing between teaching strategies (organizational, curricular and instructional) and sets of teaching tactics which it termed 'styles'. Based on cluster analysis of data provided by systematic classroom observation (not questionnaire responses) three 'primary' teaching styles were derived; a fourth was less clearly delineated and seemed more accurately described as a 'secondary' style comprizing varied mixtures of the three 'primary' ones. Though still crude compared with pedagogic phenomena such 'styles' were more easily recognizable, more firmly based on observational data and less simplistic than those employed by Bennett, by the HMI primary survey and by Black Paper polemicists.

Empirical research made a second important contribution to pedagogic debate. The studies quoted above, along with others by Bealing (1972), Ashton *et al* (1975) and Bassey (1978) helped defuse the explosive notion of 'a primary school revolution' along progressive lines. The incidence of such practices, however defined, was revealed as far less than either the advocates or the detractors of 'child-centred' ideology maintained. Only one fifth of ORACLE's teachers (of junior-aged children) adopted a heavily individualized teaching approach, only a tenth of Bennett's sample reported having a teaching style which the researchers believed corresponded to 'the Plowden definition' and less than one teacher in twenty relied mainly on an 'exploratory' approach when inspected as part of the primary survey. The rabid progressives, much castigated by Black Paper writers, had either left teaching, had reverted to less extreme pedagogic forms or, most probably, had never existed in significant numbers. This concern for penetrating and demystifying the 'black box' of the primary classroom also resulted in a number of sociological studies of curriculum, pedagogy and ideology, as illustrated by King's article in this book.

A third related development was a more considered attempt to assess the differential effects of teaching approaches on pupil attainment. It was this aspect of Bennett's work which helped bring criticism of primary education to a peak in 1976. Compared with research on similar areas in the United States, his findings, and the way in which they were presented, were strikingly unequivocal: 'The effect of teaching style is statistically and educationally significant in all attainment areas tested . . . The analysis shows clearly the general efficacy of formal methods in the basic subjects'. HMI's analysis presented a different picture. In the primary survey children in classes where a combination of exploratory and didactic approaches were used scored higher on NFER tests in reading and mathematics compared with classes where only one approach was mainly used (However, these scores were only significantly higher when compared with classes taught mainly by exploratory methods). Compared with previous studies the ORACLE project attempted to widen the basis of pupil attainment to include study skills (strangely characterized), listening skills and skills in acquiring information other than by reading. Their findings suggested that overall 'no single approach can claim to have a monopoly of desirable characteristics', though two particular styles came out best in the 'league tables' which the researchers obligingly, but misguidedly, provided. Such findings are unlikely to be accepted as definitive and strengthen, rather than weaken, arguments for much more sophisticated assessment techniques and much more sophisticated conceptualizations of primary school pedagogy. The pedagogic debate will undoubtedly continue in the 1980s.

Evaluation

The period 1974–80 was also characterized by demands for better, more publicly accessible appraisals of aspects of schooling and for greater accountability of teachers and the education service to the community at large. Such demands were often made in the context of a concern for 'standards', though the meaning of this term and the particular aspects of schooling to which it was being applied were often unclear. Neither did clarity or precision characterize discussion with the professional community, so obscuring information and making a response to public demands more difficult.

A wide definition of evaluation is adopted here and related both to other concepts and to actual developments during the period. Following Harlen, evaluation is taken to comprise 'not only the collection of information but the identification and use of criteria for making judgements about that information ... Assessment is just one way of gathering information, which involves some attempt at measurement' (Harlen, 1980a). With these distinctions in mind the demand for teacher accountability becomes an assertion that teachers are obliged to provide an account of their activities based on carefully collected information and on related judgements made in relation to explicit criteria. Two forms of accountability can be distinguished (Sockett, 1980): accountability for outcomes and results of schooling (product accountability) and accountability in terms of adherence to professional standards of integrity and practice (process accountability).

One major mode of response underpinned by a product model of accountability was to introduce more widespread assessment procedures to collect information about pupil performance. Demands for better, more regular assessment nationwide gathered strength with the publication of the Bullock report in 1975 whose first major recommendation was that 'a system of monitoring should be introduced which will employ new instruments to assess a wider range of attainments than has been attempted in the past and allow new criteria to be established for the definition of literacy' (DES, 1975, p. 513). Work was already in hand to produce tests of attainment in mathematics and, in the previous year, the DES had announced the establishment of the Assessment of Performance Unit to develop methods of assessing and monitoring, over time, the achievements of children at school. The APU became an established part of the educational scene in the late 'seventies and began to monitor the performance of primary pupils in language, mathematics and science. Its establishment stimulated less opposition from teachers than from educationists. Some of the latter, for example, accused it of attempting to establish bureaucratic rather than professional control over schooling (see the later article by Elliott) and criticized its assessment structure as 'technocratic in form, determinist in values and precariously dependent upon a costly and defect-ridden technology of test construction' (MacDonald, 1979 and in this volume). Parallel with the activities of the APU was the introduction of testing in a large number of LEA's (for example, Croydon, Redbridge, Hillingdon, Birmingham, Lancashire) to see how well schools were performing in terms of measurable pupil outcomes.

An alternative mode underpinned by a process model of accountability involved gathering descriptive data in school settings about events, conditions, activities and performances (teachers' as well as pupils') and comparing these against descriptive criteria in the form of schedules or checklists. Some local authorities renamed their advisers inspectors and stepped up the number of inspections as a way of evaluating professional performance. Some (for example, ILEA, Oxfordshire) involved teachers in devising self-appraisal schedules to assist staff in the clarification of objectives and priorities and in the identification of strengths and weaknesses. Curriculum guidlines were widely produced to assist curriculum planning, implementation and evaluation. A few schools deliberately set out to adopt models of school-based evaluation similar to Elliott's (see later article by Elliot).

The two major modes of response were not mutually exclusive, as illustrated by the HMI primary survey which conducted an appraisal using quantitative and qualitative data. Testing some pupils' performances in reading and mathematics was undertaken but the test data were only complementary to a much greater mass of qualitative data gathered in relation to detailed schedules during inspections. The report was the first publicly accessible, overall evaluation of primary education in England containing information, judgements and naming some of the criteria used in the making of such judgements.

Developments outlined above were, in part at least, responses to public concern over 'standards' – originally articulated by the Black Papers and fuelled in the mid-'seventies by the Tyndale affair, politicians, journalists and, to some extent, employers. The education service's utilization of both major modes of response will, in future, provide empirical data (both descriptive and numerical) as to levels of attainment reached by pupils and schools – one sense of the term 'standards'. But neither mode will be able to resolve the issue of 'standards' in its second sense that is, levels of competence which *should* be reached (Straughan and Wrigley 1980). Such a value-laden issue will undoubtedly, inevitably and rightly continue to be debated through the eighties, irrespective of what methods of evaluation or models of accountability are operative in schools.

Conclusion: The Issue of Control

In this chapter primary school curriculum, pedagogy and evaluation have been considered and set in a context of contraction. But contraction itself is only part of the wider social context where the problem of social control is a dominant one. Many commentators (for example, MacLure, 1979; Lynch, 1980) would agree with MacDonald (1979) that pressures on the education service during the mid- and late-'seventies were symptomatic of the 'malaise of liberal democracy . . . in a society believed to be in decline and out of legitimate control'. Arguably, as the most readily accessible of all social services, schools received the brunt of public dissatisfaction with the welfare state which had spawned an increasingly remote and proliferated bureaucracy and had been unable to satisfy growing demands for much higher living standards and for greater social justice. Certainly, from 1974, the education service witnessed attempts at reasserting demo-cratic control over its activities – through politicians bringing the curric-ulum back into the public arena, through more interventionist policies by local authority corporate managers and elected members, through the rediscovery by some school governors of their powers and responsibilities under the 1944 Act and through parental pressures for greater information about schools and for participation on governing bodies (acknowledged by the Taylor Report of 1977 and implemented in part by the 1980 Educa-tion Act).

Up till the present, power over English primary schools has been both partial and distributed: central government through the DES, local author-ities, teachers and, to a smaller extent, the local community have shared in it, but no one party has been able unilaterally to impose its will on the others. Since 1974 the myth of unbridled teacher autonomy over curriculum, pedagogy and evaluation has been exposed, though the necessity (let alone desirability) of some scope for autonomous decision-making by teachers remains (see White's article later). From time to time assertions have been made about government intentions to impose centralized control of schools. At the present time it is not at all clear whether greater leadership and coordination from the centre, extended policy-making and manage-ment by local authorities and greater community participation at local levels are producing a change in the distribution of power. Certainly, the delicate, intricate balance which has evolved since 1944 will not change overnight. Perhaps the *Times Educational Supplement* was right in predicting a long and shuffling process of readjustment between all parties concerned, with the DES and local authorities likely to gain most in terms of increased leverage (though not finely detailed control) over the system.

The future is uncertain. The golden age of the sixties is unlikely to be echoed by an 'eighties' equivalent but the issues raised in this chapter have still to be worked through. As the contributions to this book illustrate, there will be challenges enough related to influence and control, contraction, policy making, evaluation, accountability, professional development and research as well as the implications of the 'information revolution' already upon us. Meeting such challenges will, to use David Oliver's words, 'not be comfortable nor easy but neither will it be boring or lack lustre'.

References

ASHTON, P. *et al*, (1975) *The Aims of Primary Education: A Study of Teachers' Opinions* London, Macmillan Education.

AULD, R. (1976) *William Tyndale Junior and Infants Schools Public Inquiry* London, ILEA

BANTOCK, G. (1980) *Dilemmas of the Curriculum* Oxford, Martin Robertson.

BASSEY, M. (1978) *Nine Hundred Primary School Teachers* Slough, NFER.

BEALING, D. (1972) 'The organization of junior school classrooms' *Educational Research* 14:3, June, pp. 231–235.

BENNETT, S.N. *et al*, (1976) *Teaching Styles and Pupil Progress* London, Open Books.

BERNBAUM, G. (Ed) (1979) *Schooling in Decline* London, Macmillan.

BLYTH, W. *et al*, (1976) *Place, Time and Society 8–13: Curriculum Planning in History, Geography and Social Science* Glasgow, Collins.

BLYTH, W. (1978) 'The curriculum in the middle years' *Education 3–13*, 6(2).

BOYSON, R. (1975) 'Maps, chaps and your hundred best books' *Times Educational Supplement* 17 October.

BROWNE, S. (1977) 'Curriculum: An HMI view' *Trends in Education* Autumn.

BURSTALL, C. *et al*, (1974) *Primary French in the Balance* Slough, NFER.

CENTRAL ADVISORY COUNCIL FOR EDUCATION (England) (1967) *Children and Their Primary Schools* (The Plowden Report) London, HMSO.

CENTRAL ADVISORY COUNCIL FOR EDUCATION (Wales) (1967) *Primary Education in Wales* (The Gittins Report) London, HMSO.

CALLAGHAN, J. (1976) 'Towards a national debate' (The Ruskin College speech) *Education* 22 October.

COLLINGS, H. (1980) 'Falling rolls' in RICHARDS, C. (Ed) *Primary Education: Issues for the Eighties* London, A. and C. Black.

COX, C. and BOYSON, R. (Eds) (1975) *Black Paper 1975* London, Dent.

COX, C. and BOYSON, R. (Eds) (1977) *Black Paper 1977* London, Temple Smith.

COX, C. and DYSON, T. (Eds) (1969) *Fight for Education* London, Critical Quarterly Society.

DEPARTMENT OF EDUCATION AND SCIENCE (1975) *A Language for Life* (The Bullock Report) London, HMSO.

DEPARTMENT OF EDUCATION AND SCIENCE (1977) *Education in Schools: A Consultative Document* (The Green Paper), London, HMSO.

DEPARTMENT OF EDUCATION AND SCIENCE/WELSH OFFICE (1977) *A New Partnership for Our Schools* (The Taylor Report) London, HMSO.

DEPARTMENT OF EDUCATION AND SCIENCE (1978) *Primary Education in England: A Survey by H.M. Inspectors of Schools* London, HMSO.

DEPARTMENT OF EDUCATION AND SCIENCE (1979a) *Mathematics 5–11* HMI Series: Matters for Discussion, 9, London, HMSO.

DEPARTMENT OF EDUCATION AND SCIENCE (1979b) *Statistical Bulletin* 17/79, London, HMSO.

DEPARTMENT OF EDUCATION AND SCIENCE/WELSH OFFICE (1980) *A framework for the school curriculum* London, DES.

DEPARTMENT OF EDUCATION AND SCIENCE/WELSH OFFICE (1981) *The School Curriculum* London, HMSO.

GALTON, M. *et al*, (1980) *Inside the Primary Classroom* London, Routledge and Kegan Paul.

GARDNER, D. (1966) *Experiment and Tradition in Primary Schools* London, Methuen.

HARLEN, W. (1978) 'Does content matter in primary science?' *School Science Review* 209.

HARLEN, W. (1980a) 'Evaluation in education' in STRAUGHAN, R. and WRIGLEY, J. (Eds) *Values and Evaluation in Education* London, Harper and Row.

HARLEN, W. (1980b) 'Selecting content in primary science' *Education 3–13*, 8(2).

HENCKE, D. (1978) *Colleges in Crisis: The Reorganization of Teacher Training 1971–77* Harmondsworth, Penguin.

LYNCH, J. (1980) 'Legitimation crisis for the English middle school' in HARGREAVES, A. and TICKLE, L. (Eds) *Middle Schools: Origins, Ideology and Practice* London, Harper and Row.

MACDONALD, B. (1979) 'Hard times: Educational accountability in England' *Educational Analysis* 1(1).

MACLURE, S. (1979) 'The endless agenda: matters arising' *Oxford Review of Education* 5(2).

MIDWINTER, E. (1972) *Priority Education* Harmondsworth, Penguin.

NATIONAL UNION OF TEACHERS (1979) *The Cost of the Cuts* London, NUT.

PESTON, M. (1979) 'United Kingdom (England and Wales)' in *Educational Financing and Policy Goals for Primary Schools, Country Reports, Volume II United Kingdom, United States Yugoslavia* Paris, OECD.

RICHARDS, C. (1975) 'Claims' *Education 3–13*, 3(1).

RICHARDS, C. (1979) 'Primary education: myth, belief and practice' in BLOOMER, M. and SHAW, K. (Eds) *The Challenge of Educational Change* Oxford, Pergamon.

SOCKETT, H. (Ed) (1980) *Accountability in the English Educational System* London, Hodder and Stoughton.

STRAUGHAN, R. and WRIGLEY, J. (Eds) (1980) *Values and Evaluation in Education* London, Harper and Row.

START, K. and WELLS, B. (1972) *The Trend of Reading Standards* Slough, NFER.

THOMAS, N. (1980) 'The primary curriculum: survey findings and implications' in RICHARDS, C. (Ed) *Primary Education: Issues for the Eighties* London, A. and C. Black.

WHITE PAPER (1972) *Education: A Framework for Expansion* Cmnd. 5174, London, HMSO.

2
The Primary Curriculum:
The End of
Laissez-faire?

Introduction

The papers in this section do not provide a comprehensive examination of new developments in each area of the primary curriculum. They highlight developing issues of *general* importance, even though necessarily these have to be illustrated by reference to particular curriculum areas such as history or science or particular sectors such as nursery- or teacher-education. Each paper raises issues of its own but also picks up one or more of the general curriculum issues raised in the previous introductory paper that is, issues of curriculum range, structure, appropriateness, consistency, continuity, evaluation and control. Although in many respects the views offered here vary considerably from one author to another, there is a basic underlying stance which accounts for their selection in this book.

All imply that the *raison d'être* of the primary school as an educational institution is the fostering of children's intellectual development through their engagement with a carefully devised, adequately justified and widely defined curriculum. None deny the importance of other facets of children's development which contribute to effective intellectual functioning nor do they decry the value (within limits) of teacher opportunism in seizing and capitalizing upon unexpected events in the complex, only partially predictable world of the primary classroom. Nevertheless, the papers place the planning and transaction of an intellectually challenging curriculum at the forefront of teachers' concerns. Deepened understanding of subject-matter and of children's learning, greater intra-professional consultation and more clearly articulated frameworks for coordinating individual efforts are either explicitly advocated or, in some cases, implied. The papers challenge the appropriateness of a *laissez-faire* approach to the primary curriculum which leaves all curriculum decisions (or non-decisions) in the hands of individual practitioners operating in comparative isolation. They imply that *laissez-faire* is not just an inappropriate approach to curriculum decision-making but that paradoxically it devalues the professionalism of the individual practitioner by assuming a degree of individual self-sufficiency which could only be sustained if the task in question was simple, uncontentious, fully understood and self-contained. Educating young children is none of these. Almost all of the recommendations made in the papers require not just a highly developed individual sense of professionalism but an equally well-developed collective sense. As Garland stresses in his article, collective policy-making is required to coordinate, complement and reinforce the impact of individual initiatives taken by practitioners in response to the varying circumstances of their classrooms.

The first two extracts are taken from publications by the inspectorate which together provide a general description of practice as it was observed in the primary survey and a series of recommendations relating to the necessity for, and the content of, curriculum policy-making at school, local authority and, to a lesser extent, national levels. Their publication is indicative of a recent development within the education service – the assumption of a more active role by HMI in public discussion of curricular matters. Their contribution has included the publication of appraisals of practice (such as the primary survey), their attempts at isolating and clarifying key curriculum issues and their willingness to go beyond description and analysis to cautious recommendation. The goal seems to be greater coordination, coherence and continuity without replacing *laissez-faire* by its polarized opposite – rigid centralized control. The extracts included here discuss the range of the primary curriculum, the need for identifying key skills and concepts in particular areas, the necessity for greater consultation and the appropriateness of the curriculum offered to children of different abilities and backgrounds. Policy-making is seen as required at national level to establish broad agreement on the structure of the curriculum, at local authority level to identify knowledge and skills within curriculum areas and at school level to compose curricula appropriate to individual circumstances.

The third paper focuses on curriculum consistency, a theme not often discussed explicitly at conferences or in the literature of primary education but one which the author believes is fundamentally essential to an understanding of current practice and essential to consider in the formulation of future policies. Three sets of distinctions are made in relation to the concept, relevant findings from the primary survey and other investigations are presented, and recent initiatives from the Department of Education and Science (including *The School Curriculum*) are reviewed. The latter are seen as representing at national level a significant departure from the *laissez-faire* curriculum policies (or non-policies) of post-war governments and as denoting an attempt to provide greater coordination (though not detailed control) from the centre. Notions of curriculum structure, continuity and control are also seen as implicated in the discussion as to what constitutes an appropriately consistent primary curriculum. The paper attempts to challenge twin orthodoxies: that there is already a 'core' to the primary curriculum and that any extension or closer monitoring of its application would inevitably be deleterious to the education of young children and to the professionalism of teachers.

Roy Garland's article focuses on curriculum policy-making in primary schools, a new and very significant development arising partly from the necessity of responding to the recommendations of the primary survey and partly from other developments including moves towards establishing more consistent curricula and public demands for greater accountability. He views policies as 'the artefacts of professional collaboration, dispute and self-examination' replacing 'the ubiquitous yet neutered schemes of work' (p. 64). He illustrates his points with reference to a pilot study of policy creation in a small number of primary schools. He argues that policies are required not just for mathematics, language and science but especially for the whole curriculum 'in a bid for cohesion and continuity in the educational encounters we offer our children' (p. 74)

Science is one subject area which might benefit considerably from being included in a policy for the whole curriculum, provided sufficient resources and support were then made available to implement it. Jack Kerr and Elizabeth Engel's article focuses on primary science but raises a number of issues of more general importance – the failure of the curriculum development movement to bring about substantial curriculum change, the necessity to transcend the process/content polarization that has bedevilled discussion in various curriculum areas, the necessity to examine more seriously the patterns of understanding and ways of thinking children already possess and to use this information to plan teaching strategies, and the necessity for a thorough reappraisal of the place of professional studies in teacher education – a concern shared by Robin Alexander later in the section.

Similarly, whilst looking specifically at how history might be taught to young children, Joan Blyth raises points of more general interest and significance. Assumptions about what children can and cannot learn at various ages need to be constantly re-examined (especially in the 'social subjects'); the place of planned structured programmes of work in subjects beyond the 'basics' needs to be reconsidered especially with younger children; and concern for continuity needs to be extended to areas other than just mathematics and language. She is concerned to strengthen the academic content of the curriculum and to counter the view that professional training is a once-and-for-all affair.

Joan Tamburrini's article, written specifically for this collection, is an important contribution to transcending the polarities which have bedevilled primary education in general and nursery education in particular. Dichotomies such as 'academic pre-schools' and 'shared-child-rearing pre-schools', or 'child-centred' and 'teacher-centred practices' are seen as over-simplistic and unhelpful. Drawing on research evidence she contends that young children's intellectual functioning can be facilitated by tutorial intervention which does not deny the importance of children exploring and playing with materials in their own way and their own time. An active, not passive role for the teacher is implied, one based on clear intentions and on professional knowledge, not just of child development but of the kinds of skills and concepts that are educationally powerful and within the understanding of children under five.

The remaining two papers both focus on the professional knowledge required of primary teachers, especially curriculum knowledge. David Oliver argues that few schools identify and commit themselves to a distinct philosophy of education and devise policies in accordance with this. Though arguing strongly against greater curriculum consistency nationwide as discussed in the second and third papers, he believes that the approach in each school needs to be consistent. He details the theoretical basis of his own policy which is concerned not to introduce children to the substantive knowledge of various curriculum areas but to explore how experience is symbolized and structured and how knowledge claims are made and substantiated. He too emphasizes the importance of planning by teaching staff but in terms not of hierarchies of skills and concepts but of styles of thinking, symbolic systems and spheres of application. Like Joan Blyth he advocates a more demanding intellectual curriculum for children; he believes teachers can give children the confidence to make, not merely receive, knowledge structures.

The last paper in the section illustrates how the issues of structure, range, appropriateness, continuity, evaluation and control are equally applicable to the primary teacher education curriculum. After a brief review of developments within the teaching of educational and subject studies, Robin Alexander appraises the adequacy of the professional studies component, particularly in the light of the primary survey. His conclusions reinforce many of the points made elsewhere in this section. In particular he raises two fundamental questions:

(i) What sort of curriculum knowledge does a competent primary school class teacher need? and
(ii) How much of his total training should be devoted to the acquisition of this knowledge and the associated teaching skills?

Fundamental reconsideration of the content and time allocation of professional studies is called for if the college curriculum is to be more consistent with the teacher's task. His paper maps out an agenda for a genuinely radical appraisal of the relationship between professional action and professional training.

This book as a whole seeks a similar reappraisal of the relationship between professional action and reflection and between policy-making and practice.

The Curriculum*

Her Majesty's Inspectors of Schools

The Basic Skills

8.16 High priority is given to teaching children to read, write and learn mathematics.

8.17 The teaching of reading is regarded by teachers as extremely important, and the basic work in this skill is undertaken systematically. *The levels of ability of the children inevitably vary, but those who find learning to read difficult are more likely to be given work suitably matched to their abilities than the children who are more able readers.*

8.18 The survey also makes it possible to say, on the basis of the scores in the NFER reading test, NS6, that the results of surveys conducted since 1955 are consistent with gradually improving reading standards of eleven year olds. It is only in the reading performance of eleven year olds that earlier data exist for statistical comparisons to be made with the findings of this survey.

8.19 *It is vital that the careful work already being done to ensure that children become literate should continue and be further developed. Future marked improvement in the general level of performance in reading, however, probably depends on developing a more systematic approach to teaching average and more able readers to find the books they require and to use the contents page and index to decide whether to skim or to study a text thoroughly; to follow a line of argument critically; and to look out for the implications of what is written, as well as to note the explicit information the passage contains. For this to be achieved children need to be introduced to a wide range of reading material in connection with many aspects of their work.*

8.20 In writing, considerable effort is made to teach syntax and spelling. *It may be that because this work is often based on isolated exercises, the*

---

*This is an extract from DEPARTMENT OF EDUCATION AND SCIENCE (1978) *Primary Education in England: A Survey by HM Inspectors of Schools* London, HMSO. The original passage makes a large number of cross-references to other parts of the survey which have here been omitted. The original emphases are retained.

rules are too often forgotten when children write in their own words, as they frequently have the opportunity to do. What is written is often descriptive or narrative in form and, while these forms are important, by eleven years of age more children might be expected to develop an argument or to explore an idea when writing than is now the case. Furthermore, the time spent on writing should allow for the correction and improvement of initial attempts.

8.21 The children spend a considerable amount of time on mathematics and the work in this subject is better matched to their abilities than is the work in most other subjects – though the more able children often work at too low a level. In the light of these efforts, the scores achieved in the NFER mathematics test, E2, are disappointing.

8.22 *It seems clear from this part of the survey that individual assignments should not be allowed to replace all group or class work in mathematics. Teachers can, by working regularly with a group or the whole class, quicken the pace of mental response and encourage accuracy. They may also, in these circumstances, more readily draw children's attention to general rules in the work they do and so help to create a better understanding of the ways in which numbers behave. Children need to practise mental and written calculations in the four rules of number, including whole numbers and, when they are ready, decimals and fractions. They also need to use numbers in connection with practical activities. The forms of questions and the forms of answers required ought to be varied so that children are not put off by an unusual word, or combination of words or symbols. More of the examples worked by children could usefully lead to multiple answers. The work in mathematics should not be confined to the four rules of number: children in those classes where the programme included all mathematical items taught to 80 per cent of classes for the age group did better in the mathematics test.*

8.23 *The evidence of the survey bears out the view that the effective application of skills, including their use in practical activities, is important. The teaching of skills in isolation, whether in language or in mathematics, does not produce the best results.*

Other Aspects of the Curriculum

8.24 The curriculum as a whole provides many opportunities for pupils to apply basic skills, and it contains other elements that are important in their own right. The programme of most classes included work on plants, animals and man-made objects and materials. The children were taught about the historical and geographical context of the society in which they live, and the moral values that underlie it. Unless their parents asked for them to be withdrawn, they took part in religious education based on Christian beliefs. *More might be done to make all children aware of other beliefs and to extend their understanding of the multi-cultural nature of contemporary society. In the course of work on these and other matters, children acquire information and learn to respond imaginatively to what they see, hear and otherwise experience.*

8.25 *Curricular content should be selected not only to suit the interests and abilities of the children and to provide for the progressive development of the basic skills, but also because it is important in its own right.* This requires a considerable knowledge of the subject material, going far beyond that which is to be used explicitly in the classroom. The teacher's need for a thorough knowledge of the subject becomes more marked as the children get older.

8.26 *Observed practices in some parts of the curriculum show the difficulty that a considerable proportion of teachers have in selecting and utilising subject matter. Science is the outstanding example and one in which no individual item of observational or experimental work occurred in as many as 80 per cent of the classes at any age; this is the only aspect of the curriculum of which this is true. Craft is also making a smaller contribution to the work than is desirable. The lack of progression and the amount of repetition in the work in geography and history probably result from a lack of planning, though the mere presence of a scheme of work is no guarantee that a subject is well taught; over 40 per cent of the schools had schemes of work in science but there was little evidence of these programmes being implemented.*

8.27 Physical education was given about as high a priority as mathematics. Music, of which more will be said later, was also given relatively high priority. *It is interesting to notice that both of these subjects were among those for which there were frequently teachers with posts of responsibility.*

The Range of the Curriculum

8.28 It might be argued that if some parts of the curriculum are difficult for class teachers to deal with it would be better to narrow the range of the curriculum. That view does not seem to be borne out by the findings of this survey. The basic skills are more successfully learnt when applied to other subjects and children in the classes which covered a full range of the widely taught items did better on the NFER tests at nine and eleven years of age; also, for all three age groups the work of children in these classes was better matched to their abilities than was the work of children in other classes. This finding has to be interpreted with care, because the remaining classes did not necessarily have narrower curricula; the teachers may merely have been more idiosyncratic in their choice of items. *Nevertheless, there is no evidence in the survey to suggest that a narrower curriculum enabled children to do better in the basic skills or led to the work being more aptly chosen to suit the capacities of the children.*

8.29 *The general educational progress of children and their competence*

31

in the basic skills appear to have benefited where they were involved in a programme of work that included art and craft, history and geography, music and physical education, and science, as well as language, mathematics and religious and moral education, although not necessarily as separate items on a timetable. There is no justification for differentiation between the curriculum for boys and for girls because of traditional differences in social roles; such differentiation as does still occur, for example in craft work which limits girls to using soft materials, is unusual and should cease.

8.30 *It remains important to establish priorities and to keep the curriculum within realistic limits. Agreement on these matters should be sought far more than is now done with other schools in the locality, primary and secondary, and in accordance with national needs.*

8.31 *Such agreement makes it easier to ensure that the programmes of primary and secondary schools are attuned, and that there is continuity as children move from one stage to the next.*

Differences Amongst Children within a Class

8.32 Especially in the basic skills, but also in other parts of the curriculum, children are frequently divided into groups, or provided with individual assignments of work. In the basic skills, the main objective is to give work that is of an appropriate level of difficulty. In some other parts of the curriculum the groups are based on common interests or on friendship. The almost universal occurrence of grouping and individual work indicate the concern that teachers have for individual children.

8.33 The evidence of the survey shows that children's needs are more successfully catered for in some parts of the curriculum than in others; and throughout the curriculum, the needs of some children are more often met than are the needs of others. *The relative success that teachers have in matching the work in the basic skills for the slower children has already been mentioned in this chapter. Otherwise, it is broadly the case that the more able children within a class were the least likely to be doing work that was sufficiently challenging.*

8.34 One reason may be that it is difficult for a teacher to keep track of what every child in a class is doing if each is engaged in a different activity. *Certainly children who were customarily given some – though not too much – mathematical instruction in groups working from the blackboard with their teacher were at an advantage in completing the NFER test.* This advantage may have come about because a teacher could afford to spend more time explaining a process to a group than to a series of individuals, or because the group contact enabled the teacher to inject more pace into the work, or because the children learnt from each other's questions, or all three. *Some potential loss of precision in matching the work to individuals was* compensated for by other factors; in practice, the loss of precision in the grading of work for groups as compared with individuals may be negligible.

8.35 Another reason why teachers find it more difficult to match the level of work to the abler than to the slower children in their classes may be that these children are more demanding with regard to subject content. *It is particularly interesting in this connection that the work in music, for which specialist teaching, including peripatetic teaching, is most common, is the area of the curriculum in which the work of the able, average and least able children is most evenly matched to their abilities. It is also striking that classes in schools where the holders of posts of special responsibility have marked influence were much more successful than others in matching the work to the abilities of all children, including the most able.* Furthermore, the better match that is achieved in the basic skills may well occur because all the students who intended to teach in primary schools are given some training in the teaching of these skills, because carefully graded materials are available, and because dealing with children who find it difficult to learn to read is another common area of specialization in primary education.

Some Children in Inner City Schools

8.36 In recent years efforts have been made to provide for the special needs of some children in inner city schools. In the survey, inner city schools generally had a more favourable staffing ratio than similar schools in 'other urban' areas, and in some of these schools resources were noticeably better than average.

8.37 Some of the schools in inner city areas contained a larger proportion than most of children whose home language was not English, and also of those children from some indigenous families who find it difficult to gain as much as they should from their schooling. While both the HMI survey and the NFER tests indicate that standards of performance are lower than average in these schools, neither can show whether the efforts made in recent years have improved the levels of performance. *The survey indicates that children in inner city schools are more likely than others to be underestimated by their teachers and least likely to be given work which extends their capabilities. This strongly suggests that further improvement in the children's performance is possible.*

8.38 *Further study is required of how improvements may be brought about. Some research has already been undertaken in this field but more is necessary in primary schools, particularly to identify conditions that are likely to be effective in teaching children from these areas.*

8.39 *The need to raise teachers' assumptions about children's capabilities has special relevance here. It may also be that in these schools, with a preponderance of children who find learning difficult, special care should be taken to support and encourage those children who make average or good progress, not least in order that they should set a standard of work at which others may aim. This may require yet more teachers and resources. The slower children still need painstaking and thorough attention if they are to reach minimum standards of literacy and numeracy; and children who come to school with little or no English cannot be expected to make progress in school unless, as a result of careful teaching, they achieve a sufficient command of English, which is for them a foreign language.*

lum in Primary Schools:
to 'A View of the Curriculum'* 1980

Inspectors of Schools

ᴣnter primary schools at about five years of age
1ave in a reasonably social way, though they may
ng members of such a large community as a school.
ᴠe acquired the basic structures of their mother
ᴣlish, and be aware of and interested in the shapes,
tities of things about them.

Individual differences and common needs

Each individual brings a different set of experiences to bear on his schooling.
These differences arise from variety in the surroundings in which children
are brought up, from the degree of support and encouragement they have
had from adults, and from differences in what their powers of imagination
and intellect have allowed them to make of their experiences. At five,
a few have a vocabulary that is barely sufficent for their daily needs, while
at the other extreme a small minority have a wide vocabulary, can detect
fine shades of meaning and have begun to recognise written words; and
a few have started to write.

At one level of generality, all children in primary schools need to be
occupied in a programme that will enable them:

to engage with other children and with adults in a variety of working
and social relationships;
to increase their range and understanding of English, and particularly
to develop their ability and inclination to read and write for information
and imaginative stimulation;
to acquire better physical control when they are writing, or exercising
utilitarian skills and engaging in imaginative expression in art, craft,
music, drama or movement generally.

*Extracts from DEPARTMENT OF EDUCATION AND SCIENCE (1980) *A View of
the Curriculum* HMI Series: Matters for Discussion, London, HMSO, pp. 7–12
and 23–28.

Furthermore, if they are to extend their powers of language, children must be brought into contact with new experiences and ideas or look afresh at old experiences through discussion with teachers and through the use of books, role playing and audio-visual material. Studies of the beliefs and ways of life of historical characters and of people and communities who live today in other parts of the world, or indeed elsewhere in Britain, provide opportunities for language development through discussion, reading and writing. Moreover, these studies are valuable in their own right. This is especially so in a country that is multi-cultural. Learning about the nature of materials and about the needs and life cycles of plants and animals provides further opportunities for the extension and application of language and of mathematical skills and ideas. It also helps children to appreciate the world around them and provides an early introduction to the industrial and scientific age in which they live.

Some necessary differences of programme

When described in these general terms, the curricula of primary schools show close conformity. Differences that occur from class to class, and even from pupil to pupil within a class, are in the particular topics chosen for study, the methods of study employed, the weight given to each part of the curriculum and the level of difficulty to which each part is taken. There are good reasons why, to some extent, this should be so.

The first arises from differences between children, such as those described earlier. For example, a child entering school who has already begun to read soon requires books covering a wide range of topics and stories and may well be able to progress quickly with only a modest amount of supervision. Another child, before he is ready to begin to read, will need to acquire a surer grasp of spoken language, skill in noticing relatively small differences in sounds and shapes, and the habit of looking at printed material in an orderly way. Even then much patient help and encouragement may be needed if the second child is to gain in skill and confidence. To treat both children the same is to do an injustice to one.

As children make progress their interests diversify and what is a stimulus to one may be a barrier to another. If the necessary skill or the underlying idea can be presented as well in one way as another then it may create unnecessary difficulties to use the same way with all children.

Teachers as well as children differ in their abilities and enthusiasms. Schools differ in the resources available to them both because of the purchasing policies of present and past incumbents and because of the accidents of locality. A school in Lincoln is better placed to develop historical studies based on Lincoln cathedral than is one in St Albans.

The development and use of local opportunities, the special skills of teachers and the enthusiasms of children should be used to enhance the quality of work beyond what might come from a simple uniformity of practice; though such uniformity may have the advantage that the work to be covered becomes very familiar to teachers, what is done may be only a loose fit to local circumstances and soon become threadbare. When teachers make good use of their particular interests and strengths they can take children much further than is now common.

Conditions required for the inclusion of a modern language

The presence of a teacher with strength in a subject does not necessarily justify the inclusion of the subject in the curriculum, even if the children are capable of studying it. In the short term, French can be taught success-fully in a primary school where there are sufficient teachers who speak the language well enough, who know how to teach the subject to young children, and who have the resources necessary for the work. However, these conditions are only the first that must be satisfied if the time and effort spent is to be worthwhile in the long term. Additionally, there should be a reasonable expectation that the teaching will be continued even if the teachers now responsible for the work leave. It should also be possible to continue the teaching in the secondary school in such a way as to profit from what has already been done. This may be difficult and even impossible if children in other primary schools in the area have had no opportunity or substantially different opportunities for learning the language. Unless conditions are favourable in all these respects for including the subject, it is best excluded from the primary school curriculum. Plainly, there is need for agreement between schools in a neighbourhood and the LEA on whether and how the teaching of a foreign language is conducted in primary schools.

Levels of difficulty in the work

In other parts of the primary school curriculum the decisions to be taken more usually concern the range of what should be done, the choice of priorities within the range and the level of difficulty of the work. In each of these, local circumstances and the differences between individual children and individual teachers have to be taken into account, but some common requirements remain.

Skills

All children should learn to use English better as they grow older, and to read and write English with a growing sureness. Some children come to school with little or no English. It is essential for them to become fluent in English but, whatever is done to achieve this, the child's interest and pride in his mother tongue should be preserved.

A minority of children of eleven years of age can manage only simple reading texts made up of short sentences using common words. They as much as anyone require appropriate reading material on almost all aspects of the curriculum so that they may better appreciate the importance of reading. The great majority of children should learn to use books, fiction and non-fiction, in the sense that they improve their powers of comprehension, that they learn how to find the books they want on the library shelf, and that they learn to use a contents page and an index. The full range of reading skills required by the more able eleven year olds is much wider than this, and a more extensive list is given in Appendix I.

Learning to read and learning to write go hand in hand, and the majority of children should, by the time they are eight, be able to write stories and accounts of events in their own words. As they go on through the primary school many children should become accustomed to writing which involves presenting a coherent argument, exploring alternative possibilities or drawing conclusions and making judgements. Children should learn, in the course of their work, to spell the words they use, to employ acceptable forms of grammar and sentence structure and to begin to develop styles of writing appropriate to the task in hand.

In mathematics, priority should be given to acquiring familiarity with whole numbers up to 100 by gaining skills in relating them to one another – including the speedy recall of the commonly used addition, multiplication, subtraction and division facts – and by applying them to circumstances that occur in everyday life. But nearly all of the children should go far beyond that. They should begin to appreciate the simpler spatial relationships and they should make a start on work requiring a relatively explicit application of logic as with some popular games and puzzles. A more extensive range of mathematical skills that should be mastered by more able eleven year olds is included in Appendix II.

Over the course of the primary school years children should learn how to observe and to measure with increasing precision. They should also learn to use these skills with common sense; for example, when measuring or weighing, to use a degree of accuracy that is appropriate to the circumstances. They should learn to record – and to interpret and comment on – what they have seen, heard or otherwise learnt. They should gain from increasing control over their nervous and muscular systems so that they can use tools, instruments and a variety of small equipment in drawing, painting, modelling, music-making and games in such a way that they feel a sense of achievement.

Content and concepts

A wide range of skills, not least those concerned with the development of good personal relations, are relevant to the education of each child, though each makes progress at a different rate. The skills are learnt in the context of developing concepts and in the acquisition of information.

Mathematical ideas suitable and necessary for primary school children are referred to in Appendix II. Some appropriate historical, geographical and scientific concepts are discussed in the following paragraphs.

When topics are being selected for inclusion in the programme a number of factors should be taken into account. These include the characteristics of the children, the knowledge of the teachers and the availability of suitable resources and facilities. The information to be covered should be worth knowing and useful in providing further insights into some more general idea or in improving a skill. There needs also to be some agreement between teachers in a school, with teachers in the secondary schools, and with teachers in neighbouring primary schools so that if a topic is to be studied twice or more in the course of a child's school life, the second and later occasion will build on previous experience.

On the national level it can be said that all primary schools should help their pupils to appreciate that today's world grew out of yesterday's, and to acquire some sense of historical chronology, even if the topics studied are not presented in chronological order. The children should learn to distinguish between fiction and historical fact and some should begin to recognize that historical evidence may itself be partial or biased. The youngest children's introduction to the past might concentrate on the immediate circumstances of their own families and friends and the para-phernalia of daily life. But today's world cannot be understood without some knowledge of Britain's role overseas today and in former years, and reference to this should certainly be included in the later primary school curriculum in a balanced and sensitive way as a means of helping children to understand our multi-cultural society.

The lives of the children and their parents are also conditioned by the geographical circumstances under which they and others live. As they go through primary schools, children need to become more aware of local features, of the formation and characteristics of the earth beneath their feet and of the weather. They need to learn something of the major differences in the conditions under which children live in other parts of Britain and abroad, and of the consequences of those conditions. They should also learn of the importance of routes and other means of communication between human settlements.

Skills of observation, listening and touching need to be developed so that children possess information on which their imaginations can work and be expressed through painting, modelling, music-making, dancing and storytelling. They need to be developed more than is now common in such a way that children are introduced to scientific ideas about stability and change in living things and materials; about reproduction, growth and development in succeeding generations; about forms of energy sources and storage; and about factors which influence personal and community health, including safety. Children should grow to respect and care for living things. In the course of the work they should learn how to observe systematically and carefully, to note similarities and differences and to make reasonable generalizations; they should conduct, and some should learn to devise, simple experiments to test out hypotheses.

Religious education has a statutory place in the curriculum of all maintained schools and the agreed syllabus system makes it possible to provide a framework of advice and guidance for this aspect of the curriculum in county and voluntary controlled schools. However, it is necessary for schools and teachers through their schemes of work to decide how that framework is to be adapted to the capacities and experience of the particular children with whom they are concerned.

Through religious education children can begin to learn something of the characteristic practices and beliefs of Christianity and of other major world faiths, and the influence these faiths have on the life and conduct of the believer. On another level, also important in the growth of attitudes and of an appreciation of human behaviour and achievement, it is necessary to introduce children to suitable examples of literature, drama, music and the graphic arts. Of these, literature offers an especially rich source and the children should be introduced to books by the major authors who have written for, or whose books have been adopted by, children. Some of the books should have been written by authors alive today.

Summary

Current practice is such that discussion on the primary school curriculum does not need to concern itself so much with the total range of the work as with the extent to which parts of the curriculum are developed, especially for the more able children. It is only provision of observational and experimental science that is seriously lacking in many primary schools; and the teaching of French that is sometimes attempted when conditions are not suitable. More extensive discussion is required on the levels to which work could and should be taken, at least for some children, in the various parts of the curriculum; for example, the identification of the skills and ideas associated with geography and history that are suitable for primary school children should help teachers to ensure that the day-to-day programme is organized so that children become acquainted with these skills and ideas, and should help to improve continuity from one class or school to the next – whether or not these subjects are shown separately on the timetable. Working parties of teachers, LEA advisers, inspectors and others have already shown what useful guidelines can be produced for parts of the curriculum, particularly, but not only, in mathematics.

Anxiety is sometimes expressed that maintaining a wide curriculum in primary schools may be possible only at the expense of the essential, elementary skills of reading, writing and mathematics. The evidence from the HMI survey of primary education in England does not bear out that anxiety. A broad curriculum can include many opportunities for the application and practice of the skills of reading, writing and calculating. It should be planned to include them, and every opportunity should then be taken to improve children's abilities in these essential skills.

Conclusion to: 'A View of the Curriculum'*

This paper has argued briefly for a broad curriculum for all pupils up to 16. It implies a substantially larger compulsory element than now in terms of the range of studies pupils carry forward to the end of the fifth year, but with suitable differentiation in detailed content and presentation, and still with some provision for choice, to match different abilities, aspiration and need. It also seeks greater coherence and continuity in school education as a whole. It is concerned with a framework for the curriculum and therefore rightly leaves many details to be determined.

It assumes a fairly lengthy subsequent process of consultation, locally and nationally, to establish broad policies on the structure of the curriculum as a whole and to develop a range of documents further defining the parts of the curriculum and their relationship to each other. These will need to take the form of statements identifying necessary skills and knowledge. There is already useful experience on which to draw of the cooperation necessary to the local formulation of curricular statements. In a number of LEA areas, working parties of teachers and LEA advisers and inspectors have produced guidelines, particularly for mathematics; some local schemes have effectively brought schools and industry and commerce together in considering curricular content and necessary skills.

The two appendices which follow, on mathematics and reading, illustrate the forms which such statements might take. Even these two examples indicate that all statements will not be of the same type but will vary with the subject and the learning involved. That on reading, for example, would constitute part of a much longer document on the teaching of English: but much of it also could be part of a general statement on language policies common to all departments of a school. Some lists will inevitably be longer than others. It will require nice judgement to strike a balance between too restricted a statement, which might too easily settle for minimal requirements, and an over-elaborated statement which risks seeking to define too precisely how each item of learning is to be accomplished. From these analyses a school would then compose appropriate curricula for its pupils, taking into account the legitimate concerns of parents, employers and others outside the school.

In the end, whatever is decided nationally must leave much for individual local education authorities and schools to determine as they interpret

---

*This section is the conclusion to the whole publication and, therefore, contains references to secondary as well as primary education.

NB
→

the national agreement to take account of the nature of individual schools and individual pupils. It must take account of children's capacity to learn at any given stage of their maturity and identify what is intrinsically worth learning and best acquired through schooling. It must, too, allow for future modification in response to new needs in the world outside schools: decisions cannot sensibly be taken once and for all. The effort involved will be justified if it leads to developing more fully the potential of all children.

Appendix I English: Development of Reading Skills*

An essential part of the development of children's ability to read concerns the translation of letters on the page into words in the mind. Just as necessary is the growth in children's capacity to understand and use language and to relate it to experience. The following paragraphs should therefore be read as part of a wider framework for the development of children's language, involving all teachers and including:

(a) opportunities for talking, listening, writing and reading in a variety of contexts
(b) a stimulating range of literature
(c) a carefully structured approach to mastering skills
(d) consideration of how language works between people
(e) a coherent approach to language in all subjects as the medium of learning.

A curriculum should provide for the continuous development of skill in reading throughout the years of schooling, from the recognition of words to the comprehension of complicated material.

Some children entering infant schools need help in acquiring some pre-reading skills before they can make a formal beginning to reading. When these skills have been mastered, high priority should be given to teaching word recognition and to building an adequate sight vocabulary, with some understanding of phonics, so as to ensure a basic repertoire of reading skills with which to tackle written material. At the same time children should be encouraged to enjoy reading prose and poetry as a worthwhile and pleasurable activity, learning to value fiction as well as non-fiction through the use of group and individual reading books, including those chosen by themselves.

Graded reading schemes are widely used to provide young children with reading matter suited to their level of skill, but these are insufficient in isolation. 'Real' books have an important part to play from the earliest

*This Appendix relates to the whole discussion document and therefore contains references to both primary and secondary education.

stages. By the age of eight most children should be able to read, with confidence, simple sentences about familiar situations. More able eight year olds should be expected to recall the theme of a short story they have read, as well as to comprehend books of information of the kind written for young children, while gifted children of this age should be able to use adult material, at least in part.

Once children have acquired the early reading skills, they should begin to learn to predict what may appear next in a piece of writing, to use various contextual clues, to develop and extend their reading vocabulary and to use dictionaries. They should also learn how to use the contents pages of a book and its index, and the ways in which books are arranged on library shelves. These skills need to be developed in a reading context that continually underlines the pleasure and advantage that can come from reading.

By the age of eleven many pupils should be aware of the more advanced skills of reading though these require continuing development during the secondary school years if the needs of more subject-based studies are to be met. Children need to learn to read books in a variety of ways, learning how to skim and sift material, to vary the pace of reading, to process information and to discriminate between the more and the less important features. Pupils need generally to increase their range and rate of comprehension which, in turn, requires an increasing commitment to sustained reading for which the school should make due provision.

During the secondary school years pupils need to become aware not only of the overt meaning of what they are reading, but of the many kinds of oblique meaning with which it is charged: the nuances of tone and attitude, the various indicators of emotion, the contribution of imagery, the significance of structure, the effects of rhythm. Developing awareness of such factors will help them, when they are reading literature of quality, to enter more fully into the thought and feelings of other human beings in the fundamental situations that confront all of us; and, when they read some of the less good writing that is bound to come their way, to detect such features as exaggeration, bias, insincerity or·vulgarity. Unless they develop these skills, their reading is unlikely to contribute to widening their experience, sharpening their sensitivity or shaping their values. It is important to provide for them a careful balance of content, so that a wide range of novels, poems and plays is available as well as non fiction. There is value in continuing to encourage library skills and book buying, and in teachers setting an example as enthusiastic readers themselves.

A proportion of children will always require special help if they are to make even modest progress as readers. By careful selection of material and the development of teaching techniques which take note of assessment and diagnosis, these children should be given every opportunity to develop to the limits of their potential.

The outcome of a reading curriculum, therefore, should be a majority of pupils who like to read because to do so can give pleasure, can help them to find out more about things they have an interest in, and because reading can sometimes be fun. Their skill in reading should enable them to tackle a range of written material with confidence. They should have reached a stage of fluency which enables them to move from graphic symbol to meaning without having to match the symbol to a sound. Well developed critical ability should enable them to make reasoned choices of what to read and to select relevant information. They should have, as part of their experience, a sound body of well chosen prose and poetry which should include work of the best modern writers.

Appendix II The Mathematics Curriculum*

It is in the interests of the country that as many people as possible should achieve acceptable levels of competence in mathematics. It is also in the interests of the individual to reach as high a level as possible in the subject, not merely because mathematics may help a person to get a better job and do it well, but chiefly because it can help in understanding and interpreting very many aspects of the world in which we live.

The details of the approach and content of the course have to be worked out by consultation within each school; but we may take as a starting point the following objectives, which have been widely discussed over the last two years.

Approach

At every level in the teaching of mathematics the formation of concepts should have priority over the acquisition of technical skills. This is not to imply that such skills are to be neglected, but that emphasis on understanding will facilitate the acquisition of those skills which are needed.

The use of language plays a dominant role in the learning of mathematics, and teachers should be constantly asking pupils to speak and write about what they are learning, mostly in ordinary language rather than in specialized words or symbols.

Symbols should be introduced only when the need for them is perceived and pupils understand what the symbols denote. If pupils are to acquire the ability to manipulate symbols accurately and with reasonable speed, and at the same time to focus their attention on some higher purpose (such as the solution of a problem), practice is necessary. But the accurate manipulation of symbols *alone* is of limited value; pupils need also to see purpose in manipulation and to attach meanings to symbols when necessary.

*This is a shortened version of the original Appendix II – many of the references to secondary schools have been omitted.

If pupils are to be aware of the inter-relationships between mathematics and other subjects of the curriculum and between mathematics and the world of experience, and are to be able to apply their mathematics in these areas, it is necessary to stress these interrelationships constantly. Examples of the applications of mathematics in science, technical studies, geography, economics, and from industry and commerce, not only serve to help pupils make these connections but also enliven the teaching. Some mathematical ideas might best be developed in other subjects of the timetable, but in any case good liaison is essential.

Content

These are some of the attitudes, concepts and skills which pupils might be expected to acquire as they progress through school. Pupils vary greatly in their levels of achievement, but it is to be hoped that some work of appropriate difficulty will be undertaken with all pupils across the full range of ideas described below. It is to be hoped also that in the process of doing this work pupils will learn to think clearly, argue logically and communicate effectively.

Between the ages of five and eight children should begin work in the following areas:

(i)   The development of appropriate language; qualitative description, the recognition of objects from description; discriminating, classifying and sorting of objects; identifying objects and describing them unambiguously.

(ii)   The recognition of common, simple mathematical relationships, both numerical and spatial; reasoning and logical deduction in connection with everyday things, geometrical shapes, number arrangements in order, etc.

(iii)   The ability to describe quantitatively: the use of number in counting, describing, estimating and approximating.

(iv)   The understanding of whole numbers and their relationships with one another.

(v)   The appreciation of the measures in common use; sensible estimation using the appropriate units; the ability to measure length, weight, volume and capacity, area, time, angle and temperature to an everyday level of accuracy.

(vi)   The understanding of money, contributing to a sense of the value of money, and the ability to carry out sensible purchases.

(vii)   The ability to carry out practical activities involving the ideas of addition, subtraction, multiplication and division.

(viii) The ability to perform simple calculations involving the mathematical processes indicated by the signs $+$, $-$, $\times$, $\div$ with whole numbers (maintaining rapid recall of the sums, differences and products of pairs of numbers from 0 to 10).

(ix)   The ability to check whether the result of a calculation is reasonable.

(x)   The ability to use and interpret simple forms of diagrams, maps and tabulated information.

(xi)   An appreciation of two- and three-dimensional shapes and their relationships with one another. The ability to recognise simple properties; to handle, create, discuss and describe them with confidence and appreciate spatial relationships, symmetry and similarity.

(xii)   An ability to write clearly, to record mathematics in statements, neatly and systematically.

Before the age of eight for some, but between the ages of eight and eleven for most, children should continue to develop in these directions, and progress to:

(i)   The appreciation of place value, the number system and number notation, including whole numbers, decimal fractions and vulgar fractions. The ability to recognise simple number patterns (odds and events, multiples, divisors, squares, etc.).

(ii)   The ability to carry out with confidence and accuracy simple examples in the four operations of number, including two places of decimals as for pounds and pence and the measures as used.

(iii)   The ability to approximate.

(iv)   A sound understanding of place value applied to the decimal notation for numbers. The ability to carry out the addition and subtraction of numbers with up to two decimal places and the multiplication and division of such numbers by whole numbers up to and including 9.

(v)   The multiplication and division of numbers with up to two decimal places by 10 and 100.

(vi)   An appreciation of the connections between fractions, decimal fractions and the most common percentages.

(vii)   The ability to use fractions in the sequence $\frac{1}{2}, \frac{1}{4}, \frac{1}{8}, \frac{1}{16}$ or $\frac{1}{3}, \frac{1}{6}, \frac{1}{12}$ or $\frac{1}{5}, \frac{1}{10}$, including the idea of equivalence in the discussion of everyday experiences.

(viii)   An appreciation of the broader aspects of number, such as bases other than 10 and easy tests of divisibility.

(ix)   An ability to read with understanding mathematics from books, and to use appropriate reference skills.

A number of children of this age will be capable of more advanced work, and they should be encouraged to undertake it.

The above items are taken from *Mathematics 5 to 11* (HMSO, 1979), No. 9 in this series, where the ideas are discussed in greater detail.

Curriculum Consistency

Colin Richards
University of Leicester

Primary Survey

Unlike so many other documents on primary education, *Primary Education in England* (DES, 1978) bears re-examination and re-interpretation several years on from its publication. It can be read (and has been read) on a variety of different levels; its messages are directed at a variety of audiences, and its implications are both implicit and explicit. This essay concentrates on what I consider to be one of its most important underlying themes; an issue which, to my mind, has not received nearly enough professional attention and which is not just challenging but profoundly disturbing. I aim to convince readers that consistency is an important curriculum issue, but I do not seek to persuade them that any one or more particular lines of action are necessary to resolve it. The essay provides an analysis of the concept, findings from the primary survey relevant to it, possible implications at local level, and a review of recent initiatives from the Department of Education and Science which are directly concerned with its resolution.

The theme of curriculum consistency is focused upon here because tackling it is essential if progress is to be made in realizing a genuine primary education for all and partly because post-survey conferences and comment have concentrated on the survey's relatively specific implications rather than on more general, and to my mind more important, issues such as consistency. It is argued here that curriculum consistency is a short-hand term for a very important set of problems which policy-makers at *all* levels need to tackle if equality of curricular opportunity is to be a reality for all primary pupils. By 'equality of curricular opportunity' is meant the opportunity for all pupils to be introduced to some of the major concepts, skills, rules and underlying generalizations associated with established ways of knowing (both theoretical and practical) in our society.

The problem of curriculum consistency has been almost entirely neglected by those commenting on the survey's wider implications. Its consideration raises a number of thorny professional issues concerned with teacher autonomy, curriculum planning and implementation, school policy-making and local and national responsibilities for curriculum decision-making. It is linked closely with a number of recent developments such as discussions about core curricula and moves towards establishing a national framework for the school curriculum (DES/Welsh Office, 1980).

What is meant here by curriculum consistency? As far as this essay is concerned, curricula are consistent to the extent that all pupils at a particular stage, whether in the same class or different classes, are introduced to a similar set of curricular elements. Total consistency would mean that such pupils are introduced to exactly the same set of curricular elements. There would be a common curriculum, a common syllabus, though not necessarily a common repertoire of 'approved' teaching techniques (that is, not pedagogic consistency). Such a totally consistent curriculum would seem neither possible nor desirable in the English context. At the other extreme, total inconsistency would mean that pupils in different classes would be introduced to a totally different set of curricular elements; an anarchic curriculum, undesirable and even more unrealistic than its opposite. In between these extremes would be curriculum consistent to varying degrees. Those advocating some sort of core curriculum are concerned with achieving a measure of consistency such that all pupils at a particular stage, whether in the same class or different classes, are introduced to those curricular elements which they regard as essential. Notions such as 'a curriculum framework' or 'a common curriculum policy' are intended to facilitate a measure of consistency. Current discussions over a framework are not about absolute uniformity nor about its opposite, but about the appropriate degree of curriculum consistency within our schools (Thomas, 1980).

Three further sets of distinctions need to be made at this point. At least two senses can be given the term 'curricular elements'. It can refer to broad curricular areas such as established school subjects (mathematics, science etc.) and to broad areas of experience (language, aesthetics, humanities etc.). Or it can refer to more specific forms of experience offered pupils, for example, experience of collecting climatic data, of participating in singing or drama, of being given handwriting practice. Arguments for greater consistency in terms of broad areas are termed here arguments for 'coarse-grained' consistency; arguments for more specific forms of experience (but *not* highly specific experiences) being made common are described as arguments for 'fine-grained' consistency. Curriculum consistency can, also, be narrowly or widely defined that is, in terms of a narrow range of curricular elements (for example, the *three* Rs) or a wide range of such elements (for example, language and literacy, mathematics, science, aesthetic and physical education, social studies – the analysis employed in the primary survey). A last set of important distinctions relates to the 'arena' in which curriculum consistency is to be located. It is possible to argue for greater consistency *within* schools (so that children at a particular stage but in different classes are given a more consistent curriculum), within localities, within local authorities or within the national system as a whole. It is thus possible to discuss the desirability of fostering 'coarse-grained' or 'fine-grained' curriculum consistency, narrowly or widely defined, in each of these 'arenas'.

Survey Findings

How did the primary survey relate to such notions? Briefly, it provided indirect evidence of a high degree of consensus among a national sample of primary teachers as to those more specific forms of experience considered important for inclusion in the primary curriculum but, more significantly for the arguments advanced in this essay, it provided direct evidence that few such forms of experience were actually offered to all primary pupils. Its findings strongly suggested that curriculum consistency in a 'fine-grained' sense was not at all characteristic of English primary education.

The evidence was provided in the first half of chapter six, to my mind the most important and disturbing part of the survey. As a result of inspecting over 1100 classes containing seven, nine or eleven year olds, HMI identified thirty-six items (see table 1), each of which was part of the experienced curriculum in about 80 per cent or more of classes inspected. The authors of the report argued, I think validly, that because such items did occur individually in such a large proportion of classes, there must have been a high percentage of primary teachers considering each of them to be important. (Teachers' reactions to the list of items when I have discussed these on courses and conferences confirm this view). It is important to note that many curricular elements did not appear on this list; for example, there was no mention of dance, drama, spelling, punctuation, scientific experiences, environmental studies, health education or even RE lessons. Even within the list of thirty-six items 'the coverage of items varied from class to class and showed no overall consistency' (para. 6.7), although it was reported that a few items such as calculations involving the four rules of number were found in all classes inspected. When considered individually, many of the thirty-six items were lacking in up to 25 per cent of classes; for example, 25 per cent and 24 per cent of classes undertook no work related to history and geography, whether taught and learnt separately or as part of topic work. Children of the same age in different primary classes were thus being offered different selections from the thirty-six items, let alone in relation to the wide range of other items contained in HMI schedules (summarized in annex B of the survey). This inconsistency is reinforced by tables 28 and 29 in the survey (see tables 2 and 3). As can be seen from table 3 only 29 per cent of classes of seven year olds, 19 per cent of classes of nine year olds and 24 per cent of classes of eleven year olds were undertaking all widely taught items.

[A possible objection to the interpretation given in these findings is that large numbers of classes could well have tackled all but one aspect of the widely taught items. Appendix G reports; 'to be able to interpret the results it is necessary to be sure that there were not a greater than expected number of classes which satisfied all but one aspect of the group of widely taught items. This indeed did not happen' (para. G. 67).] On average only a quarter of all classes were being introduced to all thirty-six items – evidence of a lack of curriculum consistency in both its 'coarse-' and 'fine-grained' senses. [It has been argued in discussion with the author on conferences and courses that there are problems as to the validity of such findings consequent on the impressionistic nature of HMI observations, on the limited duration of the inspections (approximately one day per class by each of two inspectors) and on the time of the school year when observations were made. However, these arguments can be countered. Detailed checklists were used, the inspectors were skilled at making such judgements and account was taken of the work already completed and planned, as well as what was actually happening at the time of the inspections. Even if a margin for error is allowed, and notionally the figures in table 3 are doubled, then a claim for a lack of curriculum consistency can still be sustained.] Because during the inspections only one class in any one age-group was examined in any one school, it is not possible from the survey data to indicate the degree of inconsistency within schools. It is likely that such inconsistency did occur, perhaps to a lesser extent than across schools. Commenting upon their findings the inspectors argued:

> This would seem to suggest that in individual schools either some difficulty is found in covering appropriately the range of work widely regarded by teachers as worthy of inclusion in the curriculum, or that individual schools or teachers are making markedly individual decisions about what is to be taught based on their own perceptions and choices or a combination of these. *Clearly ways of providing a more consistent coverage for important aspects of the curriculum need to be examined.*   (para. 6.9; my italics)

Possible Implications

For those concerned to promote greater equality of curricular opportunity for primary pupils, these figures and observations make disturbing reading. For whatever reasons (and many possible, partial explanations can be advanced), there appeared to be considerable variations from school to school in the degree to which pupils were introduced to more specific forms of experience considered important by the majority of teachers. 'There is already a common core to the primary curriculum' is not a claim that can be sustained except in relation to a few 'basic skill' items such as the decoding of reading matter and operations involving the four rules of number. Alongside this variation at one level, there was also evidence of a lack of 'coarse-grained' consistency across primary classes; the primary survey, the first volume from the ORACLE research project (Galton *et al*, 1980) and the findings of the Schools Council Open Plan Schools Inquiry (Bennett *et al*, 1980a) revealed a heavy concentration on mathematics and language in primary classes with many but not all pupils being given little exposure to a wide range of ways of knowing (through science, drama, environmental studies, dance, three-dimensional construction work etc.).

Paragraph 6.9 of the survey (quoted above) implies that greater efforts need to be made to secure a more consistent curriculum. This raises a host of questions which cannot be tackled in any detail here:

(a) Who should design such a curriculum?
(b) In what 'arena' should the curriculum operate?
(c) What areas of knowledge or experience should be incorporated in it?
(d) What form should it take – aims and objectives, subjects, broad areas, lists of concepts and skills, themes, or what? Should the form vary according to the area of knowledge being considered?
(e) What proportion of time should be devoted to various aspects of the curriculum?
(f) Who should monitor its operation?
(g) What steps should be taken to see that it impinges on practice and actually affects the experienced curriculum of primary pupils?

Various lines of action could be taken; only a few of the possibilities are raised here for consideration. To help prevent within-school inconsistency, participation in curriculum policy-making could be seen as part of the professional responsibility of all staff members (see Keast, 1980). Staff could use the thirty-six items as a starting point for a curriculum review, discussing which items were essential and both adding and subtracting specific forms of experience. Policy documents could be devised for every curriculum area perhaps through the efforts of working parties, and specific guidance given on those elements considered essential. More contentiously, stricter monitoring of the curriculum could be undertaken by those with responsibility for particular curriculum areas, and more opportunities made available for members of staff to observe one another teach. Cooperative planning by teachers of the same age-group could be more strongly encouraged, perhaps even insisted upon in certain 'core' areas, though diversity in 'non-core' areas could equally be encouraged. Compulsory in-service training and staff-development weeks during the children's holidays could be instituted – though this would require changes in teachers' conditions of service. Greater use could be made of semi-specialists to help prevent too great a degree of inconsistency in classes of the same age-group where teachers have markedly different strengths and weaknesses. None of these strategies would *ensure* greater consistency – teachers and children would still be the final arbiters of the experienced curriculum – but they might help promote a greater degree of consistency in both its senses than presently appears to exist.

At local authority level more could be done to foster consultation and co-ordination among primary schools concerning the range of work attempted, the delineation of essential elements to be introduced, the assessment of standards achieved, and the deployment of staff and resources to realize these expectations. More use could be made of advisory teachers (Wicksteed, 1980) or of teachers in 'shortage' curriculum areas appointed to work in a number of primary schools. Local authority guidelines, now being produced in profusion, could be a major step towards increased coordination and consistency. If they fail to achieve this, it could become necessary to establish more definitive LEA policies; perhaps even a 'partial curriculum' (whether defined in terms of broad areas or more specific forms of experience) which would be common to all schools within an authority, though this would need to be accompanied by an insistence that each school develop its own particular strengths or emphases beyond the 'partial curriculum'. Such a radical departure from tradition could have the support of far more primary teachers than professional opinion-leaders or union leaders would have us suppose. At the very least, primary schools feeding common secondary schools could develop much closer links (as have some middle schools) to ensure that there is a definite measure of consistency in the curriculum experienced by their oldest pupils prior to transfer (and not just in subjects such as French). Equally it could be argued that some more consistent form of curriculum needs to be established at national level in an effort to see that all pupils in state schools are introduced to at least a limited set of more specific forms of experience. Suitably couched in terms of skills, concepts and, perhaps, broad themes to be introduced, rather than in terms of specific content to be taught and particular facts to be acquired, such a curriculum could perhaps foster consistency without producing uniformity in either substantive curriculum content or teaching methodology.

Recent Developments Post-survey

Each of the possible lines of action suggested in the previous section could make a contribution to tackling the problem of curriculum inconsistency in primary education. Whatever readers' personal reactions to these possibilities, there is no doubt that from 1976 onwards, and especially since 1978, the Department of Education and Science and the Inspectorate have both been concerned about the problem, more so in relation to secondary schools than to primary schools, with the magnitude of the problem in primary education being, in my view, understated in their publications.

One important development was the publication in November 1979 of *Local Authority Arrangements for the School Curriculum*, a report on the Circular 14/77 review. Here the DES summarized local authorities' responses as showing 'substantial variation within the educational system in England and Wales in policies towards the curriculum' and pointed out the need 'to see what conclusions can be drawn that will lead to a more coherent approach to curricular matters across the country' (p. 2). Under the heading 'The next steps' the report continued 'The summary of responses to Circular 14/77 suggests that not all authorities have a clear view of the desirable structure of the school curriculum, especially its core elements. The Secretaries of State believe that they should give a lead in the process of reaching a national consensus on a desirable framework for the curriculum and consider the development of such a framework a priority for the education service ... an agreed framework could offer a significant step forward in the quest for improvement in the consistency and quality of school education across the country' (pp. 6–7). In the document there was no indication as to how greater consistency was conceived – whether it was defined narrowly or widely, whether it was interpreted in its 'coarse-' or 'fine-grained' sense. Only its 'arena' was specified – what was sought was a national framework fostering greater consistency from local authority to local authority.

In January 1980 was published *A framework for the school curriculum*, a consultative document issued by the DES (*not* the Inspectorate) and intended to lead to a revised version giving guidance to local authorities, schools and teachers. Its purpose was to foster a national consensus on a desirable framework for the school curriculum, but one which would nevertheless be able to take account of local needs and developments. Quoting from *Local Authority Arrangements for the School Curriculum* it attempted to clarify the respective responsibilities of central and local government for the curriculum of schools; the former was seen as having to take 'an overall view of the content and quality of education seen from the standpoint of national policies and needs as well as the resources devoted to it'. Local authorities were also to be concerned with the content and quality of education in their areas and within any nationally agreed framework were to 'exercise leadership and interpret national policies and objectives in the light of local needs and circumstances' (paragraph 2). Authorities were to devise policies for the curriculum offered in their schools and to collect information annually about the curriculum provided. For the purpose of this essay with its concern for curriculum consistency, paragraph 17 provided a particularly pertinent quotation: 'The Secretaries of State consider ... that the diversity of practice that has emerged in recent years, as shown particularly by HM Inspectors' national surveys of primary and secondary schools, makes it timely to prepare guidance on the place which certain key elements of the curriculum should have in the experience of every pupil during the compulsory period of education'. This was a clear indication of departmental concern over the unacceptable diversity of practice at school level and the necessity for a greater measure of consistency.

What sort of curriculum framework was proposed for the *primary* curriculum? How did it relate to the questions raised earlier in this essay? The authors considered that a framework should be devised by the department itself, its partners in the educational service and the wider community, and that the 'arena' for its operation should be a national one. The areas of knowledge or experience to which all pupils should have access throughout their period of compulsory primary education should be mathematics, English, science, religious education and physical education. Other areas (the arts, social studies, moral education, health education) did not feature as 'core' elements but were to find a place somewhere; whether in primary and/or secondary education, whether throughout a stage or periodically, was not made clear. The document appeared to be arguing that the framework should take the form of a set of aims plus subject areas. Proportions of time were suggested for English and mathematics (not less than 10 per cent of school time but 'a larger part' than this in the case of English) but not for the other 'core' subjects. The monitoring of the curriculum at school level was seen as the responsibility of schools themselves (through self-assessments) and of local authorities (through their annual collection and, presumably, appraisal of information).

A number of criticisms were levelled at the framework document. It was accused of lacking adequate theoretical underpinning, of being wedded to a simplistic means-end model of curriculum planning, of being written in a vague, cliché-ridden manner and of being narrowly concerned with basic education (see Golby, 1980; Garland, 1980; Lawton 1980). Its critics pointed to phrases such as 'the efficiency of schools', 'stock-taking', 'preparation for working life' etc. which, they argued, smacked more of a commercial than an educational enterprise. Whatever the validity of these criticisms (which I think were justified) the document did represent a significant departure from the *laissez-faire* curriculum policies (or non-policies) of post-war governments and did denote an attempt to provide greater curriculum coordination from the centre. For our purposes the document was significant as representing a political response to the perceived problem of curriculum inconsistency (though that particular term was never actually used). The consistency it advocated was traditionally and narrowly conceived; not in terms of a wide range of areas of experience, such as the broad areas discussed in the primary survey, but in terms of a restricted range of traditionally labelled subjects. Despite its traditional conception and its promulgation by a Conservative administration it did take some steps towards promoting greater equality of curricular opportunity in primary education by making physical and religious education essential elements [This has to be viewed against findings such as those of the Schools Council Open Plan Schools Inquiry which reports that in some infant and junior units which were observed for two different weeks by different observes, *no* time was given to physical education, social and moral education (including religious education) or environmental studies.] It also stressed that science should form part of the experiences of every primary pupil. [It is interesting to note that in a significant (?) departure from tradition the Secretaries of State went so far as to prescribe the general form primary science should take, that is, an emphasis on the processes of science.] 'Coarse-grained' consistency was sought; no attempt was made to lay down more specific forms of experience to which primary children should have access. The framework document represented one response to the problem which forms the focus of this essay.

At the same time as the consultative document was issued, the Inspectorate published *A View of the Curriculum* in their series, 'Matters for Discussion' (HMI, 1980). This was reported as their response to an invitation from the Secretaries of State (for Education and Wales) to contribute to debate about a framework by formulating a view of a possible curriculum based on their knowledge of schools. The timing of the invitation was regarded as 'opportune in that HMI have recently completed large-scale national surveys of primary and secondary education and the published reports display evidence and raise questions about curricular provision in schools' (Foreword) especially questions of 'breadth, balance and coherence' (p. 6). The booklet supported the search for greater coordination and continuity in school education and advocated devising curricular policies at national and local levels. However, the need for curricula to be responsive to 'necessary' differences in pupils or localities was stressed; there was no hint of support for a detailed, highly prescriptive, national curriculum, 'A common policy for the curriculum in this sense cannot be a prescription for uniformity. Enabling all pupils to achieve a comparable quality of education and potentially a comparable quality of adult life is a more subtle and skilled task than taking them all through identical syllabuses or teaching them all by the same methods' (p. 2).

The questions raised earlier in this paper (p. 51) can be used as a means of analysing HMI views on a possible *primary* curriculum and of comparing these with the framework document. The Inspectorate were rather more explicit about relative responsibilities for curriculum design: DES, local authorities, teachers and the wider public were seen as sharing responsibility for the broad definition of the purposes of school education, whilst means of implementing such purposes were regarded as matters for professional judgement. The areas of knowledge to which children should have access were not restricted to the five subjects of the framework; instead each child should be introduced to elements of language and literacy (broadly conceived), mathematics, science, aesthetic education, physical education and social studies (including religious education within a multicultural perspective). HMI went on to outline some of the skills, ideas and general areas of content (for example, weather studies, family history) to which children should be introduced. Curriculum policies at two different levels were envisaged: a broad national policy on the structure of the curriculum as a whole and more detailed local ones identifying *'necessary'* (my emphasis) skills and knowledge. It was in relation to such analyses that each school 'would then compose appropriate curricula for its pupils, taking into account the legitimate concerns of parents, employers and others outside the school' (p. 23). Nowhere did HMI attempt to spell out proportions of time for particular curriculum areas, nor did they discuss how monitoring of such curricula would take place.

Compared with *A framework for the School Curriculum, A View of the Curriculum* was more rigorously argued, more generously conceived, more carefully written and more subtle in its treatment of complex issues. As Garland (1980) pointed out, it 'acknowledges complexity, takes cognizance of the schools as it viewed them and bases its arguments on a theoretical perspective and current feasibility studies' (p. 26). It was intentionally but frustratingly brief and, on occasion, vague. For example, its comments on the design and form of national and local curriculum policies, alluded to in its conclusion, needed more extended treatment. It did represent an important potential contribution to the problem of curriculum consistency. With its concern for 'common requirements', alongside its apt sensitivity to local circumstances, it advocated greater consistency widely conceived. It stroves for greater consistency in both its senses; in a 'coarse-grained' sense through its advocacy of a broad national policy and in a 'fine-grained' sense through its advocacy of local analyses identifying *necessary* skills and knowledge in relation to which individual school curricula would be composed. The qualifier 'necessary' would seem to imply persuasion at local authority level for schools to meet these *necessary* requirements. Though not even hinted at, perhaps some form of local authority 'partial curriculum', as outlined previously, might have to be a necessary concomitant of such proposals.

There was one paragraph in *A View of the Curriculum* which might suggest to readers that 'fine-grained' consistency was not a major problem as far as HMI were concerned. This began: 'Current practice is such that discussion on the primary school curriculum does not need to concern itself so much with the total range of work as with the extent to which parts of the curriculum are developed, especially for the more able children. It is only provision of observational and experimental science that is seriously lacking in many primary schools, and the teaching of French that is sometimes attempted when conditions are not suitable' (p. 11). This could be interpreted as meaning that primary teachers as a whole did, in fact, introduce children to a wide range of areas of experience except science. Examined carefully, however, the writers of the passage were arguing that, in terms of 'coarse-grained' consistency, science alone was lacking in many *schools*, though it did not indicate what proportion of the total number of schools the 'many' was. It did not refer to what took place within individual *classes*. For example, health education or drama may form part of a school's curriculum but not be offered to all children because of choices made by individual teachers. Again, on closer examination, HMI were arguing that discussion was needed *not so much* over curriculum consistency in a 'coarse-grained' sense (apart from science) *as* over the shallowness of treatment accorded curricular elements. While I can see merit in this particular line of argument, I much regret the lack of reference in the document to the 'fine-grained' inconsistency revealed by those findings in chapter six of the survey. The national and local curriculum policies advocated by HMI (see the conclusion in the previous paper) could be important steps towards reducing such inconsistency, but would need supplementing by some of the more specific strategies suggested in a previous section of this article if equality of curricular opportunity for all pupils is to be more fully realised.

1981 In March 1980 was published *The School Curriculum*, the government's promised sequel to its framework document. The new paper represented a more liberal conception of the school curriculum and had clearly been greatly influenced by the views of the inspectorate as revealed in their publication discussed above. Though often trite and sometimes pretentious, except in the sections dealing with the primary and secondary phases, the document was important – not, as some believed, because it was the final, tame, end-product of the process begun in the 'Great Debate' of 1976–77, but because it represented the first (and would almost certainly not be the last) statement of government guidance on the curriculum since 1944. In it the Secretaries of State for Education and for Wales 'set down in some detail the approach to the school curriculum which they consider should now be followed in the years ahead' (page 5). The paper reaffirmed the three-fold division of responsibility for the curriculum advocated in earlier documents: the government to determine the broad approach; local education authorities to have clear curriculum policies; and schools to engage in curricular reviews so as to match their aims and activities more closely.

As far as the 'primary phase' was concerned, the guidance given was largely 'coarse-grained' with occasional 'finer grained' elements. The curriculum was to include English, mathematics, understanding the world through historical, geographical and religious education, 'practical as well as theoretical work in elementary science', and the recording and interpretation of experience through aesthetic and practical subjects such as art, music, physical education and three-dimensional craft, including work of a simple technological kind. Lack of overall curriculum consistency in current primary curricula was implicit in the statement: 'Most primary schools already incorporate most or all of these elements in their curricula; deficiencies occur less often as a matter of policy than where space is short or teaching expertise lacking' (p. 11). Much of the discussion was in terms of skills, concepts and attitudes and, unlike the framework document, no proportions of time were suggested for particular parts of the curriculum. The monitoring of such curricula was to be shared by schools themselves and by local authorities.

The publication of *The School Curriculum* reasserted the government's proper concern for the broad structure of the school curriculum. It challenged schools to engage in curricular reviews and policy-making and local authorities to reassume responsibility for the secular curriculum which they had allowed to be lost in the period since the 1944 Education Act. The document was an important step towards creating a more consistent national curriculum. However, if such a curriculum is to be realized in either a 'coarse' or 'fine-grained' sense, it will need more than government circulars or, for that matter, increased resources (immediately demanded by the document's doubters and detractors). No policy, however carefully formulated at whatever level, can *ensure* consistency; only individual teacher's consultation, preparation and implementation can provide that.

Conclusion

The primary survey raised a number of very important curriculum issues which need to be tackled as primary education enters the 'eighties. Curriculum consistency, continuity, structure, integration and evaluation are examples of such issues. This essay has focused on the first of these and has attempted to demonstrate its importance for policy-makers in schools, local authorities and nationally.

Although the appropriate degree of consistency to aim for is 'an open and contested question' (Golby, 1980), my own standpoint is clear. Much more needs to be done to foster both 'coarse-grained' and 'fine-grained' consistency, though I am not advocating all-embracing, highly specific curricula being made mandatory at either national or local levels. This personal viewpoint is contentious and may well be a minority one at the present time, but I remain convinced that a more consistent set of experiences for more pupils for a greater proportion of their time at school is a necessary step towards realizing a more genuinely comprehensive education at both primary and secondary phases. Whether as a result of DES initiatives or professional reappraisal or wider social forces, changes in the balance of educational power and changes in the primary curriculum are likely in the years ahead. I agree with Shaw (1980) when he points out that 'if the balance must be changed the best argument for doing so is one based on justice and equity in educational provision' (p. 63).

References

BENNETT, S.N. *et al*, (1980a) *Open Plan Schools: Teaching, Curriculum, Design* Slough, NFER.

BENNETT, S.N. *et al*, (1980b) 'Open plan primary schools: findings and implications of a national inquiry' *Education 3–13*, 8(1), pp. 45–50.

DEPARTMENT OF EDUCATION AND SCIENCE (1978) *Primary Education in England: A Survey by H.M. Inspectors of Schools* London, HMSO.

DEPARTMENT OF EDUCATION AND SCIENCE (1979) *Local Authority Arrangements for the School Curriculum* London, HMSO.

DEPARTMENT OF EDUCATION AND SCIENCE/WELSH OFFICE (1980) *A framework for the school curriculum* London, HMSO.

HMI (1980) *A View of the Curriculum* HMI Series: Matters for Discussion, 11, London, HMSO.

DEPARTMENT OF EDUCATION AND SCIENCE/WELSH OFFICE (1981) *The School Curriculum* London, HMSO.

GALTON, M. *et al*, (1980) *Inside the Primary Classroom* London, Routledge and Kegan Paul.

GARLAND, R. (1980) 'Department, inspectorate and the agenda for change' in GOLBY, M. (Ed) *The Core Curriculum* School of Education, University of Exeter, pp. 21–27.

GOLBY, M. (1980) 'Perspectives on the core' in GOLBY, M. (Ed) *The Core Curriculum* School of Education, University of Exeter, pp. 3–10.

KEAST, D. (1980) 'Primary curriculum planning' *Forum* 22(3), pp. 87–88.

LAWTON, D. (1980) 'What kind of common curriculum?' *Forum* 22(3), pp. 80–81.

SHAW, K. (1980) 'Policy seen from the school' in GOLBY, M. (Ed) *The Core Curriculum* School of Education, University of Exeter, pp. 57–63.

THOMAS, N. (1980) 'The primary curriculum: survey findings and implications' in RICHARDS, C. (Ed) *Primary Education: Issues for the Eighties* London, A. and C. Black, pp. 3–16.

WICKSTEED, D. (1980) 'Supporting support' *Education 3–13*, 8(1), p. 3.

Table 1. Curriculum Items found to occur individually in at least 80% of classes inspected.

Language: Listening and Talking
(a) children taught to (i) follow instructions
(ii) follow the plot of a story
(iii) comprehend the main ideas in information given to them.
(b) children talked informally to one another during the course of the working day
(c) discussion took place between children and teachers when new vocabulary was introduced

---

Language: Reading and Writing
(a) in 7 and 9 year old classes children practised reading from a main reading scheme and from supplementary readers
(b) in 9 and 11 year old classes children read fiction and non-fiction which was not related to other work they were doing in the classroom

(c) in 11 year old classes children made use of information books related to work in other areas of the curriculum
(d) at each age children were encouraged to select books of their own choice
(e) children were given handwriting practice
(f) children undertook descriptive and narrative writing
(g) in 9 and 11 year old classes children did written work on prescribed topics related to other parts of the curriculum

Mathematics:

Work was done to enable children to learn:
(a) to use language appropriate to the properties of number, size, shape and position
(b) to recognize relationships in geometrical shapes, numbers, ordered arrangements and everyday things
(c) to appreciate place value and recognize simpler number patterns
(d) to carry out suitable calculations involving +, −, × and ÷ with whole numbers
(e) to understand money and the value of simple purchases
(f) to use numbers in counting, describing and estimating
(g) in 7 year old classes children undertook practical activities involving addition, subtraction, multiplication and division

In 11 year old classes children were taught to:
(h) estimate and use measurements of length, weight, area, volume and time
(i) work with the four rules of number including two places of decimals
(j) calculate using decimals
(k) use fractions, including the idea of equivalence, and apply them to everyday things
(l) use various forms of visual presentation including three dimensional and diagrammatic forms

Aesthetic and physical education

The programme to work included:
(a) singing
(b) listening to music
(c) two or three dimensional work showing evidence of observation of pattern *or* colour *or* texture *or* form
(d) in 7 year old classes, practice of skills in gymnastics *or* games *or* swimming
(e) in 9 and 11 year old classes, gymnastic skills
(f) in 9 and 11 year old classes, practice of skills in playing games
(g) in 11 year old classes, swimming lessons.

Social abilities and moral learning

Work was arranged to promote the following:
(a) reliability and responsible attitudes
(b) consideration for other people; for example, good manners, concern, friendship
(c) respect for surroundings and the care of materials and objects in the classroom and school
(d) participation as a member of a group or team, learning to following rules and obey instructions
(e) involvement in the development of religious ideas and moral values during the school assembly
(f) in 9 and 11 year old classes, awareness of historical change and causal

factors in relation to the way people lived or behaved in the past
[The incidence for this item in 9 and 11 year old classes was slightly
below 80%.]

(g) in 9 and 11 year old classes, work relating to at least one of the following
aspects of geography: population, agriculture, industry, transport, or
resources within or outside the locality [The incidence for this item in
9 and 11 year old classes was slightly below 80%.]

*Table 2. The percentage of classes undertaking all widely taught items in each
subject and in social abilities.*

	7 year old classes	9 year old classes	11 year old classes
Mathematics	65	76	58
English language	54	43	53
Aesthetic and physical education	73	63	58
Social abilities	65	46	61

Table 3. The percentage of classes undertaking all widely taught items for combinations of two or more subjects.

	7 year old classes	9 year old classes	11 year old classes
Items for English language and mathematics combined	42	37	39
Items for English language, mathematics and aesthetic and physical education combined	35	28	28
Items for English language, mathematics and social abilities combined	33	24	32
All items combined	29	19	24

Curriculum Policy Making in Primary Schools

Roy Garland
University of Exeter

In the warm after-glow of the Plowden Report (CACE, 1967) it was easy to accept that English primary schools were amongst the best, if not indeed the best, in the world. There appeared to be no criticisms of consequence to be made of their achievements, of their values and of the embodiment of these in practice. Visitors came from many parts of the world to observe what was considered to be forward-looking practice influenced and informed by the tenets of progressivism. This rather complacent picture, shaped not by the reality of classroom practice in the majority of primary schools but more by a romantic view of childhood and undue publicity for the practices in certain localized areas, has received sufficient jolts in the past decade finally to shatter it. Sharp and Green (1975) and King (1978) have drawn attention to discrepancies between the rhetoric that sustains progressivism and the reality which operational considerations impose upon actual classroom practice. Bennett *et al*'s (1976) investigation threw doubts on the effectiveness of 'informal' teaching methods in bringing about optimum learning in the basic skills of numeracy and literacy and official publications (DES, 1978, 1980) have drawn attention to the lack of balance in a curriculum that omits the physical sciences.

The myth that all is automatically well with primary education has departed and has been replaced by judgements substantiated by research (DES, 1978). They indicate that primary schools are characterized by good personal relationships and a concern that their pupils should be both numerate and literate. This concern has, however, tended to produce a curriculum where skills are constantly in danger of separation from the subjects they serve and has possibly drawn attention away from the needs of the more able pupils. What is also apparent is that these schools are far more complex institutions than they were a couple of decades ago. One has only to compare the curriculum suggestions in the Handbook of Suggestions for Teachers (BoE, 1937) with the factors in Annex B of the Primary Survey (DES, 1978) to appreciate how the curriculum has widened and that the range of responsibilities it is considered appropriate for their brief.

One result has been the growth of management structures that in a sense have been parasitic on an existing system of extra payments for being an experienced and sound classroom practitioner: the post of special responsibility. The creation of these structures to organize, monitor and control a more complex curriculum has been given a powerful legitimating voice in the recommendation of Her Majesty's Inspectorate in the Primary Survey (DES, 1978) where they examined the role and effectiveness of what might be termed the middle management: staff receiving enhanced payments on salary scales 2 and 3. By and large they were not over impressed with what they saw and suggested that attention needed to be paid to the duties of these teachers and the contributions that they might make to the wider workings of the school. A principal task of this particular group of teachers is likely to be the development and implementation of policies in the curriculum areas of mathematics, language and science. The phenomenon of the primary school policy on various key curriculum areas is comparatively recent and again is a response to wider influences. Primary schools have always had whole school curriculum documents: the ubiquitous yet neutered 'scheme of work' is an obvious example. These were designed to give a degree of coherence, unity and continuity to the work of the school but frequently they were arbitrarily created by the headteacher to impress curious visitors rather than to inform and guide practice. They were considered to be a professional irrelevance by many classroom teachers: a curricular placebo.

Policies are not of this nature. With schemes of work they share the characteristics of being documents that are concerned with more than day-to-day planning but they are spurs to action rather than repositories of inactive intent. The term seems new in primary school parlance: it has been possible to find guidelines, syllabuses, frameworks, suggestions, notes and checklists, but only in recent times, policies. No doubt policies will inherit some of the characteristics of all these documents but they seem to be distinct in that they represent a process during which a school has conscientiously engaged in examining an area of its curriculum. As such they are significant for they are the artifacts of professional collaboration, dispute and self-examination. They contain implications for in-service education and professional development; they represent the signs of the emergence of new career possibilities for primary school teachers as *sic!* curriculum consultants with real curricular responsibilities outside of their own classrooms.

Not much appears to be known about the growth of such policies or what might be considered good professional practice in the area. How do schools identify their priorities? How might such school-focused activities be conducted? How might the autonomy, professional interests and needs of individual teachers be harmonized with the wider requirements of the school? How can agreed policies be translated into action and what procedures might be developed to monitor and evaluate what happens? To attempt to identify in a more systematic fashion the questions *THE* that should be asked and to locate and examine policy creation in primary *STUDY* schools, a pilot investigation was instituted in 1979/80 with the intention of the work being developed in subsequent years. The investigation was sponsored as part of a university's in-service education provision and supported by a LEA and took the form of a small research orientated group of two university lecturers with background in primary education and eight headteachers of primary schools. The heads were invited to join the group. All could easily travel to the university and all had previously attended a substantial in-service course of some two terms in length dealing with primary school management. It cannot be claimed, therefore, that the group represented a typical cross-section of primary schools. In fact, the schools tended to be situated in small towns or villages in a predominantly rural region. The headteachers were familiar with the notion of curriculum management and in sympathy with the concept of research-informed action. An aim of the work was not to establish what might be typical school approaches but to explore what might count as informed practice with the ultimate intention of disseminating the information to a wider professional audience.

The group worked both explicitly and implicitly with a model of teacher and school development that celebrates praxis: the systematic and critical examination of one's own practice with the view to improvement. Within this framework meetings were held during the autumn term when on-going policies in the schools were identified and discussed and where plans for the development of the work during the spring term were made. In this term, the schools were visited on a number of occasions by the university tutors, staff meetings were attended, teachers were interviewed and case studies developed. During the summer term meetings were held at the university to discuss the findings and to explore their general validity.

The work is on-going and, under current consideration, are the issues of dissemination and the possibility of extending the group's work to other local authorities.

Inevitably given the scope and on-going nature of the project, definitive conclusions would be inappropriate; what would seem to be more apposite would be a tentative identification of a number of the issues that surrounded the policy making in these schools. In this sense the approach has some of the characteristics of the discovery of grounded theory (Glaser and Strauss, 1968) in that it seeks to move from practice to generate theory rather than verify existing *a priori* assumptions.

The issues conveniently crystallize about a number of general questions: 'How did the policies arise?' 'How did the schools cope with policy making?' 'What key factors might be associated with the progress and success of the policy creating process?'. In considering why particular policies arose at certain periods, the individuality and uniqueness of schools have to be acknowledged – although none of the schools in the small sample would claim to be anything special, each displayed differences in approach and style arising from the contingencies of their growth and development in particular communities. Yet although it is essential to acknowledge this point it was also apparent that many shared similar concerns: the development of coherent and effective policies in mathematics, language and science. A clue to the reasons why diversity of leadership style, of institutional history and particular day-to-day problems can lead to the addressing of broadly similar problems may be provided by the concepts of *planning priorities* and *curriculum priorities* (figure 1.). Interplay between these two concepts suggested explanations of the emergence of certain policies at broadly similar points in time. Planning and curriculum priorities are related in that they both point to the adoption of a new, or the reactivization or refinement of an existing, policy. They differ, however, on a number of important dimensions: planning priorities arise from the multitude of practical and contingent considerations that schools face in maintaining what might be termed an efficient service; curriculum priorities are universal in their concerns. They relate to the fact that teachers are the members of a profession with beliefs and values regarding education and what constitutes sound professional practice; they are linked to curriculum theory in that all schools have to justify their answers to certain basic questions regarding what is to be learnt, how it is to be learnt, by whom it is to be learnt and how the learning is to be evaluated. Planning priorities have two major components: contingent factors and operating factors. Operating factors point to the multitude of immediate decisions that have to be made to keep the school running smoothly. They are affected by such matters as the availability of professional and ancilliary staff, the fact that children require a high degree of supervision, that unanticipated events occur and compete for attention with more routine practices. They are located within the rise and fall of seasonal pressures, such as

Figure 1. Factors Influencing the Emergence of Primary School Policies

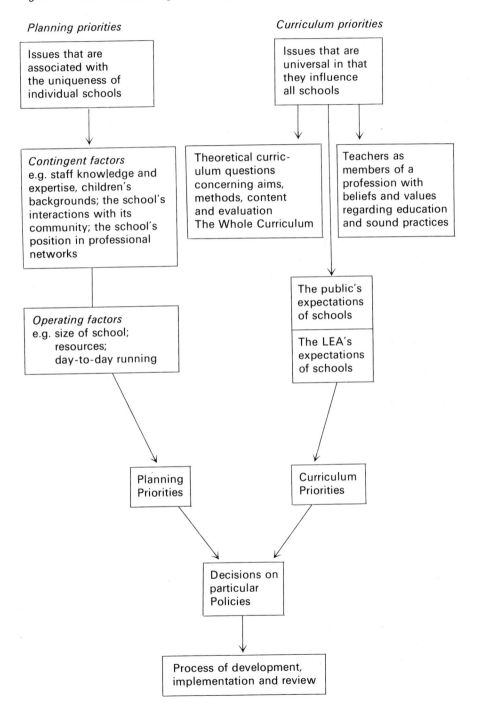

Planning priorities

Issues that are associated with the uniqueness of individual schools

Curriculum priorities

Issues that are universal in that they influence all schools

Contingent factors
e.g. staff knowledge and expertise, children's backgrounds; the school's interactions with its community; the school's position in professional networks

Theoretical curriculum questions concerning aims, methods, content and evaluation
The Whole Curriculum

Teachers as members of a profession with beliefs and values regarding education and sound practices

Operating factors
e.g. size of school;
     resources;
     day-to-day running

The public's expectations of schools

The LEA's expectations of schools

Planning Priorities

Curriculum Priorities

Decisions on particular Policies

Process of development, implementation and review

those which occur at the end of the Christmas term. The normal running of the school consumes an enormous amount of energy and time; it is accorded the highest priority. It could be hypothesized that a school's ability to generate policies of a longer term nature is correlated positively with ways in which day-to-day running is made routine so as to avoid proceeding from one crisis to another.

Contingent factors acknowledge that all schools are heirs to particular traditions and histories and are staffed by teachers with varying experience, skills, knowledge, interests, attitudes and motivation. The fact that a certain set of circumstances might be considered contingent does not mean that they are necessarily internal. An important and influential factor that differs from school to school is its position on various professional networks and its consequential relationship with other institutions and individuals. Schools can be represented on district academic councils, send members on courses, invite consultants from higher education establishments to run school-focused or school-based courses, and explain and justify their affairs to the local advisory service and the national Inspectorate. There is an element of 'entrepreneurism' regarding the exploitation of these networks: schools in the sample had enlisted the services of a local college of education to assist with the creation of a science programme; one had persuaded an HMI to run a school-based course. Within the nexus of communication and interaction, all the schools informally evaluated their own performance and identified their own needs and planning priorities: one school had decided to examine its project work with a view to establishing progression, another was concerned with the number of formal English exercises set and wished to develop a variety of methods to improve children's language skills. Several schools reported interest in assessing the place of science in their curriculum.

Particular policies are not, however, the result of purely local considerations. Teachers are members of a profession and have views on what is to be judged sound practice acquired from initial and recurrent training, and reflection upon personal experience. School policies are also a matter of public interest. All members of the group agreed that schools have increasingly to explain the conduct of their affairs to a wider lay and professional audience. Although the automatic right for others to know is contested and although ways in which this might be done, if considered desirable, have only been crudely developed, it seems reasonable to assume that schools will have increasingly to bear a wide audience in mind when policies are being formulated.

Planning and curriculum priorities are not necessarily in harmony. In this particular investigation cases were cited of a local education authority suggesting what a school's planning priorities should be. On certain occasions schools were required to produce in writing their policy on an issue such as school discipline, to discuss this with the school managers, and to send a copy to the authority. It was not known by the group why these particular documents were required and they found it difficult to fit them into any overall concept of the local authority curriculum policy or indeed to discover what happened to them once submitted. While the legal rights of the authority curriculum-wise are not in dispute, they are subject to interpretation. There appears to be a natural history in the development of school policies arising from a delicate inter-play between an assessment of internal and external factors. If a powerful and legitimate institution 'jumps the queue', the results could be dysfunctional if it turns the school away from what are seen as the real issues. Low priority is given to this type of demand and the result appears to be a shadow exercise where paper policies are concocted. The cost is a diversion from concentration on the issues the school perceives as pressing. This periodic demand from the authority seemed particularly oppressive to the head of a small school who had to meet every request personally with no way of delegating responsibility.

The possible ways in which the imperatives of policy making emerge have been explored: what of the strategies and tactics that these heads adopted? As Nias (1980) has pointed out, the style adopted by headteachers varies, as does the priority they give to the various management tasks which institutions face in order to maintain themselves. In Nias's terms, the headteachers in this sample appeared to be positive in their leadership: they did not let issues drift without clear direction, neither did they rule by fiat but set considerable value on consultation, cooperation and staff involvement. A major decision made, however, by the head alone concerned the overall strategy of a concurrent or consecutive development of policies. In the former case a number of issues, for example, language and science would be dealt with simultaneously, in the latter the whole attention of the staff would be concentrated on one curriculum area usually for the period of a term. Evidence does not exist in this investigation of the comparative effectivenesses of the approaches, but the consecutive approach seems to be more associated with established heads while those who were more recently appointed seem to prefer the speed but extra work load of concurrent development. Not unexpectedly, given the leadership style of the heads, developments were not left to chance but were orchestrated. The heads, indeed, had definite views on the constitution of a sound policy and they took positive action to attempt to bring it about. The action had a number of elements: the development of staff skills, information gathering and piloting ideas. This orchestration was applied with tactics that emphasized gradualism, building on existing strengths and consultation. It was tempered by an assessment of the morale and general well being of the staff: perhaps the quintessence of successful policy making are these judgements by the headteacher on what is necessary, practical and opportune.

The development of staff skills is related to an issue raised earlier: the emergence of middle managers in the primary school. The heads invariably encouraged one of their staff to take responsibility for a curriculum area. An interesting symbiotic relationship then developed with the member of staff taking initiatives, convening and chairing meetings, circulating documents and materials and giving advice but within the ambience of the head's general approval. None of the teachers had had any training for their newly emerging role and, given the nature of primary school teaching, few had opportunities during the day to plan or discuss or consult: all had full-time class teaching commitments. New skills had to be learnt on the task: this point is likely to be repeated in any primary school that develops in the directions discussed in this article and it does pose pressing questions regarding in-service provision for this group.

In the actual process of policy development, all the schools made conscious efforts to increase the amount of information available to them. A variety of practices were evident: reviewing books, testing apparatus, attending courses, generating school-focused and school-based courses, visiting other schools, arranging for visits by local advisers and advisory teachers and tapping the strengths of the local further and higher education institutions. This might be viewed as a particularly interesting and encouraging finding, for curriculum development seems often to be guided mainly by the personal experiences, enthusiasms and prejudices of the participants rather than by a more knowledge-based approach. A concomitant phenomenon was the trying out of new ideas without a necessarily ideological commitment to making them work: one school was assessing the advisability of combining or separating environmental studies and science, another was considering whether to continue to use a particular schools' broadcast as a contribution to its language policy.

Primary schools have, in the past, tended not to document their work in ways that could inform the outsider of their aims, values and priorities and convey the particular demands, tribulations and rewards of their endeavours. In these schools there was a degree of documentation originated by others than the head but the teachers did not write about their jobs: they talked about them in a way that perhaps is not easy for the uninitiated to appreciate. If, as seems likely, we are moving towards creating meaningful, professionally binding yet constantly evolving curriculum policies, then permanent records of the guidelines and the ways of working that have been currently agreed upon are going to be necessary. These schools would not, however, necessarily agree. Attempts to encourage the compiling of systematic accounts of the process of development were resisted on the grounds of the bureaucratic nature of the undertaking, and doubts as to whether the extra effort involved would be justified. One head was firmly of the view that paper products were of secondary importance when measured against the value of the discussions in which his staff were engaged.

There was evidence of a possible contradiction or at least a paradox in the work of these schools. Mention has been made of the efforts to make informed judgements regarding the introduction of new ideas by collecting relevant information. These efforts, characterized by a degree of opportunism as well as preplanning, were frequently evident. Efforts, however, to apply similar techniques to the on-going monitoring and evaluation of existing policies were not so evident. It could be that the assumption is that, once the initial gradient of initiation and implementation has been climbed, the policy will reach a plateau of institutional stability and will maintain itself in a relatively unchanging state. Alternatively, the concept of policies may be so new that a sufficient time lapse has not occurred to make such monitoring meaningful. Only one school in the group appeared to be preparing to embark in a systematic fashion upon such an enterprise. In this case there was action not because of any crisis but because the head considered it part of good professional practice.

In these schools it has been suggested that the heads played a major and significant role in policy development by their choice of strategy, orchestration, style and sense of timing. But although seemingly exuding authority, power and patronage, they are dependent on the good will and cooperation of their staff. What views do the classroom teachers hold on the current concern with whole school curriculum policies? Do they consider it to be an enfringement upon their legitimate universe of professional decision-making or as a guide in areas of uncertainty? The evidence available is based on interviews with some dozen teachers in two of the schools and its likelihood of providing definitive answers is small. It does, however, provide a number of pointers towards issues and some interesting areas for further investigation for one of the missing voices in the whole-curriculum debate has been that of the class teacher; for ideas to flourish in schools it will be necessary for them to become part of the teachers' vocabularies of action. Ideas are more likely to be implemented by those who help to generate them. All the teachers interviewed would appear to be in this category: they had had opportunities to contribute to the on-going policy debate within their school.

Given the fact of teacher involvement it is not surprising to find their attitudes positive and supportive of curriculum policy making. They tended however to link the moves in this direction with forces external to the school rather than as examples of teacher initiative. Several pointed graphically upwards when discussing this point with a comment that it was someone 'up there'. Others spoke of the plethora of offical reports and also of the fact that the ending of selection at '11 +' had temporarily left a void in external assessment of primary schools. Given that policies were seen as a response, opposition to the concept would be understandable. The teachers, however, saw them as helpful: it was useful to know what was expected of one; they could provide guidelines that would prevent duplication of work. They were considered to be particularly useful for less experienced teachers or those new to the school. Although the teachers accepted the principle, they had views regarding the characteristics of a good policy: it should be flexible and non-directive and should not infringe on their right to select their own teaching method. If policies were of this nature then it was considered that teachers had no right to opt out: professional autonomy was acknowledged to have limits. Dangers were, however, identified: children's interests could be ignored; spontaneous and opportunistic teaching might suffer. It was also considered that such documents could mislead if they were to be interpreted as an exact record of a class's work rather than representing a statement of general intent.

Previously, if a teacher required definite advice or support on any aspect of the curriculum from needlework through music to language and mathematics, he or she approached the head. Leadership in curriculum issues had not devolved. A move towards the more formal consultation of colleagues is an innovation but, nevertheless, one that was welcomed by the heads who freely acknowledged that it was impossible to keep up to date in every area of the curriculum. The teachers interviewed accepted the legitimacy of the newly emerging role of curriculum consultant. They considered, however, that the person involved should still have responsibilities for a class: credibility would grow from being a good class teacher rather than from an ability to produce policy statements. It was considered that there should be close liaison with the headteacher who should retain ultimate responsibility. The consultant should act as a coordinator, facilitator and adviser and should work closely with colleagues: there should be no unilateral decisions made but the agreement of the staff should be sought. Interpersonal skills and professional sensitivity were not enough: knowledge of the subject and its current development were essential, and an ability to produce teaching material based on them desirable. It was also considered desirable that the consultant should obtain wider perspectives on the school's needs by teaching classes other than their own. The broad picture that emerges from the interviews is of teachers giving general approval to policy development because it created the security of guidelines, provided opportunities to counter the professional isolation endemic in teaching, and contributed to professional development.

Earlier mention was made of the concept of curriculum priorities: part of these priorities is likely to be a concept of the whole curriculum. If the case is accepted for the development and monitoring of policies across various constituent elements of the curriculum to curtail duplication and to aid continuity, it is proper to ask how might particular initiatives and decisions relate to the total pattern of a school's activities. To date there have been relatively few attempts to examine this complex question. Two of the most penetrating and sustained theoretical analyses in recent years have been those by Dearden (1968) and Wilson (1971). Dearden emphasized a knowledge-based approach while Wilson developed the essentially moral claim that we should give primacy to the pursuit of the interests of children albeit in a systematic and disciplined fashion. Although written from differing perspectives both are united in their concern to illuminate the totality of a child's educational experiences from a philosophical viewpoint.

Other attempts to develop the concept of the whole curriculum have been made by Schools Council (1972) but the issue has been given a sense of urgency with the publication not only of the Primary Survey (DES, 1978) but by the increasing interest of central government in the curriculum field (DES, 1980). The pressure for an explicit statement of whole curriculum policy by schools has come in the main from outside bodies: this is really not surprising. We can appreciate and understand what is happening in schools by examining tradition, yet what is at stake is not solely pedagogical: social, cultural, economic and the political issues of accountability are involved. What occurs in schools matters! Schools will need to take cognizance of these pressures: however formidable the task of formulating and implementing a concept of the whole curriculum might be, it cannot go by default: to have no policy is a policy. All schools have an implicit model of the curriculum built within the priorities they afford issues and their modes of operation. Intelligent and informed policy making requires that the model is made explicit.

There is evidence of the difficulties that class teachers experience in articulating their concept of the relationships of their work to the whole (Keast, 1974). The operational demands of the day-to-day running of a class provide little opportunity or incentive to adopt a holistic viewpoint. The practice of staying with a particular class rather than gaining experience by professional mobility across the whole spectrum of ages results in a limited knowledge of the totality of curriculum experiences and activities offered by the school or of their sequencing and continuity. A ubiquitous form of within-class organization that has been categorized by Bennett *et al*, (1980) as the 'split half' also mitigates against seeing one's work as a whole: at its simplistic it results in 'basics' in the morning and 'frills' in the afternoon.

The Primary Survey (DES, 1978) contains a view of the curriculum that stresses cohesion and deprecates teaching knowledge or skills in isolation. The inspectorate's view of the curriculum is unfortunately buried in the document: it is however implicit within the schedules (Annex B) which were used in inspecting classes. It would appear to owe much to the seminal work of Hirst and Peters (1970) on the concept of a liberal education. It is a view which stresses structured experience rather than self-directed discovery and which points towards the importance of the application of knowledge and skills. At its heart is a celebration of the central task of education as fostering knowledge and understanding. The model contained within the Survey has five main areas: language and mathematics which are seen as spanning the whole of the curriculum; aesthetics including arts and crafts, music and physical education; experimental and observational science; social abilities including history, geography and religious education. In human affairs alternatives are not always apparent but they are always possible. It does seem likely, however, that the model will be realized in practice. This result is possible because of a combination of the prestige and authority of the inspectorate, the unquestioned acceptance of the theoretical basis on which their suggestions rest and the current demands supported by central government that schools should articulate their purposes. The emergence of the model in practice will be gradual: the growth of publicly articulated views of the whole curriculum will require skills of management and leadership from headteachers and a degree of professional reorientation on the part of teachers.

It has been argued that policy making represents a new and significant development in the history of primary education and that it is one that is likely to take root. It represents a method of coping with change and a flood of new ideas and knowledge by the incorporation of the values and shared perceptions of a staff into an agenda for action. It provides opportunities for the talents, understandings and insights of teachers to be available to the whole school rather than just their own class and as such has a powerful potential for professional development and consequences for in-service education. It has also been suggested that particular policies must be wedded to a concept of the whole curriculum. Unless this occurs, any particular curriculum policies, not withstanding the enthusiasm and commitment with which they were developed, will run the risk of being free-floating and independent entities. Primary school teachers have supported a concept of integration that aimed to break down subject barriers within the classroom. The concept of the whole curriculum with its dependent issues of policy development is another variant of integration that subsumes individual classes in a bid for cohesion and continuity in the educational encounters we offer our children.

References

BENNETT, S.N. et al, (1976) Teaching Styles and Pupil Progress London, Open Books.
BENNETT, S.N. et al, (1980) Open Plan Schools Slough, NFER.
BOARD OF EDUCATION (1937) Handbook of Suggestions for the Consideration of Teachers and Others Concerned in the Work of Public Elementary Schools HMSO.
CENTRAL ADVISORY COUNCIL FOR EDUCATION (1967) Children and Their Primary Schools (Plowden Report) London, HMSO.
DEARDEN, R.F. (1968) The Philosophy of Primary Education: An Introduction London, Routledge and Kegan Paul.
DEPARTMENT OF EDUCATION AND SCIENCE (1978) Primary Education in England: A Survey by HM Inspectors of Schools London, HMSO.
DEPARTMENT OF EDUCATION AND SCIENCE (1980) A Framework for the School Curriculum London, HMSO.
GLASER, B.G. and STRAUSS, A.L. (1968) The Discovery of Grounded Theory New York,

Weidenfeld and Nicholson.

HIRST, P.H. and PETERS, R.S. (1970) *The Logic of Education* London, Routledge and Kegan Paul.

KEAST, D.J. (1974) 'Exeter middle schools: Their emergence and curriculum' Unpublished M.Ed. Thesis. University of Bristol.

KING, R. (1978) *All Things Bright and Beautiful: A Sociological Study of Infants' Classrooms* London, Wiley.

NIAS, J. (1980) 'Leadership styles and job-satisfaction in primary schools' in BUSH, T. *et al*, (Eds) *Approaches to School Management* New York Harper and Row.

SCHOOLS COUNCIL (1972) *Education in the Middle Years* London, Evans Brothers.

SHARP, R. and GREEN, A. (1975) *Education and Social Control: A Study in Progressive Primary Education* London, Routledge and Kegan Paul.

WILSON, P.A. (1971) *Interest and Discipline in Education* London, Routledge and Kegan Paul.

*Should science be taught in primary schools?**

Jack Kerr
University of Leicester
and
Elizabeth Engel
NFER

A positive answer to the question posed in the title of this article is conceded at the outset, but a detailed response must surely depend on the resolution of a number of problems. First, what precisely do we mean by primary science? Has the approach as represented by the Nuffield Junior Science and Science 5–13 Projects resulted in more scientific investigations in classrooms? Is the time appropriate to re-examine the current orthodoxy which lays so much more emphasis on ways of behaving scientifically than on science itself? At the five to eleven year stage, should the case for a more ordered and deliberate introduction of essential scientific concepts be given further thought? Do we know how children learn to behave in scientific ways? How adequate is the provision for the preparation of primary school teachers, at both initial and post-experience stages, to cope with scientific activities in their classrooms? Attention must be focused on these important questions if planned scientific experiences are to become accessible to young children.

Although we believe it is essential to provide opportunities for children of all ages to enjoy scientific experiences, translation of this conviction into practice is known to be far from simple. And the dichotomy (which has always been a dichotomy in theory only) between, at the one extreme, science as a means of acquiring skills and attitudes characteristic of the discipline and, at the other, science as learning information has not neces-sarily provided us with a useful framework for practice. Wynne Harlen (1978) has analyzed the alternative approaches to primary science and attempts to find some guidelines for avoiding the errors of both extreme

---

*This is an edited version of the article which appeared in *Education 3–13*, 8(1), (1980), pp. 4–8.

positions. The questions we have posed need to be re-examined, but perhaps a de-emphasis of the processes/content polarization and a conscious avoidance of extreme views of science may provide a more useful context for this re-examination.

Assessment of Progress in Primary Science

Judged on the basis of published material alone, the reader might conclude that the past twenty year period has been one of unusual progress and innovation. Apart from the mass of commercially-produced books, kits and resources of all kinds, since 1964, at least six project teams in Britain alone have been actively developing curricular materials for teachers to stimulate and support scientific activities and experiences with young children. Many reports have been published by the Association for Science Education, the Department of Education and Science, the British Association and other bodies. The Interim Report of the Schools Council's Impact and Take-Up Project (Steadman *et al*, 1978) suggests that in quantitative terms the outcome of all this activity has been disappointing. The Nuffield Junior Science Project materials were familiar (that is, 'read parts or know well') in only 18 per cent of a random sample of 279 primary schools. According to the headteachers, 13 per cent of schools in the sample were using the materials but only 7 per cent of the teachers agreed that they were doing so. The Science 5–13 Project was known to 30 per cent of the same sample, 36 per cent of the headteachers claiming the books were used, as against 22 per cent of their teachers. Science 5–13 books were actually seen by members of the project team in 50 per cent of the schools visited. It is interesting that when about six hundred teachers were asked which national curriculum project was 'best known', Science 5–13 ranked very highly – fourth out of 107 projects listed. In Ashton's study (Ashton *et al*, 1975) based on data collected in 1969–72 – 1513 teachers rated 72 aims of primary education in order of importance. That the child should 'know some basic scientific procedures and concepts' was ranked 62nd; 'know basic facts of sex and reproduction' 63rd; and 'understand how the body works', 64th. Yet scientific activity in the classroom would be a powerful means of achieving other, more highly-ranked aims in Ashton's study. For example, 'to make reasoned judgements and choices' was 23rd in importance of the same 72 aims; 'a questioning attitude to his environment' ranked 24th; 'inventiveness and creativity', 30th; and 'to observe carefully, accurately, and with sensitivity', 37th. This discrepancy, between the ranking of aims which specifically mention science and the ranking of more generally expressed aims which in fact describe important aspects of scientific (and, of course, other) activity, is interesting. It may be that many primary teachers simply do not recognize the particular contribution science could make to the achievement of aims which they themselves rank highly, or it may be that they would prefer to try to achieve these aims in non-scientific contexts in which they feel more comfortable. The most recent report on the state of science in primary education in England is based on a survey of 1127 classes in 542 schools by HM Inspectorate. They found that the 'work in observational and experimental science was less well matched to children's capabilities than work in any other area of the curriculum' ... 'only a small minority recognized the important contribution which science could make to children's intellectual develop-ment'...and...'the ideas and materials produced by curriculum develop-ment projects have had little impact in the majority of schools' (HMI, 1978, chapter 5, iv, p. 58).

In summary, the evidence suggests that many primary teachers are aware of the existence of important curricular developments in primary science, they rank highly objectives which science educators would recog-nize can be achieved through planned scientific activity, and yet there seems to be precious little scientific activity going on in our classrooms. Apart from inspired work by a minority of schools and teachers' centres, it is clear that our efforts to spread science teaching in primary schools over the past decade have been largely ineffective. Why is there so little visible progress? Is it simply that the pace of any educational change is always painfully slow? Are there any other reasons?

A Reassessment of Policy

Factors commonly thought to impede the improvement of science at the primary stage include:

(i)   the poor science background of teachers, resulting in lack of confidence to attempt work in science;
(ii) failure of headteachers to recognize the potential contribution of science to the curriculum; and
(iii) inadequate provision of simple apparatus and materials.

These obstacles to change will be looked at later, but there may be a more fundamental reason why progress has been so slow.

The writings on child development of Isaacs, Dewey, Piaget and others had a powerful influence on most of us in the 1960s. The case for more openness, more activity and more concern for the individual child won over the Plowden Committee, whose work was in progress at the same time as the Nuffield Junior Science Project. This project team followed suit, and recommended that children should be allowed to investigate the environment by working at self-appointed tasks to develop skills of observing, questioning, exploring, interpreting findings and communi-cating, across the curriculum. The team argued that at this stage starting to *do* science was more important than science itself. The so-called 'process approach' to primary science had arrived. Few noticed the much-less publicized Oxford Primary Science Project (Redman *et al*, 1969) supported by the Ministry of Education which produced its report in 1969, a little later than Nuffield Junior Science. The Oxford group argued that it was impossible to ignore the fact that 'children will bring science into the school' and it was vital to include the contribution of science in the interpretation of the environment. Children must be given an understanding of some of the essential ideas used by scientists. Four main concept areas – energy, structure, chance and life – were explored by methods which were not *in fact* dissimilar to those recommended by the Nuffield group. But to no avail. The all-embracing child-centred philosophy dominated discussion about the whole of the primary curriculum, and generally precluded consideration of materials such as the Oxford project which delineated content areas for scientific exploration.

The process-content debate, referred to earlier, has been with us since the start of science teaching. It figured in varying degrees in Henry Armstrong's campaign for discovery methods a hundred years ago, the general science movement of the 1950s and all the Nuffield Science Teaching Projects. But at no time did we try to lay so much emphasis on process and attitude objectives as in recommendations for primary science a decade ago. This sophisticated orthodoxy – for this is what the process approach has become for teachers – was so deep-rooted that, until recently, few people were prepared to appear so heretical as to question it. Could it be that progress in primary science has been limited because the *general* principles controlling primary policy have been applied unbendingly in the case of science? In Harlen's paper, referred to earlier, she lists examples of 'guidelines to content' to meet the process criteria (pp. 622–624), but at the same time emphasizing that 'the content objectives must not be allowed to replace the process and attitude objectives'. The same shift to a more practical balance, albeit tentative, is detectable in the HMIs report and, more overtly, in a recent article by Norman Booth, 1978). At present the content of primary science is left almost entirely to chance, a state of affairs which puts a considerable strain on conscientious teachers who lack sufficient background and experience of science. We conclude that if science *should* continue to be taught in primary schools, an adjustment of policy is desirable. Perhaps we should begin by forgetting all about the process-content dichotomy, and look more closely at how the child acquires scientific skills and attitudes as well as an understanding of essential concepts, and then at what the teacher is required to do about it.

Children's Scientific Ideas

The fact that learning depends on the learner successfully relating new experience to what is already known is crucial to all theories of cognitive development, and is an idea familiar to teachers. It follows that what a learner brings to a learning situation is of great importance. Irene Finch (1971) makes a very interesting distinction in this connection. She suggests that teachers of English show interest in children's own ideas and opinions, but by contrast, science teachers frequently give the impression that children's ideas are not worth much consideration beside those of great scientists. She goes on:

> But the English teacher is not, and cannot, be aiming at producing a class of Shakespeares, and we cannot be aiming at producing a class of scientists ... Somehow we must arrange for children to produce useful scientific ideas in our lessons, and to get credit and kudos for them. (p. 407)

Many teachers would agree, and some science educators (for example, Driver and Easley, (1978); Deadman and Kelly, (1978)) have suggested that there is a need to look more fundamentally and in detail at pupils' own understandings and ways of thinking about scientific ideas, and to use this information in planning teaching strategies. Thus the traditional Curriculum/Pupil model would be reversed; pupil understanding would be investigated *first* and then gradually incorporated into teaching and curricular planning. As with classical botany and zoology (on which the modern study of these subjects is founded), it may be that the first job is description and classification.

But is this any more than good teachers have always done? Good practice has always included listening carefully to individual children's ideas and then beginning from the vantage point of the learner's own experience. This is quite true, but we believe that research can provide valuable support for this approach.

There are indications from the small body of qualitative research into children's understandings that *common belief patterns* emerge. Frequently these patterns, which may be totally 'wrong' ideas or may represent a partial understanding, persist despite instruction. This seems to be particularly true for scientific notions which defy 'common sense'. (For example, the fact that all matter is made up of molecules and atoms, or the fact that sideways pressure at a given depth in a fluid is the same as downwards pressure.) Sometimes the alternative explanations offered by children are unanticipated, and even bizarre. Documentation of these common patterns of understanding in children of different ages (and, ideally, in the same children at different ages) should yield useful information on developmental trends and on individual pupil differences.

Two examples of investigations with young children may perhaps serve to illustrate the points made so far in this section. Nussbaum and Novak (1976) interviewed fifty-two seven to eight year olds in an attempt to elucidate their ideas on the 'Earth' concept. The interviews, which included the use of models and drawings, began with a set of questions which included: How do *you* know that the Earth is round? Which way do we have to look in order to see the Earth? Why don't we see the Earth as a ball? etc. From analysis of the data, Nussbaum and Novak identified five common patterns of children's thinking about the Earth, ranging from primitive notions of a flat earth with no concept of space to a notion of a spherical planet, surrounded by space and with things falling to the centre. They concluded that the problem of developing a conception of cosmic space is central in learning the Earth concept, and yet this aspect is not emphasized by teachers or in textbooks. Similarly, they thought there was a need to explore ways of helping young children to understand that 'down' directions are towards the centre of the Earth. Many children who 'know' that 'a person on the other side of the Earth does not stand upside down, and does not fall off because gravity pulls him towards the Earth' still do not completely comprehend the meaning of this statement.

Using a similar approach, Albert (1978) identified eleven 'thought patterns' which underlie the concept of heat found in children from four to nine years. Just one of her findings will suffice as illustration. The adult conception of heat implies that cold, warm and hot are a single dimension. Albert found that the four, five and six year olds in her sample did not consistently distinguish between 'hot' and 'warm', even though they used both terms. But at the age of eight children began to distinguish clearly between 'hot' and 'warm', at the same time regarding them as different instances of the same dimension. They did this by reflecting on how *they* act on and react to objects at different temperatures. For example, Ron (age nine) pointed out: 'Like hot is sort of burn you, and warm is just feeling nice'. Teachers of older children will be aware that the idea of 'cold' as an entity, and a separate one from 'hot', is held quite frequently up to fifteen years (and probably beyond!).

Many primary teachers would accept the need to take account of the learner's perspectives. If the approach outlined above could demonstrably identify difficult areas, isolate problems (perhaps ones which impede any further development of understanding) and suggest ways of overcoming them, teachers are likely to respond positively. Over-generalizations are no use – justice must be done to the rich variety of children's ideas.

To summarize, it has been suggested that descriptive studies of children's understandings could be accessible and very useful to teachers. If research can identify common belief patterns, some of the 'spade work' will have been done for teachers. These patterns would not be considered as 'norms' or 'stages', but would certainly alert teachers to the possible perspectives their pupils may bring to learning. A build-up of information from studies of this kind, one conceptual area at a time, is bound to be slow (but then most 'instant' educational solutions turn out to be ephemeral). The *application* of information gleaned from these studies must be investigated by classroom-based research, preferably by teachers themselves. One thing is quite clear. It is obvious that the requirement for primary teachers to be well-trained in science will become no less urgent if this approach is adopted.

Professional Training of Primary Teachers in Science

How adequate is the preparation of primary teachers at both initial and post-experience stages to meet the demand for scientific activities in their classrooms? As far as initial training is concerned, attention given to science is *less* than it was twenty years ago. A survey of thirty-six of the 109 training colleges in England and Wales was carried out in 1960 for use at a British Association conference on 'The Place of Science in Primary Education', the proceedings of which were published in 1962. (Kerr, 1962) At that time, about three-quarters of the students 'were getting some science instruction', 40 per cent of the colleges required all primary students to attend science courses, and 45 per cent allocated thirty hours or less for primary science. Two provided over 100 hours. This was thought by the delegates to be a highly unsatisfactory picture. What would they have thought about our present provision?

Since the introduction of B.Ed. degree courses in colleges, the majority of students are given the most scanty professional training in science. Many are given none at all. The fact that the study of curricular areas, other than English and mathematics, usually operates on an options system is partly responsible for this deterioration. The preparation of primary teachers to cover all the areas of the curriculum has been a major problem for decades. Part of the intention of setting up separate Professional Studies Departments and Educational Studies Departments in the majority of training institutions was to enrich professional training and underline its importance. In fact, too often the consequence has been quite the opposite. Universities and the CNAA have imposed their views of what kind of knowledge is academically acceptable for the award of degrees, and the development of professionally-relevant courses (seen by the teaching profession to be necessary) has been neglected. McNamara and Desforges (1978) claim the time is ripe to abandon the disciplines of education at the initial training stage and develop 'the teaching of professional studies as an academically rigorous, practically useful, and scientifically productive activity' (p. 17). Through a project funded by The Nuffield Foundation, they aim to work out a more clearly-articulated rationale for professional studies, one which is informed by practical knowledge (which they call 'craft knowledge'). The project seeks to develop professional skills through the generation of classroom-based theories of instruction and teacher behaviour. The Science Teacher Education Project (Haysom and Sutton, 1974) was a move in this direction; that is towards building theory from professional practice. Given the present pattern of teacher education programmes, the professional preparation of teachers is unlikely to be improved until the aims of these projects are taken seriously.

Opportunities for the further professional training of primary teachers in science, especially at teachers' centres, have been generously provided until the recent financial cuts. These courses and workshops have been actively supported by teachers. School-based courses, using the staff as the 'unit' rather than individual teachers, seem to be the most promising method of bringing about change.

Looking to the Future

It is clear that progress will depend on the tempering of theoretical 'ideals' (which are anyway rather subject to fashion) to take realistic account of practical constraints. Some of these constraints, such as the low level of scientific training of many primary teachers, may be very unpalatable. To ignore them is simply escapist. Sometimes the contrast between consultative reports from 'experts' and teachers' opinions is striking. In a recent evaluation of a health education course in some Sheffield primary schools, it was found that the project appealed to teachers precisely because it was prescriptive, in terms of content especially, and because it offered the necessary in-service training and resource back-up.

The recent shift from the practice of producing only teachers' materials for primary science to preparing materials for use by pupils is another example of a realistic response to practical constraints. Local curriculum development groups and commercial publishers have been turning out children's science work cards and assignment sheets for some time. The HMI's report (p. 59) acknowledges that 'the discriminating use of carefully-chosen' pupil material can 'help to sustain work in science'. The Director of the most recent Schools Council project, 'Learning Through Science', plans to produce pupil materials, although as a team they are wedded to the idea of getting children to show initiative and to devise some of their own methods of carrying out investigations.

Seemingly, these advisers perceive the danger of worksheets becoming the syllabus. We would agree with this view. It would be an extreme and totally retrograde step to finish up with a prescribed science course for primary schools. Even so, if we expect primary teachers to plan scientific activities for children, more understanding of children's scientific ideas is needed, more rigorous and relevant professional training in science for all primary teachers must be introduced, headteachers must be persuaded of its importance, and the resources for the children to engage in these activities must be provided.

References

ALBERT, E. (1978) 'Development of the concept of heat in children' *Science Education*

62, pp. 389–399.

ASHTON, P. *et al*, (1975) *The Aims of Primary Education: A Study of Teachers' Opinions* London, Macmillan, Schools Council Research Studies.

BOOTH, N. (1978) 'Science in the middle years' *Education 3–13*, 6(2), pp. 37–41.

DEADMAN, J.A. and KELLY, P.J. (1978) 'What do secondary school boys understand about evolution and heredity before they are taught the topics?' *Journal of Biological Education* 12(1), pp. 7–15.

DRIVER, R. and EASLEY, J. (1978) 'Pupils and paradigms: A review of literature related to concept development in adolescent science students' in *Studies in Science Education* 5, pp. 61–84.

FINCH, I.E. (1971) 'Selling science' *School Science Review* 53, pp. 405–410.

HARLEN, W. (1978) 'Does content matter in primary schools?' *School Science Review* 59, pp. 614–625.

HER MAJESTY'S INSPECTORATE (1978) *Primary Education in England: A Survey* London, HMSO.

HAYSOM, J.T. and SUTTON, C.R. (Eds) (1974) *Science Teacher Education Project* London, McGraw-Hill.

KERR, J.F. (1962) 'Training for learning through investigations' in PERKINS, W. (Ed) *The Place of Science in Primary Schools* London, The British Association, pp. 33–44.

MCNAMARA, D. and DESFORGES, C. (1978) 'The social sciences, teacher education and the objectification of craft knowledge' *British Journal of Teacher Education* 4(1), pp. 17–36.

NUSSBAUM, J. and NOVAK, J.D. (1976) 'An assessment of children's concepts of the earth utilizing structured interviews' *Science Education* 60, pp. 535–550.

REDMAN, S., BRERETON, A. and BOYERS, P. (1969) *An Approach to Primary Science* (The Oxford Primary Science Project) London, Macmillan.

STEADMAN, S.D., PARSONS, C. and SALTER, G.B. (1978) *An Enquiry into the Impact and Take-up of Schools Council Funded Activities* London, Schools Council Publications.

Teaching young children about the past*

Joan Blyth
City of Liverpool College of Higher Education

In a recent editorial Colin Richards (1979), wrote of the concern of HMI to strengthen academic content in the primary school curriculum. He emphasized the awareness of the 'neglect of these central concerns in many classes, especially in relation to science, craft, history and geography'. This article attempts to focus on this 'neglect' in the teaching and learning of historical material among young children aged five to seven. At this stage of school life 'historical material' means any people, events and ideas concerned with a period before 'now' for the children. This could be 'yesterday' or palaeolithic man. In the words of David Attenborough (1979)' all living things are influenced by messages from the past'. So are young children, whether consciously or unconsciously, and to them the past is important to help them to understand themselves in time, and to help them to relate more sympathetically to other people, especially their parents and grandparents. These ideas are supported by Margaret Donaldson (1978) who believes that other people's past helps the self-centred child to 'decentre'. This article has two main purposes, in the first place, to look at present practice, its underlying assumptions and what happens in the classroom, and secondly to suggest some possible approaches to replace or improve upon them.

Present Practice

Underlying assumptions

Three assumptions appear to influence teachers of young children in relation to historical material. One is that their training at college supplies them with the philosophy and tools of their trade for a lifetime. This

*This is an edited version of the original article published in *Education 3–13*, 72, (1979), pp. 42–47.

training is child-centred rather than subject-centred, it favours the child progressing at his own pace and not undertaking new learning tasks until he is 'ready', in the teacher's view, or wants to (in his own view), and it accepts that intellectually the young child is easily satisfied. Therefore the day's programme concentrates on language and number, art work and physical education. Any reference to the past is incidental, unprepared and decided on by the individual teacher. Story-time, at the end of the day, when we are all tired, is one of the few opportunities to introduce historical material and this is not likely to be a programme with any purposive historical content at all. A skilled teacher may also use the past in role-playing and dramatic work. Assuming that young teachers start their careers with such clear guide-lines, it is not surprising that publishers do not produce suitable books, pictures, games and resources. The Gittins Report (1967) warned of the dangers of the non-specialist trying to use historical material with younger children. The Environmental Studies 5–13 Project (1973) found difficulty in supplying their pilot schools with material about the past and saw a need for support from an historian or archivist in the preparation of material.

Another, almost unspoken, assumption is that young children will actually be damaged emotionally and intellectually by the 'pressure' of the 'academic approach'. Children should not have to listen too long to the teacher and be imprisoned by a planned and structured programme of work, beyond language and number. This assumption is conveyed to the children who believe that hard thinking will damage their brains for future schooling. At the end of a period of work in a first school with six-year olds, one of my brightest pupils said that she had enjoyed the work on the past but feared that she had 'used up her brain' and would not have enough left for her junior and secondary schooling! This second assumption is closely related to the third, which is that history is too difficult for young children to understand. This may partly arise from the old-fashioned view that history is all facts and dates, and the young teacher may have exhausting memories of preparing for 'O' and 'A' Level history papers.

This third assumption, that the nature of history is 'facts', dies hard and this to some extent may be the fault of specialist historians in relation to younger pupils. Yet historians would agree that all facts can never be known and that 'hunches', in the words of Professor Jerome Bruner (1963) or sensible guesses, are most important tools for the historian. Another difficulty about teaching for the past is the language used by historians to describe events and people of the past. This seems unnecessarily difficult when young children cannot even use everyday language correctly and the learning of two different vocabularies appears an additional burden. In addition, concepts, especially those of chronology and time, are even more obvious problems. On the other hand Gustav Jahoda (1963) thinks that at five years old 'the ordering of events into earlier and later begins to emerge' and that the child of five can understand the words yesterday, to-day and to-morrow'. A more recent view supporting this is that of John West (1978) who writes 'Recent practice by inspired and skilful infant teachers should persuade us that even seven years of age is unnecessarily late to begin to develop young children's awareness of the meaning of "Long, long ago" and "Once upon a time"'. Thus it is the responsibility of historians to interpret their discipline and its nature anew to teachers of young children, to broaden its scope and relate it more obviously to the 'here and now' of children's understanding.

Classroom Practice

These three assumptions are established, strongly felt and are part of the 'raison d'être' of the teacher of young children. They lead in most classrooms to unplanned introductions of historical material as it comes into story-time as myth or truth, or on national historic occasions such as a coronation, the Queen's Jubilee, a royal marriage or a school centenary when ready-made teaching resources are cheap and easily accessible. Such material may also be discussed incidentally during 'news' if some children have watched an historical TV programme, or discussed more thoroughly a weekly TV programme watched in school and supported by a good pamphlet (for example, *How We Used to Live* – social life in the nineteenth century). The weaknesses of this 'hit and miss' approach are many. There is often confusion in children's minds between myth and truth, and teachers in different years repeat the content taught if a careful watch is not kept on schemes of work. Children do not gain any historical continuity if all stories are 'one-off', and unless they undertake some activity of their own, the work is just 'listening to teacher' and the material may not be related to the children.

Yet there are some outstanding enthusiasts in using the past with young children and the freedom allowed traditionally to primary teachers has borne much fruit in these cases. In three cases known to me, the teachers were in positions of authority in school and so influenced the whole school. In two cases the teachers provided their colleagues with correct and scholarly historical information which involved them personally in much hard work. In one of these cases the school's centenary (1876–1976) was used as a big historical project for every class in the school and each class contributed to the display, and made its own 'Book of Learning 1876–1976'. In the other case the head teacher used local historical sources to help his colleagues to teach the local history of the town, and the children wrote stories and poems and made models using this material for detailed information (Newton, 1970). In a third case, in a small all-age village school, the head teacher based all the children's work for a period of time on the model of a lake village or at another time on a frieze of Roman Britain (Marshall, 1970).

Other able teachers have used historical artefacts of the nineteenth and early twentieth centuries for discussion of historical evidence and sequencing of material (West, 1970). The history of a town has been pieced together by young children asking older people to answer a simple question-naire and bringing these older friends into the classroom (Le Fevre, 1969). Certain museums pay particular attention to working with young children and using the genuine artefacts from the museum to teach about the past. At the Bethnal Green Museum of Childhood Imogen Stewart helps young children to use her collections of dolls' houses from 1673 and dolls from 1750 and she feels strongly that 'things should not be avoided because children do not understand them', that is, in the first place.

Views as to classroom practice vary. On the whole government reports have not been pessimistic about what is being done in this area and what it is possible to do. The Hadow (1933) and Plowden (1967) Reports have not been very concerned to discuss historical material in the five to seven age range but the Primary Education Handbook of 1959 (Ministry of Education, 1959) believes that true stories should be mingled with fantasy stories and should not be separated in the child's mind. But it did suggest the teaching of family history and the use of artefacts, if children and teachers could be given help with the work. Although finally not favourable to the use of historical material in this age-range, the Gittins Report empha-sized the need for discussion about the past between teacher and child. This is supported by Joan Tough's work on the importance of talking with children (Tough, 1976) and also by the Russian psychologist LS Vygotsky (1962) when he writes 'verbal intercourse with adults thus becomes a powerful factor in the development of the child's concepts'. The HMI Primary Survey makes no particular reference to the five to seven age-range but generally thinks that history is taught 'superficially' in four-fifths of schools, giving children little idea of change and evidence, and that there is 'lack of planning in the work'. On the other hand teachers of young children who have worked out original and stimulating approaches are enthusiastic in their talking and writing, and together with some research workers, believe that more successful work could be done with historical material than is at present the case.

Possible Approaches

The teachers mentioned earlier in this article are dedicated people who probably spend too much of their leisure time preparing historical material for their classes! This part of the article is concerned to help the less dedicated, or those dedicated to other areas of the curriculum, to give their classes a satisfactory diet of the past. For these teachers it is hoped to start them thinking about the historical content of their work (that is, what of the past should they teach?), the possible teaching techniques to help children to overcome the problems of understanding the past (that is, methodology) and finally the resources more readily available to provide activity for children.

What 'past' to teach

The essential thinking behind the appropriate scheme of work is dependent upon the organization of the school, the interests and knowledge of the teacher and the local environment. During these early years all schemes should be flexible and historical material may not be used in all terms. But there should be some scheme linked with work to be done in later years and so avoiding unintentional repetition. Teaching the past has been found most satisfactory in vertically grouped schools as the seven year olds can help the younger children, especially in discussion. In order to understand the difficult concept of time, Gustav Jahoda (1963) has suggested working backwards, from 'now' to 'then'. An example of this could be starting with the children themselves in the present and in their own locality and broadening out in the second year to 'Children in Victorian Times'. Throughout the two years, either told or read, the building up in word books of historical vocabulary (for example, the meaning of 'century', 'monarch', 'coach', 'battle') and all the time constant reference to simple time-lines on the walls of the classroom. During one term, stories from the past could be introduced during three or four separated weeks grouped according to topic (for example, 'soldiers in ancient times', 'famous queens', 'children of the past'). With this background, a possible scheme might evolve. (See figure 1).

Figure 1.

	Term 1	Term 2	Term 3
Year 1 Aged 5–6	Myths through stories.	Stories of the past grouped in topics ——— role playing.	Study of artefacts brought by teacher and later the class.
Year 2 Aged 6–7	Family History.	Local History of own village, town, area.	Local visits and a patch of national past related to their own locality.

This scheme may seem rather parochial except for the extension allowed by the stories, yet it provides time for discussion and activity related to the child's own knowledge, lays a foundation for a development of local and national themes in later schooling and keeps the child's thought on change and evidence rather than facts. It also has a unity, as family history, artefacts, local history and visits can obviously and easily be linked.

J. Blyth

How to teach it

Techniques of teaching such a scheme are more difficult when children are only just learning to read and write. The obvious technique is that of discussion which requires good class control and great patience, both from teachers and children. This may be difficult for inexperienced teachers. In my work with six-year olds I used three approaches. They were the use of artefacts, a museum visit and family history (Blyth, 1978). The children and I each brought an 'old object to school, we felt them, named them and then tried to put them in order of oldness from various pieces of evidence. We could have developed this further to collect them into categories of objects such as books, toys and jewellery in order to develop concepts further. This links with Gustav Jahoda's remark about 'ordering of events' beginning at the age of five, quoted earlier in this article. This technique requires 'hunches' on the part of the children, supported by knowledge of likely chronology on the part of the teacher. Many of the objects brought by the children were too close to each other in time to distinguish age-sequence but the wedding-dress of my great-grandmother (1857) was certainly agreed by all to be 'very, very old' especially compared with toys brought by two of the boys (Christmas, 1975). With such young children I should have gained more help from parents, or better still, provided obviously different artefacts borrowed from the schools museum service. These borrowed objects would have had the advantage of being genuine evidence as well as being more varied (for example, stone age axe-head, Saxon brooch, Victorian sewing box, Second World War gas-masks, etc.). Yet the six-year olds had confidence to make guesses and consider evidence.

My second approach, which was the most successful, was a visit to the city museum, situated in a genuine Tudor building. This involved preparation for the visit, the visit and the follow-up. These three parts took place on three consecutive mornings. To my surprise a 1611 Speed Map, wall-size, became the real teaching medium. Town walls, gates, churches, the castle, sea and land seemed obvious to all the children and we found the Tudor house we were to visit on the map. I provided a simplified rough sketch-map for each child to complete and this also proved easy. This bears out Dr Tough's advice that children should be introduced to maps and diagrams as early as possible (Tough, 1976). The visit to the museum rather overpowered the children who had never been before and they saw a plethora of 'old objects', including feeling the actual stones of the medieval town wall. On our return to school, the next day, we discussed what 'old objects' each had seen and why they seemed old. We also tried to put them in order of age, as we had done with their own artefacts, but this proved difficult, especially in the absence of the actual objects. Yet they realized that walls, buildings and fireplaces were 'old', as well as smaller objects.

The third approach was that of family history starting from my own life and family, and developing into their lives and families. Intense interest was shown in my life and family and much discussion evolved which I tape-recorded. Recollection was their stumbling-block when it came to making up their 'life-lines' as nothing of importance seemed to have happened to them! The contrast between my thirty-five years and their six staggered them! Constructing their 'family plans' on the model of mine proved easier, and as with mine, we worked from right (recent time) to left (earlier time) of the page. The horizontal family tree has been found easier for young children to understand than the usual vertical one. Many years ago Sir Fred Clarke (1929) wrote that the word 'grandfather' had more meaning in teaching historical time than dates.' In the same way 'Tales of a Grandfather' by Sir Walter Scott may still inspire teachers of stories of the past. During this work on families I found that the children understood family relationships very well and were good at giving evidence for what they said. Time and age concepts were more difficult to grasp but even these were developing at the end of the nine weeks in which I taught them. All the children, for example, seemed more conscious of what person or object was 'older' or 'younger' than another. Although I did not use role-playing and drama to any extent owing to lack of space, this could be a most stimulating and normal technique for young children, especially after a true story has been told from true historical sources giving adequate detail for miming and role-playing. If done well this can stimulate imaginative historical thinking (Fines and Verrier, 1974).

Help for the teacher

In these days of economy, resources for new forms of teaching are inadequate and many excellent young and experienced teachers are doubtful about implementing new ideas without good and accessible support which will not mean working into the night once more. Artefacts from museums and homes are fairly easy to collect and quickly presented displays can be made of these, with labels made by the children where possible. Children, however young, can lend a hand in mounting a display. Old maps and photographs of the locality may be bought cheaply from the local museum and/or record office. Many parents and older friends and relatives constitute useful oral evidence and can be tape-recorded. Local buildings, even the school itself, are resources. Pictures of all sorts, posters and postcards from museums and art galleries, and slides made from books may all be used individually, in groups or as a class. John West, who is researching into these techniques, writes 'it seems evident that *powers of observation* are high at six to eight years' (West, 1978). He uses period pictures to accompany artefacts; a nineteenth-century fan could be used with a picture of nineteenth-century ladies using fans at a ball. This practice is supported by the 1933 Hadow Report which believes that the child of six can 'read' a picture to the extent of knowing what is happening in it; he may need more help from the teacher with an historical picture. TV programmes with pamphlets are usually excellent but cannot be built into a scheme of work as they are not always repeated, especially at convenient times. Many more suitable books, very well illustrated, are badly needed. In the 1960s Longmans published a series for five to seven year olds called 'Little Books' and one set was concerned with historical topics. These are small books to hold, using bold type face and are well-illustrated. A and C Black have published a series called 'People' Around Us' and the first two books (Wagstaff, 1978), accompanied by photographs, a book of mastercopies for duplicated sheets and a teacher's guide may now be bought. Above all, in these early days teachers talking with children is one of the best resources.

Having looked at what is happening in schools to-day and suggested possible approaches to introduce more structured and academically rigorous work using historical material, it is important to emphasise that all this work is strengthening the basic teaching of language and number, at the same time as developing expressive activities. Above all the new content for the teacher to master is minimal. Just as all children do not master language and number without considerable effort, and some never do, so the same will happen with this new area of the curriculum. Because an area of work is difficult it should not be avoided. In the words of one psychologist 'there is a gap between what they (children) can do and what they actually do (Bryant, 1973).

References

ATTENBOROUGH, D. (1979) 'Life on earth' BBC series, Spring.

BLYTH, J.E. (1978) 'Young children and the past' *Teaching History* 21, June.

BOARD OF EDUCATION, CONSULTATIVE COMMITTEE (1933) *Infant and Nursery Schools* London, HMSO.

BRUNER, J.S. (1963) *The Process of Education* New York, Vintage Books.

BRYANT, P.E. (1973) 'What the young child has to learn about logic' in HINDE, R.A. and HINDE, J.S. (Eds) *Constraints on Learning* London, Academic Press.

CENTRAL ADVISORY COUNCIL FOR EDUCATION (Wales) (1967) *Primary Education in Wales* London, HMSO.

CENTRAL ADVISORY COUNCIL FOR EDUCATION (England) (1967) *Children and Their Primary Schools* London, HMSO.

CLARKE, F. (1929) *Foundations of History Teaching* Oxford, Oxford University Press.

DONALDSON, M. (1978) *Children's Minds* London, Fontana.

FINES, J. and VERRIER, R. (1974) *The Drama of History* London, Clive Bingley.

HER MAJESTY'S INSPECTORATE (1978) *Primary Education in England: A Survey by Her Majesty's Inspectors of Schools* London, HMSO.

JAHODA, G. (1963) 'Children's concept of time and history' *Educational Review* 15(2), pp. 90 and 101.

LE FEVRE, M. (1969) 'Introducing history to young children' *Teaching History* 1(2), November.

MARSHALL, S. (1970) *An Experiment in Education* Cambridge, Cambridge University Press.

MINISTRY OF EDUCATION (1959) *Primary Education: Suggestions for the Consideration of Teachers and Others Concerned with the Work of the Primary School* London, HMSO.

NEWTON, E.E. (1970) 'An Evertonian spilling over' *Teaching History* 1(4), November.

RICHARDS, C. (1979) 'A different shade of green' *Education 3–13*, 7(1), Spring.

SCHOOLS COUNCIL (1973) *Environmental Studies 5–13: The Use of Historical Resources* Schools Council Working Paper No. 48, London, Evans/Methuen.

TOUGH, J. (1976) *Listening to Children Talking* London, Ward Lock, p. 79.

VYGOTSKY, L.S. (1962) *Thought and Language* Cambridge, Mass. and New York, MIT Press and John Wiley.

WEST, J. (1978) 'Young children's awareness of the past' *Trends* Spring, p. 9.

WEST, M. (1970) 'History and the younger child' *Teaching History* 1(4), November.

New Directions in Nursery School Education

Joan Tamburrini
Roehampton Institute of Higher Education

Polarization

One of the most detrimental influences on educational thought and practice is the tendency to polarize practices. Polarities are useful when they draw attention to valid distinctions that may have been neglected, but their danger is that practices and their underlying assumptions and values are usually oversimplified, sometimes to the point of caricature. The result is that myths are perpetuated and both theorists and practitioners are driven into defensive entrenched positions when what is required instead is unprejudiced reconsideration of old practices and consideration of new ones.

In recent years a polarization of the purposes and practices of nursery schools has emerged which not only militates against unbiased thinking about early childhood education but is also potentially dangerous in terms of political repercussions in preschool provision. The purposes and practices of nursery schools have been polarized as providing either education or a shared child-rearing support system. Marion Blank (1974), for example, has drawn a distinction between two types of preschool: 'shared rearing preschools' and 'academic preschools'. The former, she suggests, stems from the desire of women to have support services in the rearing of their children while the latter originate with the concern to prevent future academic failure. Thus the two institutions differ in terms of purpose. The major purpose of the shared child-rearing preschool, she asserts:

> is not to change, educate, alter or modify the child along particular lines, although this may occur. Rather it is to provide, during the hours of the day when the children are in school, a secure benign environment that is compatible with the interests and predispositions of the young child.

By contrast, in the 'academic preschool':

> ... the central goal is not day care, but education ... it is a basic alteration in the child's level of functioning so that not only all present academic learning, but all future academic learning will be enhanced.

The implication of Blank's analysis is that the traditional British nursery school engages not in education but in child-rearing. Education goes on in schools whose more formal structured programmes are typified by those based on the Bereiter and Engelmann programme or the Peabody Language Development Kit.

In a reply to Marion Blank, Tizard (1974) rejects this polarization, but she does so, not to produce a more elaborate, non-polarized conceptualization of nursery school practice but, instead, in order to reject the distinction altogether. Paradoxically, by doing so she arrives at a similar position to Blank's in her view of the traditional British nursery school when she claims that:

> the curriculum of the nursery school can hardly be distinguished from that of the home.

The main distinction between parents and teachers as educators, she claims:

> is ideological – that is both parents and teachers provide the same kind of learning experiences for the child, but the teacher formulates her objectives and has theories about her methods.

Tizard's purpose is a worthy one. She expresses anxiety about the implications for practice of Blank's distinction, particularly in terms of the tendency for 'most adult-child contacts (outside the nursery school to be) down-graded to "child-rearing"', rather than for child-rearing to be seen as a pervasive process in which 'all adult-child contacts are potentially important and fruitful'. Nevertheless, to blur the distinction between what does or should go on in a nursery school and what goes on in the home, the day nursery or in child-minding deprives the nursery school teacher of a professional role, even though Tizard expresses a desire to avoid doing so.

Tizard's argument rests on two major points. First she argues that both upbringing and education go on in the home, and second that much of what a child learns at home and at school is incidental or unintended rather than the intended outcome of an attempt to educate. These arguments would seem strange if they were applied to children of compulsory school age, but parents do to a greater or lesser degree attempt to educate older children and all schools have a 'hidden curriculum' which produces incidental or unintended learning. It would seem that Tizard, like Blank, bases her argument on the fact that the traditional nursery school curriculum is more informally structured than that of the compulsory schooling sector.

Research Findings

Tizard and Blank are by no means the only theorists to argue that traditional nursery schools are not primarily educational institutions. Van der Eyken (1977), for example, has also argued that the nursery school ethos does not 'place the emphasis where it belongs – on educational needs'.

Van der Eyken's evidence for this claim is drawn largely from the findings of the survey conducted by Taylor, Exon and Holley (1972) for the Schools Council. The survey was carried out among 578 teachers. Part of the questionnaire completed by the teachers was concerned with the main purposes of education. There were five aims focused on intellectual development, social and emotional development, physical development and the creation of an effective transition from home to school. Each of these aims was derived from discussion with teachers. Another section of the questionnaire was concerned with objectives, that is with more specific goals related to these aims. Thirty objectives were derived representing a range of capabilities, skills, attitudes, values and dispositions, and were related to the four developmental areas – social/emotional, intellectual, physical and aesthetic – included among the aims. The teachers were required to place each of the five aims in rank order from one to five in terms of the priority they would give it relative to the other aims. The section dealing with objectives required the teachers to rate each one on a five point scale.

Van der Eyken's report of the findings of the survey claims that 'the teachers gave a considerably greater weighting to the social and emotional development of children, and considered that intellectual development was, if a choice had to be made, the least important'. Concerning the objectives Van der Eyken reports that 'once again, intellectual or cognitive development took a low priority'.

Before examining Van der Eyken's reporting of the findings, some reservations concerning the survey itself need to be kept in mind. First, with regard to aims, a choice of priorities had to be made: if a teacher was reluctant to place the aims in rank order believing each of them to be equally important, she had either to rank them in spite of her reluctance or to fail to return the questionnaire. Second, this section required only a ranking of the aims not a statement of the reason for the ranking given. Let us suppose a teacher conceives intellectual development to be of supreme importance, but believes that attempts to bring it about will be fruitless unless favourable social and emotional factors predispose a child to be receptive to the teacher's efforts. She might then give social and emotional development a higher ranking than intellectual development for that reason. As Van der Eyken himself says, 'so much depends on how the respondents interpret the questions'.

The same criticism cannot be made of the section of the questionnaire dealing with objectives, since teachers were not required to put them in rank order but instead had to rate each one on a five-point scale. It was found that objectives concerned with the child's psychological awareness of himself and others was most likely to be emphasized. Next came areas concerned with school expectations, physical development and general social awareness, with creative, aesthetic objectives only a little way behind. Finally came intellectual or cognitive objectives. However, in interpreting these results it is important to note that, as Taylor and his associates emphasize, some objectives serve more than one area of educational intentions. For example, 'to help the child understand and recognize the feelings, needs and attitudes of others' has an intellectual component as well as one relating to self-other objectives.

Even if these reservations were not valid, Van der Eyken has overstated the case. It is in the section dealing with objectives that the cognitive domain emerged with the lowest score, and this was in contradiction to the ranking given to intellectual development in the section on aims, where it emerged not last but second in rank order. In addition, as Taylor and his associates with more caution than Van der Eyken point out, 'no great gulf separates any of the objectives from any other. All are considered important, though it is reasonable to infer that some will be given priority, depending on the child and the circumstances'.

Taylor, Exon and Holley conclude that these unresolved complexities and contradictions, indicated in their research, are 'likely to have arisen from the difficulties of translating broad statements of educational intent into specific aspects of practical action'. What does seem certain from the Schools Council survey is that most nursery school teachers have a strong resistance to 'formal' curricula, to structured programmes exemplified by the Peabody Language Development Kit or the Bereiter and Engelmann programme. Instead they favour a curriculum based largely on children exercising choice of activity from a wide range of materials, few of which are tightly pre-structured. Within this context, according to Taylor and his associates, 'cognitive objectives are seen as only a little less important than social and emotional ones'.

A more powerful source of evidence that nursery school teachers may give relatively low priority to cognitive development comes from studies of practice. Thomas (1973) observed a small sample of children for a complete day, recording every response uttered by and to them and noting their activities and the time spent on each. She found that the teachers accepted minimal verbalization from children and that their own verbal exchanges with a child rarely extended either his language or his thinking. In addition the experiences and pattern of activities tended to be repetitive. In sum, little attention seemed to be paid to intellectual objectives in general and to developing language in particular.

Another study of nursery school teachers' practice, particularly their use of language, was carried out by Tizard, Philps and Plewis (1975). Twelve preschool centres were studied. Four were day nurseries rather than schools and, since the staff were not teachers, need not concern us here. Of the remaining eight institutions four were 'traditional' nursery schools and four 'had departed from tradition to the extent of including a special language programme in the school day'. The results showed significant differences between these two types of nursery school. In the schools with a language programme staff spent more time interacting with the children and these interactions had more 'cognitive content' than those of staff in the 'traditional' schools. There appears to have been some match between the beliefs of the staff concerning the functions of the institution and their behaviour:

> in those centres where the staff saw their main function as looking after children whilst their mothers worked or providing them with an opportunity to play with other children, the staff interacted less with the children and in a more supervisory capacity than did staff in centres with avowedly educational aims.

A more recent study by Tizard (1979) examined video-tapes of the same children in their nursery schools and at home, and concluded that there was more connected discourse in the latter.

One should, however, be wary about drawing a firm conclusion from these studies that nursery school teachers have a relative lack of concern for intellectual development and for extending children's language. None of the studies finds that teachers' exchanges with children do not have cognitive content, but rather that the proportion of such exchanges is relatively small. Sylva, Roy and Painter (1980), in their study that was part of the Oxford Pre-school Project, certainly found instances of exchanges involving 'tutorial' dialogue. Unfortunately these instances were infrequent. What we do not know is whether this state of affairs reflects a relative lack of concern with the cognitive domain or whether it is the result of managerial demands in the ecology of the typical nursery school. Bruner (1980) in his overview of the Oxford Preschool Project suggests this may be the case:

> Teachers talking non-managerially with children can and do produce long and rich dialogues. But management duties must preclude such dialogue. And for chillingly good reasons when one computes the statistics of the situation. Take the typical preschool group ... It will contain, say, twenty-five children and three adult staff. The study by Sylva, Roy and Painter computes that, on average, a child will talk conversationally three minutes in an hour with an adult. Assume that for each child each hour this constitutes three three-turn conversations with an adult ... This makes about twenty-five connected conversations for each adult each hour ... Is it realistic to expect much more conversational activity from a teacher in preschool settings as organized?

Some support for the suggestion that the problem may be a managerial one comes from the Oxford Preschool Project evidence. It finds that staff-child ratio is a potent factor determining the quality of staff-child interaction. The centres studied were divided into those with good staff-child ratios (1:8, 1:9 and 1:10) and those with excellent ones (1:7, 1:6 and 1:5). It was found that:

> children in centres with excellent ratios are more prone to conversation. Interestingly, they speak less to one another but twice as much with staff members. The magnitude of the difference is surprising, as there were not twice as many adults around to serve as conversational partners.

Fostering Intellectual Development

Whether the comparative infrequency with which teachers in traditional nursery schools seem to engage in dialogues where the intention is to stimulate and extend children intellectually is the result of cognitive objectives not being given priority or to managerial demands, it is nonetheless important that this state of affairs changes. If it does not, Tizard's claim, that nursery schools do little more than other agencies in educating young children, and attempts by politicians and administrators to close down nursery schools or to replace teachers with staff who have had no teacher training will be difficult to combat. It would be an equally sad state of affairs if Tizard's claim were to affect change in the direction of nursery school teachers being driven to adopt a curriculum consisting primarily of formal, highly structured programmes of the kind they have previously rejected. The remainder of this chapter will be concerned with evidence about the ways that young children's intellectual functioning and development seem to be most facilitated. It will be argued that the evidence suggests that the conventional wisdom of nursery school teachers, that the curriculum should be one in which children's intentions are given a central place, is well grounded, but that within such a context a teacher needs to interact with children in ways that require knowledge and skills of a professional kind, making nonsense of the notion that a formal curriculum is concerned with education whereas an informal one is not.

The work of Piaget has dominated the psychology of intellectual development for several decades. There is not the space here to go into details concerning his work. The important thing to note is that his description of the thinking of preschool children is mainly in terms of their incompetence; of how, that is, they cannot yet reason. The major characteristic of young children's thinking, according to Piaget, is that they are unable to 'decentre', that is they focus on a limited aspect of an object or situation, resulting in false conclusions or 'illogical' thinking. Just a few examples must suffice to illustrate this. The young child cannot put himself at the point of view of another person when it is different from his own: he 'centres' on his own point of view. If the shape of some malleable substance is changed, (if a ball of clay, for example, is rolled into a sausage shape) a young child believes the quantity has either increased or decreased. He does so because he centres either on the increase in length and ignores the decrease in width or *vice versa*. Young children generally centre on similarities between objects and ignore dissimilarities. Piaget's example is of a child who, on a walk, saw first one slug and then another slug and concluded they were the same slug. Conversely and paradoxically, a child may sometimes centre on dissimilarities and ignore similarities. This leads him to conclude, for example, that there are several suns because he has seen the sun in different places. This account of young children's thinking is in terms of incompetence; of what they cannot yet understand; of how they cannot yet think. It creates a problem for those concerned with the education of young children, when their traditional wisdom has been that it is important to start with what a child can do and understand; with his competencies rather than his incompetencies.

There is now, however, a considerable amount of evidence that, given certain conditions, young children's intellectual capabilities are greater than Piaget's tests might lead us to believe. Tamburrini (1981) has argued that it should not be inferred from this evidence that Piaget's tests are invalid, but rather that Piaget's tests assess some overall generalized competence that will be shown by a child in all relevant contexts, whereas there are some specific contexts where a child will think at a higher level than he does in a standard Piagetian test. What the characteristics of these contexts are must therefore now be examined.

First, it would appear that, if we want a young child to function intellectually at his most capable, we must ensure that the way we ask him to express his understanding is appropriate to his level of understanding and development. A comparison between children's responses on Piaget's standard tests for egocentricity and those in a test devised by Borke (1978), which modifies the standard test only slightly, illustrates this principle. Egocentricity is the term Piaget uses for the inability of the young child to put himself at the point of view of another person when it is different from his own. In Piaget's test the child is shown a three dimensional model of three mountains each of which has a feature clearly distinguishing it from the other two. The child is required to select from photographs of the mountains from different points of view the one representing the perspective of a doll which is placed *vis-à-vis* the mountains in a position different from that of the child. On this standard test few children under the age of seven are able to select the correct photograph. Most young children select the photograph representing their own point of view. Borke modified the test in a simple way. Instead of selecting from photographs the child had to demonstrate the point of view of the doll by turning a turntable. Many children of four and some of three years of age were able to do this correctly.

A second condition favourable to children thinking at their most capable is the familiarity of the materials involved. In a further modification of Piaget's 'mountains' test for egocentricity Borke substituted for the three mountains a three dimensional model consisting of miniature people and animals in familiar domestic settings. As in the previous experiment the turntable was used instead of a selection of photographs. Under these conditions even more young children were able to give a correct response than in the other experiment by Borke discussed above.

A third important condition affecting the level of young children's thinking is one particularly stressed by Donaldson (1978) involving the extent to which they understand the intentions of the participants in a situation. She reports an experiment carried out by McGarrigle which again involved a minor modification to a standard Piagetian test. One of Piaget's tests for conservation of number involves showing the child two rows of five objects, say counters, aligned so that each counter in the second row is placed underneath the corresponding counter in the first row. The experimenter then spreads out the second row and the child, who has agreed that there was the same amount of counters in each row when they were aligned, is now asked whether there is still the same amount. In McGarrigle's version of the task the rearrangement was ostensibly the result of accident rather than of the intentional act of an adult. This was achieved by introducing a teddy bear, called 'naughty Teddy' who rearranged the elements. In this modified version more young children gave the correct response than normally happens in the standard test. Donaldson comments that in the standard test the young child tries to make sense of the experimenter's intention in terms of his experience of adults' intentions in his everyday transactions with them. If an adult arranges some objects, asks if they are the same amount, rearranges them, and then again asks if there is the same amount, a young child is likely to assume that the answer must be that the amount has changed, because in his experience adults do not carry out an action on things if their state is to remain the same as it was before.

A fourth condition affecting young children's understanding is, perhaps obviously, the complexity of relationships involved in a situation. For example, Light (1979), investigating egocentricity or role-taking abilities in a group of four year old children, used a number of tasks varying in complexity but each one requiring the child to identify another's point of view that was different from his own. One of Light's tasks used a three-sided pyramid with a different toy illustrated on each of its faces. The child was required to say which toy the experimenter who sat opposite him could see. In a more elaborate version of the task a doll was used and placed in each of five positions from two of which it would 'see' only one toy and from the other three of which it would 'see' two toys. The child was required to identify the toy or toys the doll would 'see' from the various positions. Out of a group of sixty children only five gave the correct response on all trials in the second task, whereas twenty-three did so in the first task.

These findings lend support to the conventional wisdom of the traditional nursery school that children need to explore and play with materials in their own way and in their own time. Further support for this practice comes from a comparative study carried out by Sylva, Roy and Painter as part of the Oxford Preschool Project. A comparison was undertaken between preschool centres in Oxfordshire and in Miami, Florida. In the Oxfordshire schools a large range of equipment was available from which, for the most part, a child selected what he wanted when he wanted it. By contrast, in most of the Miami centres a limited range of materials, such as three Rs materials, was laid out at any one time, and choice was firmly controlled by the teacher for large parts of the day, even in some cases in so-called free play periods. Sylva and her associates found that the Miami children were not stretching themselves intellectually as much as the Oxfordshire children, and this was in spite of the greater emphasis in the Miami centres on school-like activities and in spite of the much greater frequency in them of prescribed work as compared with the Oxfordshire centres.

While the evidence suggests the need for children to have ample opportunity to explore and play with materials in their own way and in their own time, it would be wrong to conclude that all the adult needs to do is to provide appropriate materials and then to adopt only a supervisory role. Evidence is beginning to accrue of differences in children's social experience that are associated with differences in their intellectual functioning. This evidence supports the view that nursery school teachers should adopt an active rather than passive role with respect to the cognitive domain.

In the investigation by Light mentioned above, there were individual differences among the sixty four-year old children in relation to their ability to role-take. He used a number of role-taking tasks among which there was sufficient intercorrelation for him to obtain a composite score for each child. These scores were then related to other factors including aspects of maternal style. One of these aspects was the mothers' teaching strategies with respect to a simple task. The mothers were first shown how to arrange some coloured blocks in a prescribed pattern. They then had to teach the task to their children, and the way in which they did so was observed by the experimenter. Two different maternal styles emerged, one in which the mother corrected an error immediately a child made it, and the other in which correction was delayed until a child was himself aware of a problem because the difficulties arising from an error were clear to him. In other words the second style synchronized more with the child's perceptions than the first one did. A significant association was found between competent role-taking and the maternal style involving deferred correction.

Another aspect of maternal style explored by Light concerned social control and was based on the distinction made by Bernstein in terms of a personal/positional dimension. Bernstein (1971) has suggested that in a 'person-oriented' family a child's awareness of self and others develops and differentiates as the motives and intentions of the family members as individuals are realized in their speech to one another. By contrast, in the 'positional' family reference is to status or position and a child learns a less differentiated role. Light was able to analyze transcripts of his sample of mothers in an open-ended interview that included questions about social control. He found a great variation in the frequency with which personal rationales in relation to social control of the child were given. These comments, Light says, 'get below the surface of the child's behaviour and consider things from the point of view of the child's feelings, intentions and character'. Light found a positive correlation between a frequent use of person-oriented rationales by the mother and good role-taking abilities on the part of the child, which was particularly notable when compared with the absence of a significant relationship between the use of such rationales and the child's IQ.

In Light's study these differences were not associated with social class differences, partly, perhaps, because his sample drawn from Cambridge and its environs was not strongly differentiated in terms of conventional social class distinctions. However, social class differences have been found in other studies of maternal teaching styles and of parents' language in different social class groups, (for example, Brophy, 1970; Hess and Shipman, 1965).

The traditional nursery school gives a central place to children's play. Other preschool services also emphasize play: the term 'Preschool Play Group' speaks for itself. In the study carried out by Sylva, Roy and Painter, however, there seemed to be a reluctance among staff to see children's play as varying in quality and in value. This may well spring from the fairly widespread assumption that play is such a natural and universal phenomenon that it will occur in spite of what adults do. It is probably reasoned that any intervention will destroy the spontaneity of play and that, since it is a 'natural phenomenon, all play is of equal value.

There is now, however, considerable cross-cultural evidence (see Feitelson, 1977) to suggest that make-believe play varies in extent and quality depending on the attitudes towards play of the adults in a community. El'konin (1966) has concluded that make-believe play does not develop spontaneously but, instead, arises in interaction with adults who suggest it.

The findings of cross-cultural studies of children's play have led to a number of tutoring studies whose primary purpose was to improve the imaginative quality of children's play through adult modelling. Freyburg

(1973), for example, carried out a study with a group of eighty five-year old children from low socio-economic class families. The children were evenly divided into a control and experimental group, and the children in the experimental group were given eight twenty minute training sessions in small groups of four children at a time. They were taken to a room equipped with a large table on which were spread pipe-cleaners, a variety of fabrics, clay, Playdoh, bricks, Tinkertoy sets and a wide variety of wooden shapes. During each of the eight sessions the investigator introduced a theme based on the children's interests and began to enact small plots in which pipe-cleaner figures were made to talk and to engage in make-believe roles. The children were encouraged to adopt a role using play equipment of their own choosing. Compared with the control group the experimental group improved significantly in the imaginativeness of their play and in the degree of concentration shown in it. Moreover when the children's play was reexamined two months later these changes had persisted.

Some other tutoring studies have, in addition, examined other outcomes of adult modelling for imaginative play. Several have found that experimental groups who have been tutored not only improve in the quality of imaginativeness in their play but, subsequently, also achieve higher scores on a creativity test than children in the control group. Golomb and Cornelius (1977) even found that children tutored for play performed better in Piagetian tests than did children in the control group.

Smith and Sydall (1978) have suggested that it is not the specific tutoring for play so much as adult interaction which is effective in producing these outcomes. This is to some extent borne out by the findings of the study carried out by Sylva, Roy and Painter. Two aspects of children's play were examined; its cognitive complexity and the degree of concentration shown by the children. Cognitive complexity was examined in terms of the sequential organization and elaboration in a bout of play and concentration was assessed in terms of duration of a bout of play – a 'bout' being a sequence of activity having a coherent thread. It was found that there was an upward shift in the complexity of play associated with adult interaction of any kind, but particularly when the interaction involved the adult in a tutorial capacity; that is 'when she deftly expands the child's scope of action or conception, often using the concrete task as a take-off point for discussion in a more abstract or imaginary vein'.

In sum, research into differences in maternal style and their outcomes and into the effect of adult interaction on the quality of children's make-believe play and some cognitive outcomes suggest that nursery school teachers need to do more than provide a rich range of materials with which children generate and direct their activities. They need also to adopt a role which includes interacting with children in a way that synchronizes with their intentions and purposes.

It would seem then that the task for the teachers is three-fold: first, she needs to diagnoze a child's intentions, second, to comment on or elaborate them in some way that has cognitive potential, and third, to ensure that the child understands her, the teacher's, intentions. Each of these three components in an interaction require considerable knowledge and skill on the part of a teacher.

When a teacher is concerned with children between the ages of three and five years, diagnostic skill is not something she should expect to 'come naturally' as it seems to in the studies of the mother-infant dyad such as Schaffer's (1971). Diagnosis on the basis of the child's language is a highly professional matter. Tough's project for the Schools Council on Communication Skills has categorized the various functions, some more cognitively loaded than others, that a child's language use may serve. Even when a teacher has studied these functions, diagnosis is no simple matter. As Stannard (1980) emphasizes in his comments on the work of Tough, it is not always easy to determine a child's intention from the language he uses, as often what a child says will serve more than one purpose: a statement about some object or event may at its face value serve to communicate information about that object or event, but it may also be concerned with maintaining the personal identity of the speaker.

In addition, the diagnosis of language is often only a first step in assessing a child's level of intellectual functioning. For example, a statement by a child that serves a clear purpose of maintaining personal identity may not inform a teacher whether that child is capable of role-taking, of taking another person's point of view. To elicit such information, further dialogue is necessary and successful dialogue, in this instance, requires knowledge of the development of role-taking abilities.

There are many occasions, however, when it is not from what a child says but from what he does that a teacher needs to assess his level of development. Correct assessment requires more than 'common-sense' or everyday experience of children. It requires professional knowledge. The development of children's drawings illustrate this. Younger preschool children draw what they claim to be representations of the human figure that are usually unrecognizable as such, with elements totally separate – facial features, for example, appearing outside the head. Slightly older children draw features enclosed within the head of a figure that is tadpole-like, having no torso. At this stage arms are often omitted but legs seldom are. The 'common-sense' layman's assumption accounts for these differences in terms of the child's manual coordination abilities. As Goodnow (1977) has shown, this is a false explanation. Correct assessment requires a knowledge of children's drawing strategies that should be part of a teacher's professional training. Similarly the ability to diagnose correctly a child's development with respect to classificatory concepts, from how he arranges miniature animals and objects in the sand tray or with respect to mathematical concepts from his play in the 'home corner', requires professional knowledge.

Diagnosis of a child's intentions or level of development is, of course, of nothing more than academic interest unless it is followed by an attempt to extend that child's understanding or to elaborate his intentions into educationally fruitful activity. It has been argued here that the nursery school curriculum should be one in which a teacher's interactions with her pupils synchronize with their intentions and levels of understanding. Thus, skilful extension requires skilful diagnosis. But professional knowledge of what constitutes a worthwhile curriculum in educational terms at this stage is also necessary. If, as Bruner has suggested, the managerial demands in a nursery school are considerable, a teacher, when not dealing managerially with children, has to decide where it would be most educationally profitable to engage in tutorial dialogue. Even though a teacher has provided materials that she considers have the greatest potential for provoking educationally fruitful activities, children will generate problems and activities that will differ in their educational potential. A child who has discovered that he can use constructional materials to build an edifice that remains stable if it is symmetrical has encountered a problem of considerable mathematical importance. If a teacher first makes explicit for him his formulation of the problem and his solution, then directs him to an activity with the balance scales and an assortment of objects and, yet later, confronts him with how to account for an asymmetrical structure that balances, he may well begin to understand that it is equal distribution of weight rather than symmetry that determines balance. The decision to interact with this child rather than with a group of children who, at the same time, are using the same equipment to symbolize objects at a make-believe tea party would be justifiable on educational grounds. On another occasion a group of children holding a make-believe tea party that seems to lack elaboration or imaginativeness may well be the ones who should be selected for attention in terms of a tutorial dialogue to improve the imaginative quality of their play.

In sum, the education of preschool children requires professional knowledge of both child development and of the kinds of skills and concepts that may be acquired by children in that age range and that are educationally powerful. The fact that the context in which this takes place is not that of a formal curriculum, but an informal one in which a large proportion of their activities are generated by the children does not mean that teachers are merely engaged in a shared child-rearing exercise. On the contrary, a high level of professional expertise is required to educate young children within an informal curriculum where there is a synchrony between children's intentions and the educational dialogues a teacher initiates.

J. *Tamburrini*

References

BERNSTEIN, B. (1971) 'Social class, language and socialization' in BERNSTEIN, B. (Ed) *Class, Codes and Control, Vol. 1* London, Routledge and Kegan Paul.

BLANK, M. (1974) 'Preschool and/or education' in TIZARD, B. (Ed) *Early Childhood Education* Slough, NFER.

BORKE, H. (1978) 'Piaget's view of social interaction and the theoretical construct of empathy' in SIEGEL, L.S. and BRAINERD, C.J. (Eds) *Alternatives to Piaget* London, Academic Press.

BROPHY, J. (1970) 'Mothers as teachers of their own preschool children: the influence of SES and task structure on teaching specificity' *Child Development* 41, pp. 79–94.

BRUNER, J. (1980) *Under Five in Britain* London, Grant McIntyre.

DONALDSON, M. (1978) *Children's Minds* London, Fontana/Open Books.

EL'KONIN, D. (1966) 'Symbolics and its function in the play of children' *Soviet Education* 8(2), p. 35.

FEITELSON, D. (1977) 'Cross cultural studies of representational play' in TIZARD, B. and HARVEY, D. (Eds) *Biology of Play* London, Heinemann.

FREYBURG, J.T. (1973) 'Increasing the imaginative play of urban disadvantaged kindergarten children through systematic training' in SINGER, J.L. (Ed) *The Child's World of Make believe* London, Academic Press.

GOLOMB, C. and CORNELIUS, C.B. (1977) 'Symbolic play and its cognitive significance' *Developmental Psychology* 13, pp. 246–252.

GOODNOW, J. (1977) *Children's Drawing* London, Fontana/Open Books.

HESS, R.D. and SHIPMAN, V.C. (1965) 'Early experience and the socialization of cognitive modes in children' *Child Development* 36, pp. 860–886.

LIGHT, P. (1979) *The Development of Social Sensitivity* Cambridge, Cambridge University Press.

SCHAFFER H.R. (1971) The Growth of Sociability, Harmondsworth, Penguin.

SMITH, P.K. and SYDALL, S. (1978) Play and non-play tutoring in preschool children: Is it play or tutoring which matters?' *Child Development* 48, pp. 315–329.

STANNARD, J. (1980) 'Communicating communication' *Education 3–13*, 8(1).

SYLVA, K., ROY, C. and PAINTER, M. (1980) *Childwatching at Play Group and Nursery School* London, Grant McIntyre.

TAMBURRINI, J. (impress) 'Some educational implications of Piaget's theory' in MODGIL, S. and MODGIL, C. (Eds) *Piaget: Controversy and consensus*, Praeger.

TAYLOR, P.H., EXON, G. and HOLLEY, B. (1972) *A Study of Nursery Education* Schools Council Working Paper 41, London, Evans/Methuen.

THOMAS, V. (1973) 'Children's use of language in the nursery' *Educational Research* 15(3), pp. 209–216.

TIZARD, B. (1974) *Early Childhood Education* Slough, NFER.

TIZARD, B. (1979) 'Language at home and at school' in CAZDEN, C.B. (Ed) *Language and Early Childhood Education* Washington D.C., National Association for Young Children.

TIZARD, B., PHILIPS, J. and PLEWIS, I. (1976) 'Staff behaviour in preschool centres' *Journal of Child Psychology and Psychiatry*, Vol. 17, No. 1.

VAN DER EYKEN, W. (1977) *The Preschool Years* Harmondsworth, Penguin.

The Primary Curriculum: A Proper Basis For Planning

David Oliver
Evesham Church of England First School

The School Context

Children in our primary schools are taught by hardworking and conscientious teachers who share with the general public a view of the purposes of schooling in the early years, which gives pride of place to making their pupils competent in maths and language and which relegates other areas of knowledge to a subsidiary place in their scheme of things (Ashton *et al*, 1975). The ORACLE project's review of fifty-eight classrooms found that two-thirds of the time in school was given over to the teaching of maths and language (Galton *et al*, 1980). Similarly Bennett, *et al*, (1980) found that, even in open plan schools, 70 per cent of junior teachers adopted the split day approach to curriculum organization, whereby basic skills were taught in the morning – when children were popularly supposed to be at their most receptive – and the rest of the curriculum in the afternoons. On average in infant open plan classes 36.7 per cent of the time was given to language and 15.8 per cent to maths; in junior classes the figures were 30.7 per cent and 17.1 per cent respectively. At the extremes the total allocated to these subjects was never less than 37.6 per cent and could be as much as 72.5 per cent in infant classes and in juniors could range from 25.8 per cent to 74 per cent of the time available. In the light of this information it is not surprising that HMI found that the majority of junior pupils across the age and ability ranges received inappropriate teaching in the humanistic disciplines, history, geography and aesthetics (DES, 1978). What was at first sight surprising and for most people much more disturbing was that an equally high percentage of able pupils were offered work in the field of maths and language which was no more appropriate to them than the rest of the curriculum is to the majority. Less surprising but no less disturbing was that less than one third of our children received an adequate grounding in both observational and experimental science. The message from such inquiries is clear. Most primary teachers are failing to provide a suitable education in the majority of curriculum areas for the majority of pupils and they are failing not because they are carelessly radical but because they are not radical enough. It is not that too many schools are like William Tyndale but that too few are willing to identify and commit themselves to a distinctive philosophy of education.

School and Society

Some years ago Judge (1975) argued that it is possible to define what it is that society reasonably and consistently should expect of schools and for teachers to place emphasis in their teaching upon those skills, competences and bodies of knowledge which the reasonable man expects most pupils of a given age to master. The evidence of the research quoted above suggests that schools have been able to do just this and that it is because of their success in implementing a consensus curriculum that they are failing either to teach the brightest children effectively, even in the skills they regard as basic, or to devote adequate planning and resources to other equally important areas of knowledge.

As Judge made clear, the assumptions that underlie a consensus curriculum are that the society of tomorrow will be the society of today and that the skills generally possessed and valued by today's man in the street will be the skills required by our pupils when they leave school in not less than five years time and possibly as many as fifteen or twenty. Both of these assumptions are indefensible. Schools do, of course, exist in a social context; they do require the support of the society in which they operate and try so hard to serve. All curriculum planning must take this fact into account. But the valued curriculum of today may not be the valuable curriculum for tomorrow. The ability to do long calculations by hand is, for an exponentially increasing number of people, a less useful skill than the ability to define the limits between which the result of a given calculation must lie or to check quickly on the appropriateness of an answer provided by an electronic calculator. In this context the ability to approximate up and down, to extract digital roots and know the ring structure of odd and even numbers are much more valuable than the ability to set out meticulously columns of figures in order to manipulate awkward quantities the nth decimal place.

When thinking about their responsibility to society, what teachers need continually to bear in mind is the often overlooked fact that for better or worse social patterns are subject to change either as a result of external conflict or internal pressures – sometimes slowly, often rapidly along a variety of dimensions; demographic, technological and ideological. Change along any one dimension is always and unavoidably associated with change in all the others. For teachers, in a time of falling rolls and reduced commitment to public expenditure, this message ought not to need spelling out. Less money and fewer pupils means smaller less well equipped schools; fewer teachers with less equipment means changed organization and a reduced curriculum resulting from a reduction in the amount of expertise available and in the availability of what expertise there is. Effective teaching must be based on a recognition of this fact of organic change and curriculum content be derived from attempts to identify the direction and pace of this change in the society to which both pupils and teachers belong, in an effort to equip the latter to function effectively as participant members of that different society which will exist when they leave school. This does not mean just making the best of a bad job. Education is necessarily dynamic and if we choose to deny this central truth we may feel happier and more confident but we will be deluding ourselves and failing our pupils.

Implications of Change

From this uncontentious recognition of the fact of change several significant propositions logically follow. First, that education must be forward looking; a valuable system of schooling will not be created by returning to the outmoded ideologies and related curriculum of yesterday's dead society or by declaring a moratorium on curriculum development. A clear consequence of this is that to a greater or lesser extent good educational practice will be out of step with the society in which it operates, and its worth may well not be self-evident to the normal member of the public, educated as most will have been in a previous system for a past age. Further, those schools whose teachers accept that change is inevitable and attempt to anticipate that change are, in themselves, necessarily agencies of change, making what they see as a real possibility more likely to come about. They are, thus, political institutions open to challenge both in terms of the likely correctness of their forecasts and of the desirability, if not of initiating, at least, of accelerating a shift in that direction. It is, therefore, the case that any political system, whichever party is in power, must take a real interest in what happens in school. Given that there is, inevitably, a large measure of uncertainity as to what could or will in fact occur and deep disagreement as to what is to be counted desirable, there will, unavoidably, be a degree of tension between educationists and those in power. This will be expressed in terms of a struggle over curriculum control, in an effort to direct and influence the pace of this change. Teachers are, willy nilly, political activists. Because they cannot be certain about what could or will happen, it follows that mistakes will occur frequently, that any curriculum which is future-orientated not only runs the risk of being, but will almost certainly be in some ways, misdirected. It also follows that the imposition of a prescribed curriculum, either in whole or in part, on all state schools will be disaster mitigated only in proportion to the degree that this common element accurately anticipates the nature of change in society or represents a relatively insignificant fragment of the total curriculum.

The only way to guarantee that, within any society, there exists a pool of expertise, practical and intellectual, capable of responding positively and expansively to changed circumstances is by encouraging the development not of one or two but of a wide range of different curricula subjected to a variety of critical scrutinies from many different points of view. There should be a place in such a system not only for the sort of school advocated by Black Paper contributor Stuart Froome but for those such as the much maligned Tyndale school. It is as well to remember that some of the parents of pupils at that establishment actually valued the education their children received and also to ask who saw to it or felt any obligation to see to it) that these children continued to receive the eduation their parents felt was benefiting them when all the controversy had died down? The freedom of the majority depends ultimately on their willingness to safeguard the freedom of the minority. Together with variety must go real freedom of choice – all parents must be enabled to choose, from the range available, the type of schooling their children are to receive and not simply be forced to use the one that the state sees fit to provide. In other words all parents should have, as of right, the privilege at present granted to a few persons on religious grounds, of not attending the local school. We must, as a profession, resist (at other than a very general level) formulating a more explicit consensus about what education is intended to do, as proposed by HMI (1980) and reject totally any moves in the direction of a national core or framework curriculum, as proposed by DES (1980) especially when these moves are paralleled by proposals, such as those made by the Central Policy Review staff, to rationalize the number of agencies responsible for overseeing the curriculum at national level. There are other no less powerful reasons for resisting any changes of this kind; in particular, that they are an obvious and obnoxious form of social control being, in effect, an attempt by those with privilege and power to limit both the aspirations and the ability to realize higher aspirations of those without. How else does one explain the redirecting to the private sector of scarce public funds to educate the gifted pupils of the deserving poor unless it is assumed that the curriculum imposed either by mandate or financial constraint on state schools will be second-rate, a curriculum for serfs rather than for free men? A consensus curriculum will further reduce freedom to choose not only the type of schooling our children have but the kind of life they will lead thereafter.

The urgency is made all the greater in the light of the realization that one aspect of social change will be in the intangible area of values and attitudes. Whilst I, for one, would not wish to argue that there are no fixed values, I would, with many others, be reluctant to claim that my values are either the only values or necessarily the best. Equally, even if we did wish to claim that our values were the best, I would suggest it is self evident that the holding of the same general values can lead to a wide range of conflicting specific behaviours. Those people who advocate abortion are at one with those who oppose it on setting a paramount value on the worth of the individual and their rights. It may be that the fundamental values do not change but what is beyond dispute is that our understanding of what constitutes behaviours expressive of these values is subject to radical reappraisal. A moral agent is first and foremost an autonomous rational being acting in accordance with his conscience. It follows that schools need to see to it that in inculcating a respect for basic values they do not merely insist on a thoughtless conformity to specific and transitory patterns of behaviour from their pupils. As in other areas, variety is the only way of guaranteeing the degree of receptivity to new ideas which is the hallmark of both an open and a tolerant society. In this as in so much else teachers seem either unwilling or unable to confront the issue squarely. Ashton (Ashton *et al*, 1975) found that teachers set more store by conformity than by independence, stressing, together with industriousness and a sense of purpose (whose purpose? we may ask), self control, obedience and the pursuit of social acceptability rather than trying to encourage their pupils to become socially effective through making their own decisions and formulating their own opinions.

To summarize the argument so far, schools exist today to equip pupils for life tomorrow and so will inevitably be nonconformist agents for change, subject to a wide range of pressures both from those people who feel any change to be threatening and from those who wish to prescribe the course of future events. In facing up to the possibility of change, schools cannot opt out of even the most sensitive areas of enquiry, for a change in one aspect of society means change in all other aspects. A teaching sequence looking at the building of a new by-pass or motorway ought inevitably to lead from economic considerations to a consideration of individual, as opposed to sectional, interest; to the value placed on non-productive intangibles and, in the process, raise both contentious and unresolved issues with wide and, for many people, uncomfortable implications. Even seemingly practical decisions in school, such as the use of unpaid volunteers to do ancillary and supervisory duties, are in the end political and so, ultimately, moral statements. For this reason, any curriculum which is worthwhile will be objectionable to some people. Teachers need to face up to the fact that they cannot please all of the people all of the time, but perhaps they could at least persuade most of the people that whatever they are doing is motivated by a genuine concern for their pupils and is directed by a clearly formulated philosophy of education against which the adequacy of their practice can be assessed. Much of the present anxiety about what is happening in our schools results from parental experience of the damaging effects of industrial action by some teachers and from a failure of the more imaginative and innovatory to give a clear account of the thinking which underlies their practice. Those teachers recognized by the members of the Plowden committee (1967) as successful were not articulate enough, offering not useful descriptions of what they were doing or reasons for doing it but expressions of benevolent aspiration, having at best only a tenuous relationship to the educational practices going on in their classrooms. At a time when teachers' benevolence is no longer taken for granted, and in the absence of articulate rationales from teachers, it is scarcely surprising that other people not directly engaged in teaching but equally concerned with the education that children receive in school seek to impose clearly defined conditions of work and a prescribed curriculum.

Teaching and Knowledge

I believe that one reason for the inability of primary teachers to give a clear account of what they are doing is that they attempt to derive their practice from an inappropriate theoretical basis. Teaching is first and foremost concerned with the transmission of knowledge. Effective practice must therefore be grounded on an adequate epistemology, or theory of knowledge. Teachers do not merely need to know what they teach but to know what it is to know what they teach. All teaching is in fact an expression, in terms of practical behaviour, of such a theory but it is usually ill-formulated, incomplete and often inconsistent. Such a theory will necessarily be realist, assuming that there is an external world made of persons, objects and so forth of which it is possible to be aware and so to affect and be affected by.

Philosophers distinguish between two types of knowledge: practical, *know how*, knowledge; and propositional, *know that*, knowledge. Propositional knowledge is further sub-classified into *empirical* knowledge and *a priori* knowledge – the truth of the latter is absolutely assured but tells us nothing about the world, since it is basically an explication of the meanings carried in a symbol system. Empirical knowledge, being derived from our limited experience of the world, can vouchsafe new knowledge about reality, but this knowledge is never either necessary or indubitable.

Unfortunately it is far from clear that this distinction is either valid or pedagogically useful. It seems to me self evident that every time we carry out a practical action we are demonstrating not just know-how but making explicit our belief in a proposition, stating a hypothesis about the world and subjecting it to a test. Similarly the possession of propositional knowledge means that the person possessing it will be disposed to behave in a limited number of ways which, in the light of that knowledge, he recognizes as appropriate to that situation. Not that whenever we act we consciously rehearse to ourselves a proposition about the world, though we certainly may do, or that we have consciously formulated such a proposition, although if called upon to do so we most probably could. Nonetheless something equivalent to such a proposition must surely be part of our mental equipment whenever we display the ability to act. Knowing how to do something necessarily must entail knowing that something. It also follows that knowing that something entails having some related know how.

Both knowing that and knowing how to do something require that the knower has an internalized model of reality and the ability to make explicit aspects, but aspects only, of this not necessarily well formulated knowledge. In other words, knowing is associated with the ability to represent and communicate the structure of the context of action by means of a publicly accessible system, if not of symbols at least of tokens and signs. The models we are able to construct are a function both of the means of collecting data at our disposal and of the latent symbol systems available to us for structuring this data. The structure that we imagine we perceive in the world is, to some degree, derived from those systems, relating only those features which are susceptible to representation within them. As Whorf (1956) puts it 'We dissect nature along lines laid down by our native languages'. A given symbol system be it linguistic, mathematic or graphic in form is, as Wittgenstein (1953) was fond of saying, 'a way of life'. Although it is widely recognized by linguists and philosophers that symbol systems do influence our perception, it is a view which conflicts with the common sense opinion that our perception determines the subject matter for our symbol system to represent. Nonetheless, I would suggest that the levels or kinds of awareness we have are a function of the conceptual schemas and related symbol systems at our disposal. Einstein, for example, was able to improve on Newton not as a result of having more data to structure but by having at his disposal a different system of geometry which made it possible to relate this data in a more powerful way. Poincaré (in Passmore 1968) was surely correct when he claimed that our descriptions of the real world are conventions, if not totally free, nonetheless creations imposed on reality by the human mind. For any given set of facts an indefinite number of explanations is possible and these explanations are not given nor discovered but invented. This means that we have applied, can apply and in all probability will continue to apply, totally inappropriate conceptual structures to the world.

Having a right to claim to know involves having an awareness of both the power and the limitations of the conceptual structures and related symbols we use, and being able to recognize the appropriateness of the symbol systems for the purposes we have.

One of the main focuses of schooling will, if this analysis is accepted, be to explore what we can know and to what degree we can have confidence in our knowledge derived from an exploration of symbol systems, learning both what can and cannot be encoded in a given system and how to use the code. If we accept the idea that all of our knowledge of the structure of reality is tentative and conventional, to a large degree implicit in our symbol systems, we will be extremely cautious about imposing rigid standards of correctness.

Many psychologists have fallen into the unfortunate habit of assuming that because young children use language in idiosyncratic ways they have somehow failed to acquire true concepts, possessing instead something other, pseudo concepts or whatever. It is obvious, however, that the child who consistently labels all furry animals of a certain size 'pussy' does not have a false or inadequate conception of cat, rather he has made use of this label to fix his perception of a larger category of objects and is demonstrating his possession of a valid concept of broader kind, such as small mammal or pet. He is quite properly using the most appropriate word available to him to structure his experience of the world, including only some objects of his perception in the class 'pussy' and rejecting others. Whilst he may learn very quickly to confine the use of 'pussy' to only cats, he may, as a result, lose his ability to deal with this now unlabelled broader category of objects. It is of course important to establish the fact that there is a socially accepted usage; we cannot go around using words in private ways if we are to operate effectively in a social context. But it does have very real dangers if, in the process, the labels become too rigidly fixed and the consensus usage becomes regarded as inviolate, thus inhibiting new ways of connecting realms of experience. Often it would be as well to ask not if a certain usage is correct but whether it is useful.

Types of Thinking

The distinction between poorly and well formulated knowledge implied in the previous section has little to do with standard usage but much to do with the distinction between what is variously called intuitive and analytic, open and closed, lateral and vertical, loose and tight thinking. Being unconscious and uncontrollable, intuitive thinking cannot be the guarantor of knowledge, but it is the source of hypotheses. Because of its untidiness, it is much, but wrongly and needlessly, neglected in school. For, while intuition is imperfectly understood, some things about it can be stated with a fair degree of confidence; first, that such thinking, while neither incorrigible nor orderly, is based on relevant, but not necessarily complete, knowledge; secondly, it is incomplete and probabilistic; further it seems to be in some way visual, associating separate items in the manner of a dream. Often intuition provides the only way of approaching a new category of experience and is essential for tackling many of the problems of daily existence. Bruner (1974) has argued that for the young child approaching an unfamiliar area of knowledge the choice is either to do nothing or to use the less than rigorous techniques of intuition. Intuitive thinking is not more primitive or less satisfactory than analytic thinking, it is complementary to it. In an age when the capacity of machines for carrying out analytic algorithms is outstripping man's, his powers of intuition will be increasingly important both to give the machines worthwhile tasks to perform and to sense the rightness or wrongness of their results. Bruner was undoubtedly correct to stress the need to train our pupils to operate beyond the sphere of formal intellectual involvement so that they have the ability and confidence to postulate tentative conclusions on the basis of insufficient evidence and to inquire after new evidence in order to reduce the conjectural element in these conclusions.

The role of analytical thinking is to enable precisely this inquiry after new evidence. Analytical thinking is conducted by means of symbol systems, is commonly supposed to be mechanical and algorithmic, orderly and predictable. Various attempts have been made, most influentially by Bloom and Kratwohl (Bloom and Kratwohl *et al*, 1956), to arrange levels of analytical thinking into a hierarchy of difficulty. In Bloom's taxonomy the lowest level of knowing was that of remembering, developing through comprehension, application, analysis and synthesis, to evaluation. Kohn (1963) proposed an alternative six-category hierarchy at two levels of sophistication – the first consisting of perception, association and concept attainment, involving respectively the ability to differentiate, label and categorize; the second level consisting of relational, critical and creative thinking. Sanders in similar vein suggested memory, translation, interpretation, application, analysis, synthesis and evaluation. There are common features that all these analyses share, an obvious one being that there is not so much a hierarchy within a single type of thinking as a progressive shift in emphasis from intuitive through analytic back to intuitive thought processes. A further assumption, implicit in such hierarchies, is that low order abilities can be exercised independently of those at a higher order. This second implication, whilst obviously convenient, is unfortunately fallacious. Observation entails judgement and evaluation, application involves not only comprehension and observation but evaluation and analysis, and so on, through the lists.

Sequencing

It simply is not the case, therefore, that we can develop an adequate overall teaching sequence either on the basis or within the framework of these hierarchies. Progress in learning is not to be measured as a clamber up a ladder of neatly ranked skills, it is to be measured in terms of the learner's ability both to receive and to produce material at all skill levels across an increasingly widening area of experience. As Fordor (1972,

1976) has pointed out a child's thinking develops not in logical power but in a progressive extension of the sort of content to which specific computational processes can be applied. The effort of teachers to impose such hierarchies is counter-intentional for in the process the sense of problem is lost and such teaching cannot be informed by the idea of the tentative nature of knowledge statement – their permeability as Bernstein (1973) calls it.

Any hierarchical model of planning, even at the individual topic level such as that offered by Gagné (1964), is open to similar criticism and is useful only in so far as we do not take it literally. The insistence on mastery of low order skills before progressing to high order skills fails to take account of the fact that such mastery may be dependent on first acquiring higher order skills; that often the possession at a crude level of a high order skill is required to make a start in learning. Further, such a hierarchy fails to recognize the open nature of mastery, or understanding. Mastery is a relative not an absolute term and levels of mastery are capable of being refined. The problem is that the whole can only be understood if we understand the constituent parts whilst these parts, in their turn, can only be understood if we understand the whole. The teacher is not concerned with developing complete mastery and understanding of a given skill or concept but with developing an adequate degree of both to enable further learning to take place, in the light of which, understanding of previously learned material will be refined.

Nor is difficulty obviously an intrinsic quality of material so much as a quality of a relationship between the learner and the material; it is a phenomenological attribute. Viaud (1968), in his discussion of intelligence, went so far as to suggest that we cannot make theoretical predictions as to what constitutes a complicated task for a particular human being. Nonetheless, if used with proper insight, the task of analyzing a body of competence into a system of subskills can be of assistance in enabling a teacher to respond flexibly and appropriately to the responses made by individual pupils. We can and need to recognize potential sources of difficulty in both the nature of the task and the nature of the learner. The intrinsic difficulty of a task is a function of the amount of information the learner has to assimilate to accomplish it; that is, in terms of the actual quantity of data and the category ranges being considered, the temporal range through which and the spatial range across which they are being related. But even very simple bits of information may be outside the capabilities of a given learner and what will make a given piece of data difficult for them will depend on their physiology, experience and purpose. It is no use asking a blind man to distinguish between a Rembrandt and a Turner, or a person from a non-graphic culture to make sense of pictures. Purposes, experience and physiology each affect the other; we only have those purposes which we feel able to achieve and this sense of ability depends on experience of past achievement and this level of achievement is itself dependent on our bodily make up. These two aspects of difficulty are summarized in figure 1.

Figure 1.

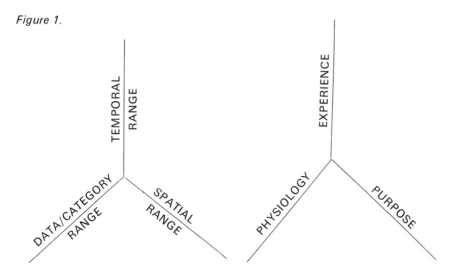

From these considerations, it follows that new material needs to be introduced holistically to the new learner's perceptual field. It needs to be expressed in a range of forms with which he is already familiar, he is able to perceive and receive, and are explicitly related to his real life experience and congruent with his existing purposes. The work of Gestalt and other psychologists has clearly demonstrated the necessity of keeping within the learner's perceptual field both the problem and its means of solution. Our task as teachers is to help the learner develop greater physiological acuity, broaden his experience and enlarge his sense of need and purpose. In part this task is to provide him with those symbol systems which can reduce complex material to manageable proportions, and to do this not by using text book examples but the lived experiences of the learner as examples of more general categories of phenomena. Teaching of this kind is multi-dimensional. If we are to teach map reading, for example, we must explore, if only incidentally in some non trivial way, the nature of communication, to see what maps can do that words, numbers or pictures can't and what they cannot do that those other means of communication can. This means exploring our own intentions and commitment to others and leads, in fact, to a consideration of our existential authenticity.

Contemporary Practice: A Critique

We can, on the basis of the foregoing discussion of both the social context in which schools operate and the nature of knowledge, thinking and learning, begin to develop a critique of present thinking about education at all levels, but especially the primary level. We can see that the obsession with consensus and consistency is both unrealizable and unnecessary. We can see, too, that a neatly ordered syllabus – however convenient it might be for those who see the key to good teaching as the maintaining of records of pupils progress (for example, Southgate, 1978) – is itself based on a mistaken view of the relationship between different types and levels of thinking and of their relationship to age and development levels. A record to be valuable must assume both a final goal and a means of measuring progress towards this goal. I have a private nightmare that one day the checklist will rule, that teachers will be saying 'Sally or Simon has mastered 397 of the 400 sub skills that make for efficient reading' but that the pupil in question will still be unable to read. There is no final clearly describable goal or set of goals, no crock of gold at the end of the educational rainbow; knowledge is not fixed but shifting; there is no body of required facts, skills or concepts relevant for all people in all places at all times. Such phrases as numeracy, literacy, oracy, and so forth, may sound like such goals but what is effective numeracy or literacy? While fixed in the discipline, the actual skills will be subject to reassessment in terms of their utility and logical necessity, as they are related to living and to developments in our awareness of the disciplines. Maths teaching has already withnessed radical shifts of emphasis – for example, in the early teaching of set theory based on late nineteenth and twentieth century developments in mathematical theory (Nuffield Foundation, 1969). Geography is in the process of a similar upheaval (Cole and Benyon, 1969); physics has long since ceased to be determinist (Popper, 1973); and orthodox Christian theologians no longer require us to believe either in an incarnation or a God (Cuppitt, 1980). Whenever teachers have responded to these shifts, the result has been to introduce curriculum content which has been outside, and often in conflict with, the reasonable man's store of knowledge and for which he could see no relevance.

Does this, therefore, leave us with the uncomfortable conclusions that we can have no way of assessing the effectiveness of schools or of prescribing a general pattern of education and that we have to resort instead to a kind of cultural relativism? Does this mean that we can only compare schools with a similar style of teaching or which have addressed themselves to similar problems or which operate in the same social context, assessing their practice in terms of how clearly they have formulated their underlying philosophy of how thoroughly they have anticipated criticism and of how closely their practice corresponds to this theory? Do we simply shrug our shoulders when the results are totally inappropriate? Certainly, if this degree of tolerance coupled with a demand for rigour were acceptable, only good could result from it. But I do not think that we either can or need to reject all standards of a more universal kind; on the contrary, I would suggest that implicit in relativism is an appeal to just such standards and that, without them, relativism itself is impossible. To make judgements even of an apparently relativistic kind we have to go beyond the type we are studying – for, if we did not, the standard of excellence would be the standard of conformist or hackneyed rather than innovative work. In point of fact, in all spheres of human activity, it is the original, the creative breakthrough which we see as excellent, not the average, the mediocre or the norm – but an innovation cannot be judged within the confines of the social consensus operating, it must be judged against some more absolute objective standard however imprecisely formulated. Surely the importance of creative insight is not going to be denied in education. To teach children about the restructuring insights that men of vision in all fields have achieved and yet to insist that our teaching styles and curriculum content be judged in terms of their consistency with a normative consensus standard would be a most flagrant example of cognitive dissonance. And yet these were precisely the kinds of criteria applied by HMI in the 1978 Survey (HMI, 1978).

The argument outlined so far has implicity suggested some more adequate criteria for judging the education offered primary pupils. Good teaching must be future-orientated, must respect and attempt to develop the existential authenticity of all the participants, must be skill – rather than information-centred and must adopt a critically open attitude to knowledge claims, whatever their source. In particular, it will be concerned to explore how we symbolize and so structure experience in order to make and substantiate such claims. In the early stages it will, because of its concern with authenticity and experience, take as its subject matter the shared experiences of the participants. It will be innovatory but, as innovation in itself is no mark of excellence, it is not to be valued for its own sake. What is to be valued is innovation motivated and constrained by a commitment to the pupils and to the society to which they will belong as full participants. The one dreary feature of present discussions on education is the inability of those engaged in it to see the need for radical change. The primary curriculum envisaged by HMI is traditional in the extreme. Despite a plea elsewhere to keep the curriculum in realistic limits, they advocate the inclusion of history, geography, moral, religious and physical education – as well as language, mathematics and art and craft. Others have argued that a curriculum so structured is inappropriate – basing their objection on a fallacious view of knowledge as forming an indivisible integrated whole.

Whilst I have made it clear elsewhere (Oliver, 1978, 1980) that I hold no brief for this particular line of argument, I would suggest there is room for considerable streamlining of the primary curriculum. An effective basic curriculum should be concerned to take, as its content, areas of experience shared by the participants, methods of structuring this experience and levels or styles of operation within the structuring symbol system. It should be concerned not with the width of informational content but with identifying styles of reasoning appropriate to different categories of experience, partly on the grounds that other agencies such as the media can, in fact, convey information more effectively and, partly, that such information is remarkably susceptible to revision. Consequently we should not seek for an encyclopaedist in every classroom or an academy in every staffroom, but we should require of our teachers that they have the necessary epistemological sophistication to distinguish between *a priori* and *empirical* knowledge, know when mechanistic causal explanations are appropriate, when probabilistic explanations are the best that can be achieved, when there is a need to appeal to purpose and intention, when all that is possible is a functional description and when a sequential account of stages in a process will lead to appropriate insight. It is not on this account necessary for them to know much science, history, geography or etc. but it is necessary for them to appreciate how workers in these disciplines proceed to make sense of experience.

A case study

To illustrate the argument above, a study of copying in the classroom can be the basis for introducing a wide range of coding systems and related concepts in the process of generating significant propositions relevant to areas of study as diverse as aesthetics, ethics and geography. In a given class of pupils engaged in illustrating a poem, the resultant products, besides being recognizably products reflecting unique personalities, will, in many cases, share common features, not all of which can be explained by reference to the task. Some pictures will emphasize this aspect, others a different aspect, some will be seen from one perspective, others from another. Nor will this distribution of features be random. The taking on of ideas from one person by another will be constrained by the relative spatial location of the parties, the availability of physical resources, the value placed by the imitator on the innovator, the ability of the copyist to emulate the innovator and so on. The distribution of different styles can be mapped, showing the source and spread of ideas and the boundaries between cultural groups. These can be correlated with the physical layout of the classroom and with less tangible factors like friendship groups or perceptions of expertise. In fact a classroom can be studied in the same way that Hagerstrand or Tornquist studied diffusion in Sweden. Such a study on a limited scale can give insight into the two key principles of geography, the distance principle and the location principle identified by Ambrose (1970). Further, pupils can be introduced to the concept of personal and cultural style, the value of originality and the role of imitation and its ethical implications in the arts and life. Pictures can be ranked by pupils in order of preference and different orderings can be compared graphically and in table form, levels of agreement and disagreement can

Figure 2.

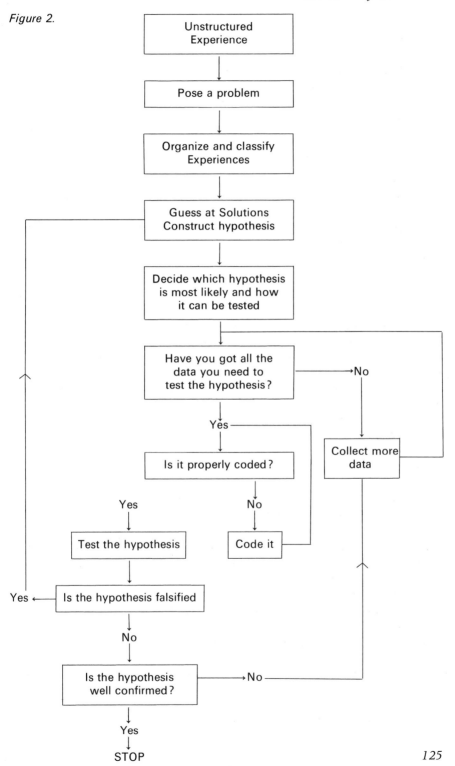

be identified and explanations sought for in terms of how different people perceived the task and how far their solutions were seen as appropriate by others, and so the class can proceed to identify different peoples' value systems.

We can model this sort of teaching sequence in a flow chart such as that in figure 2. The unclassified experience in this case is drawing, the problem is how to account for difference and similarity in product. The solution proposed could be that neighbours copied from neighbours or that friends worked together; in fact, the more hypotheses that can be generated the better. They should be generated by the pupils in open discussion and, in the process, the ways in which each hypothesis can be verified or falsified should also be discussed and the sorts of data needed to make those tests identified. Coding would, in the example, consist of mapping the classroom, the cultural regions and friendship groups and testing to see how far one relates to the others. If it is found that only children at the same table have similar pictures, the implication would be that proximity is the determining factor, if, on the other hand, this does not explain all cases of similarity, then the way forward is to look for a modified hypothesis. It is only after undertaking work of this kind that pupils are properly equipped to study examples at a larger and more significant scale. The logic of the curriculum is to start with what the child can experientially encompass and has the skills to handle before looking at examples which, whilst they can be seen to be isomorphic with that experience, have contingent details that distract attention from the under-lying structure and distort the focus of the learning pattern.

Modelling the Curriculum

It is only after having structured their own experience and having it enriched by experiencing the difference between model and reality that pupils are ready to study critically much that is traditionally taught in schools. It will be seen that, while such a teaching strategy cannot be summarized in schemes of work, it is not without purpose and structure and a check on effectiveness is possible. The formal curriculum can be adequately modelled in ways such as shown in figure 3. It is not claimed that the model, as it stands, is definitive of the form such a model would take. Clearly, the types of symbol system identified are crude and, within each broad category, a wide variety of sub-classifications could be made and would at some stages need to be made. For example, visual systems could be separated into graphs, networks, diagrams, maps and pictures; a further distinction could be drawn between metaphorical and literal systems as well as between qualitative and quantitative. Nor is it claimed that the classification of spheres of application is the best that could be made, simply that it is sufficient for the purpose of planning an adequate

Figure 3.

STYLES
OF THINKING

1	Modifying the Model
2	Applying Model in new context
3	Synthesising Data ie Model making
4	Inferring beyond Data
5	Relating Data
6	Encoding & Displaying Data
7	Collecting Data
8	Identifying a Problem/Question

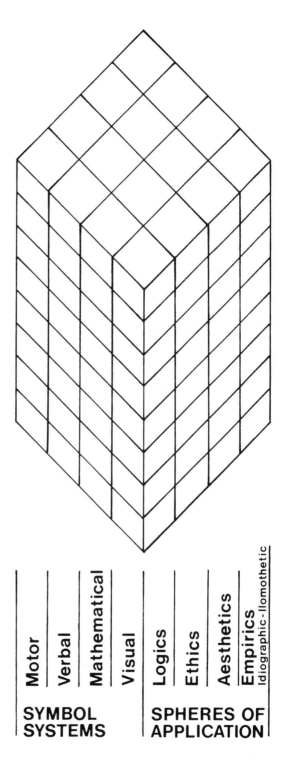

Motor
Verbal
Mathematical
Visual
Logics
Ethics
Aesthetics
Empirics
Idiographic - Ilomothetic

SYMBOL
SYSTEMS

SPHERES OF
APPLICATION

primary curriculum. An alternative set of content categories could be one's self as an individual, others' selves, society the animate world and the inanimate world. In any of these cases it is not suggested that complete coverage is either possible or necessary. It is an essential premise that any discipline which is an example of any one of the spheres of application can act as an initiation into the mode of thinking appropriate to that sphere.

In applying the model, the teacher is not asked to introduce pupils to all areas of aesthetics, for example, but to give them a chance to operate in some effective way in this field. A gifted musician may well confine himself legitimately to enabling pupils to respond aesthetically by making and responding to music, thereby neglecting the visual arts. Similarly, it is argued that biology will serve as well as physics as an introduction to the nomothetic method of explaining the empirical world and that any study of man as a member of a group to the idiographic style of explanation. Rather than having to provide vicarious substitutes for experience across the whole field of knowledge forms, the teacher's task is to identify key methods of inquiry and help pupils to use these to structure their own experience. Data and content will be provided to a large measure by pupils themselves; the teacher's job is to use this data to develop facility with symbol systems and styles of thinking, so filling in each cell of the matrix not in the course of a single project but during a protracted period of teaching time. How the exploration of copying as discussed earlier could be analyzed in terms of the model is illustrated in figure 4 and demonstrates the value of the model as a means of monitoring curriculum balance. The model could be modified to accommodate different emphases in value – if, for example, it was felt that motor symbols should not have equal status with verbal, or logics with empirics – but such modifications do not invalidate the basic structure offered. In such a style of teaching, the emphasis will be on group work, discussion and criticism. In essence, the aim is to simulate the way research is conducted at the frontiers of knowledge, the intention being to avoid rote learning of tricks which have later to be unlearned and which form barriers to later learning.

In structuring real experience the tidiness of the model contrasts obviously with the chaos of life as it is lived; by confining our attention to the model world of text books we inevitably fail to give our pupils an insight into the contrast between reality and its representation. This is not to suggest that there will not be occasions when worthwhile learning will makes use of some precoded, vicarious rather than direct experience as its initial stimulus, but in such cases the learners should be presented with the coded data of a kind related to that derived from their own experience, from which others have drawn conclusions, rather than being presented with these conclusions and encouraged to structure data for themselves before considering the structures imposed on it by others. It is only after the pupils have learned that structures are invented by other people much like themselves and are open to criticism and modification that they

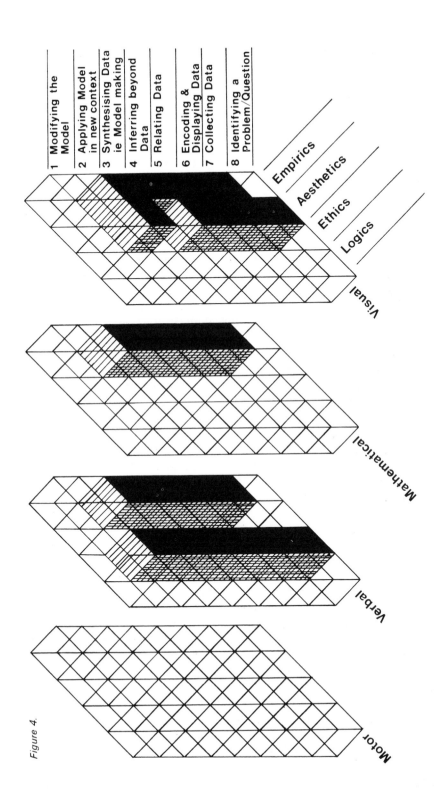

Figure 4.

1 Modifying the Model
2 Applying Model in new context
3 Synthesising Data ie Model making
4 Inferring beyond Data
5 Relating Data
6 Encoding & Displaying Data
7 Collecting Data
8 Identifying a Problem/Question

Empirics

Aesthetics

Ethics

Logics

Visual

Mathematical

Verbal

Motor

are ready to read and handle standard textbooks in the appropriate way. In the primary school there can be no place for watered down versions of secondary textbooks which are themselves watered down versions of standard works. Such simplified texts serve to give the work from which they are indirectly derived the spurious authority of Holy Writ and place it beyond the critical consideration it requires. The primary child should be presented not with canonical reconstructions of the past in history, for example, but with the evidence on which such reconstructions are based and, only after suggesting (however inadequately) what can be inferred, should be shown not one but a variety of reconstructions to criticize.

Such a teaching style is extremely time consuming and breadth of coverage must inevitably be sacrificed in the interests of depth. However, given that other agencies exist which fulfill the informing function more effectively than school, this is not the failing that many might think it to be. In fact the justification is precisely that, because other agencies do exist and because the amount of information published by them is increasing exponentially and the structure imposed on it subject to frequent revision, the school's function is not significantly to provide more information but to equip pupils to handle the information they will receive. Schools cannot continue to regard the mass media with suspicion and ignore rather than take positive advantage of their existence. Equally, because of this width of coverage, teachers need to select examples of problems from as wide an area as possible. Whilst it is not being claimed in this paper that the curriculum outlined either by implication or with reference to specific examples is the only valid response to the current socio-educational context, it is contended that only by focusing on styles of thinking, types of symbol system and spheres of application, in some such way as that described, is it possible to envisage schools fulfilling a necessary function in a society such as ours. Such a curriculum must be concerned with the development of a wide range of skilled behaviour and informational content selected on the basis of its appropriateness for stimulating the development of these skills. There is no body of essential information in an area with which all people need to be acquainted, but there are skills without which no individual can function autonomously or authentically. These they need to have developed to a higher level of mastery than is at present regarded by people in all walks of life as adequate. There is nothing particularly new in all this but it certainly requires stressing again and again because the message is neither received not understood by other than a very small minority of hard pressed teachers.

Conclusion

To conclude, the basis of teaching is epistemology and any other focus can, if not contained within this idiom of activity, only prove damaging. I am aware that the concepts of childhood, readiness and intelligence which play a key role in most teachers' thinking about their job have not been used in this paper; for my part I believe that each of these concepts have had a deadening effect on education and have functioned not as stimuli to innovation but as excuses for failure and as rationales for offering our pupils a restricted and restricting curriculum. But that's another story. Skill-focused teaching starts from data not conclusions, experience not books, and is open not closed. Young people are ready to do far more than we give them credit for and by diagnosing what they can do, rather than what they cannot, and teaching from this area of competence we can give them the confidence to make, not merely receive, knowledge structures. Traditionally our education system has been authoritarian and fact-centred, obsessed with maintaining control rather than encouraging discipleship. Teachers must be concerned to develop in their pupils an attitude which is at once responsible and critical. They must be taught to frame questions in such a way that a line of investigation is defined so that solutions to the problem expressed may be found. To do this there has to be a shift towards open-ended teaching and learning situations. We must aim at assisting each child to form his/her own mental model of the world so that (s)he will be able to organize and structure information into coherent and consistent bodies of knowledge easily stored and readily recalled when needed and be willing to share ideas with others.

Symbol systems are only of value as means of communication. The basis of communication is trust and confidence, confidence in ourselves and trust in others that we have something to communicate which is worthwhile and to which they will respond with consideration. Developing the style of work described in this curriculum means establishing close and caring relationships with one another in the classroom and the school; it is not arid and pedantic but fertile and imaginative. Such a style of teaching removes from the teacher the need to maintain an impossibly high level of informedness or from schools the need to purchase costly sets of text books and expensive commercial apparatus for specialist teaching. It further preserves the status of the general class teacher and the present high value placed on personal relationships while demanding a major change in teachers' view of knowledge which threatens the existing distribution of authority and status. In so far as the profession is prepared to consider such an option, it demonstrates its awareness of the role of schools in the modern world. In so far as it fails to respond to this demand, it abdicates responsibility and should not be surprised if others less directly involved take control not simply of what but how teachers should teach, deciding the content of the curriculum, the details of the syllabus and the resources to be used. We need not and should not allow this to happen, but it will be no use protesting unless we can demonstrate that it is teachers, not some other agency, who have the experience, expertise, courage and concern to make the best decisions not for the past but for tomorrow. Above all we need to stress the need for variety in educational provision. It is complementarity not consistency which should be the criterion of adequacy in provision at all levels from the local to national. The pursuit of consensus is logically inconsistent with the quest for balance in the total curriculum. Balance is the equilibrium of matched conflicting forces, is unstable and requires constant adjustment to changing circumstances; it is uncompromising. In a world where the centre no longer holds, it is balance not reluctant agreement which should be our goal. Life in a society where people have the degree of openness of mind to welcome disagreement, the self confidence to make public their true convictions and a commitment to rationality and to valuing others will not be comfortable nor easy but neither will it be boring or lack lustre.

References

AMBROSE, P. (1970) 'New developments in geography' in WALFORD, R. (Ed) *New Directions in Geography* London, Longman.

ASHTON, P. *et al,* (1975) *The Aims of Primary Education: A Study of Teachers' Opinions* London, Macmillan.

BENNETT, N., ANDREAE, J., HEGARTY, P. and WADE, B. (1980) 'Open plan primary schools: Findings and implications of a national inquiry' *Education 3–13,* 8(1).

BERNSTEIN, B. (1973) *Class Codes and Control Volume III* St Albans, Paladin.

BLOOM, B.S. and KRATWOHL, D.R. *et al,* (1956) *Taxonomy of Educational Objectives: Handbook 1 – The Cognitive Domain* New York, David McKay Co. Inc.

BRUNER, J.S. (1974) *The Relevance of Education* Harmondsworth, Penguin.

CENTRAL ADVISORY COUNCIL FOR EDUCATION (1967) *Children and their Primary Schools* London, HMSO.

COLE, J.P. and BENYON, N.J. (1969) *New Ways in Geography* Oxford, Basil Blackwell.

CUPPITT, D. (1980) *Taking Leave of God* London, Student Christian Movement.

DEPARTMENT OF EDUCATION AND SCIENCE (1978) *Primary Education in England: A Survey by HM Inspectorate of Schools* London, HMSO.

DEPARTMENT OF EDUCATION AND SCIENCE (1980) *A Framework for the School Curriculum* London, HMSO.

FODOR, J.A. (1972, 1976) quoted in JOHNSON LAIRD, P.N. and WASON, R.C. (Eds) (1977) *Thinking* Cambridge, Cambridge University Press.

GAGNÉ, R.M. (1964) *Conditions of Learning* Second Edition, London, Holt, Rinehart and Winston Inc.

GALTON, M., SIMON, B. and CROLL, P. (1980) *Inside the Primary Classroom* London, Routledge and Kegan Paul.

HAGERSTRAND, T. (1967) *Innovation Diffusion as a Spatial Process* Chicago, University of Chicago Press.

HER MAJESTY'S INSPECTORATE (1978) *Primary Education in England* London, HMSO.

HER MAJESTY'S INSPECTORATE (1980) *A View of the curriculum* London, HMSO.

JUDGE, H. (1975) Articles in *Times Educational Supplement.*

KOHN, C.F. (1963) 'Basic concepts of geography and their development in the classroom' in FENTON, E. (Ed) *Teaching the New Social Studies* New York, Holt, Rinehart and Winston Inc.

NUFFIELD FOUNDATION (1969) *Nuffield Mathematics Project* London, Chambers and Murray.

OLIVER, D.K. (1978) 'Skill-centred teaching: An alternative to integration' in RICHARDS, C. (Ed) *Education 3–13* Driffield, Nafferton Books.

OLIVER, D.K. (1980) 'Primary education: A radical alternative' in RICHARDS, C. (Ed) *Primary Education: Issues for the Eighties* London, Black.

PASSMORE, J. (1968) *A Hundred Years of Philosophy* Harmondsworth, Penguin.

POPPER, K. (1973) *Objective Knowledge* London, Oxford University Press.

SOUTHGATE, V. (1978) 'Reading: Three to thirteen' in RICHARDS, C. (Ed) *Education 3–13* Driffield, Nafferton Books.

TORNQUIST, G. (1970) *Contact Systems and Regional Development*, Lund.

VIAUD, G. (1968) *Intelligence: Its Evolution and Forms* London, Hutchinson.

WHORF, B.L. in CARROLL, J. (Ed) (1956) *Language, Thought and Reality: Selected Writing of Benjamin Lee Whorf* Cambridge, Mass., MIT Press (see also Bernstein 1973 *op. cit.*).

WITTGENSTEIN, L. (1953) *Philosophical Investigations* Oxford, Basil Blackwell and Mott.

Teacher Education and the Primary Curriculum

Robin J. Alexander
University of Leeds

College and School: Match or Mismatch?

This article considers the relationship between two curricula – the primary school curriculum and the teacher training curriculum. That there should be a relationship nobody doubts – the one prepares people to operate effectively in the other: the question is, what sort of relationship? Using the word which HMI very much made their own in the primary survey (HMI, 1978) it could be argued that there should be, at the very least, a 'match' between the needs of teachers and what colleges provide.

However, match is not a straightforward concept, for a number of reasons. Even if courses are indeed matched to the practices and expressed needs of serving teachers, is it certain that these necessarily or inevitably meet the needs of the children? In conventional assertions about the 'irrelevance' of college courses to children's needs there are at least two tacit assumptions meriting query: one is that schools simply by virtue of being 'where the action is' meet children's needs and the other is that college staff by being away from the action have neither the right nor ability to define those needs independently.

For, of course, the notion of 'needs' itself is acutely problematic. All statements of needs in the educational arena – including those which make strongest claims to value freedom, the empirically-based lists of 'developmental' needs featured in many student psychology texts – are statements of value, opinion, ideology, not fact. In the classroom the nature of the teaching activities and their control by one adult define, *de facto*, the children's needs. With no other adult present and a tradition of quasi-autonomy, the definition can go unchallenged, or at least can be legitimated by something called 'professional judgement'. But if teacher educators, who are also professionals but inevitably view children and educational processes differently (if only in a more generalized, less situation-specific way) come up with alternative statements about needs, are these less legitimate if they differ from those of practising teachers? The assumption of absolutes, let alone consensus, in the discussion of educational needs seems naïve and dangerous.

Even if an attempt is made to resolve this difficulty by ignoring values and beliefs and basing training courses firmly on schools 'as they are', what are the chances of achieving 'realism' when every school is different and what goes on in each might be described differently by different observers? Is it possible to produce a picture of schools culled from this diversity of actual and perceived practice which is sufficiently coherent to serve as a basis for planning? Even the very word 'primary' as a label for 3–13 provision suggests a unity and uniformity which are quite misleading. This is the longest (and arguably the most important) stage of compulsory education. It covers a considerable range of children's development, and it includes a great diversity of types of school – nursery, first, infant, junior, JMI, middle. 'Primary', as a label, is useful only in the most superficial sense – the quasi-legal sense of defining a stage of schooling. To see it as implying anything further – for instance that there is a coherent educational philosophy and practice for all schools within the primary stage – is unwise. 'Start with schools as they are' has become something of a slogan in the teacher education world lately. Down-to-earth, no-nonsense 'realism' always provides a potent rallying point (especially so in a situation where plurality and complexity can paralyze action), but it is misleading to suggest that defining schools as they are is any less problematic than saying how schools ought to be. The debate about the Lancaster report (Bennett *et al*, 1976), the HMI survey (HMI, 1978) and the ORACLE findings (Galton and Simon, 1980 and, with Croll, 1980) demonstrates this clearly. If only we *did* understand 'schools as they are' the teacher trainers' task would be greatly simplified.

However, the problem does not end here since, whatever the pressure towards present-oriented course planning, teacher training is nothing if not future-oriented: even the probationary year is four to six years away for course planners and three to four years away for the new student and much can change even in that short period, particularly when national and local policy have such a strong impact on schools as at present and are conducted on such a hand-to-mouth basis. But course planners need to look further ahead than this, to have some notion of where schools and society might be heading: whose crystal ball do they gaze at? Do they adopt the neo-Malthusian pessimistic projection of economic, even global catastrophe, or the micro-chips with everything paradise of the colour supplements (or neither)? Or do they abandon all futurology as pointless? (They do not, of course: all vocational courses embody assumptions about the future however present-centred they might claim to be, if only the assumption that nothing will change).

Finally, in thinking about the future, do the teacher educators adopt a reactive stance or a deterministic one? Do they identify ways in which teaching might improve and prepare students to contribute to this? Do they, more fundamentally, view the educational process as one which enables children to adapt to change which others (presumably educated elsewhere) introduce, or as one which gives children the means to influence their own destiny? Is it schools as they are, as they might be or as they ought to be, society as it is, might or ought to be, and is the teacher to be a conformist, a reformer or a revolutionary? These are some of the general problems associated with the search for 'match between primary school needs and teacher training curricula. In practice, course planners just have to exercise a choice, knowing that by someone's definition of schools', teachers' and children's needs all courses lack 'match'. Of course there are also clear practical reasons why college courses and tutors often come in for considerable criticism from the profession (some of them justifiable in anybody's terms) but much of the difficulty boils down to this problem: that achieving match between the needs of children, teachers and schools on the one hand, and the character of college courses on the other, is not just a practical, organizational problem, but a matter of competing values, ideas, opinions, beliefs, some of which are irreconcilable. There is, thus, no way that the training institutions can win. There are, however, ways that some of the inconsistencies between the college curriculum and the teacher's task can be partly alleviated; this article is concerned with some of these inconsistencies – especially those that concern the teacher's role in relation to the primary curriculum. Whatever the attraction of the new realism in teacher education – that is, working towards the achievable target of training for the first few years of teaching rather than for life – the course must also lay foundations for subsequent development. Since it is my hypothesis that despite the considerable strength of primary schools in certain directions there is a notable inadequacy in relation to *curriculum conceptualization, appraisal and renewal*, I shall argue that it is in this area that there is the most substantial 'mismatch' between initial training courses and professional needs.

The Teacher Education Course: Innovation without Change?

A college course adds up, or should add up, to a coherent view of the nature of the teacher's task, to a view of the 'needs' of the professional and, by extension, to a view of the nature of teaching, learning and curriculum in the schools where the teacher will eventually work. So that, when trends in primary teacher education courses are examined, it should be possible to detect without too much difficulty the 'professional profile' of the primary teacher and the implicit 'model' of the primary school towards which they are directed. The match between these and the 'real world' of primary schools can then be considered.

Just before the publication of HMI's own survey on the B.Ed. (DES,

1979), Peter Chambers undertook an analysis of a large number of B.Ed. courses produced in the course planning explosion which followed the James Report (Chambers, 1979). He found that, although many courses on the face of it looked and claimed to be different from the first much criticised B.Eds. which appeared in the mid 1960s, the old underlying structures and assumptions were remarkably persistent and the genuinely innovatory courses were few and far between. There are clear reasons why this should be the case – the conservatism of validating bodies for one, and the conservatism of college staff for another. More pervasively, the academic structure of the colleges limited the extent of change and, in turn, was limited by the nature of staff experience and qualifications and by the deep institutional divides between the academic subject experts, the educational theorists, and the 'practical' professional studies tutors.

Despite different labels, the main elements still tend to be variations on the following pattern rooted in the McNair Report (Board of Education, 1944), developed by the Robbins Report (CHE, 1963), reflected in the B.Eds established from 1965 onwards and confirmed by the James Report (DES, 1972):

(a) one or two 'main' or 'main' plus 'subsidiary' subjects which are studied at a fairly advanced academic level and are seen as providing the student's 'personal' higher education;
(b) education theory;
(c) curriculum or professional studies – that is, the school subjects one is to teach and how to teach them;
(d) school experience.

The innovations and variations are more often than not *within* these categories rather than *between* them. Where there is innovation which actually crosses boundaries, it tends to involve the low status area of professional studies (which is increasingly related more closely to school experience and/or education theory) rather than the high-status area of the academic subject. The major shifts within the academic area have been towards a greater element of interdisciplinarity, multi-disciplinarity and the use of a 'unit' structure to permit greater flexibility and more variable student choice. Within the education theory area more thematic approaches have been developed rather than separate courses in psychology, sociology and philosophy of education. Thus, courses include units entitled 'The Young Child', or 'Classroom Studies' – or even 'The Curriculum' – each of which can be psychological or sociological, or philosophical, or a combination. Also, attempts are being made to link the education theory to practical work in schools so that, for example, discussion of children's cognitive development may involve students in undertaking simple Piagetian tests of conservation with children.

The major shifts within professional studies have been:

(a) the introduction in a number of courses of curriculum non-specific teaching skills resulting from a closer analysis of the teaching task than hitherto – that is, the students don't just do courses in the teaching of reading or maths, but may have discrete practical teaching units (the more sophisticated successors to courses on blackboard work display etc.);

(b) linked to this a greater use of techniques such as simulation, role play and microteaching;

(c) shifts in the curriculum emphasis of professional studies in response to reports like Bullock, James and Warnock. Most notably this has produced an increase in the time devoted to the teaching of spoken and written language, reading and mathematics; more recently, since the primary survey, science is getting closer attention.

Finally, the fourth area, school experience, has seen two shifts. One is towards a greater structural and temporal flexibility – thus, instead of three block practices, there may be day attachments, half-day attachments, short blocks, long blocks and various combinations of these. The other is a change in the use of the school from the simple sink-or-swim teaching practice to its use as a setting for observation, for small-scale enquiries, for individual and small-group rather than whole-class teaching. The underlying concept has changed – the school is not simply a place where students practise what they have been taught in colleges, but is where they actually learn and study: the intended school-college relationship is now reciprocal.

'Personal' and 'Professional'

Curriculum should have meaning as well as form or structure. What meaning does this changing teacher education curriculum have, what view of the teacher's role does it represent, and how consistent does it seem with what goes on, or what might go on, in primary schools? The basic divide between 'personal' or 'academic' and 'professional' is still there, and indeed most people do not even question it but move straight on to the arguments about 'consecutive' and 'concurrent' courses – about '2 plus 1', '2 plus 2', '1 plus 2' etc. – purely structural questions which ignore issues of purpose and meaning. But this most deeply-rooted of all assumptions in teacher education needs to be questioned. The assumption is that the teacher needs a personal education which is intellectually demanding and personally satisfying, regardless of what sort of school he is to teach in, and that this 'personal' education is provided only by the study in depth of the academic subject or subjects. The latter half of the last sentence must be questioned, for it implies that the non- 'academic' 'professional' part of the course is a mere 'training' with little intrinsically educative value. Some have questioned it, and a few colleges have abandoned the main subject for primary students, arguing that the whole degree should be both professionally and personally educative and that professional study can be rigorous and 'degree-worthy'. Many teachers take this view, resenting (understandably) the way the academic subject dominates the student's course and attention. The college response, however, is usually not to question the personal/professional dichotomy but to juggle with the sequence.

However, it is also worth looking at the matter from a different standpoint. Equating 'personal' solely with 'academic' might be untenable, but does this mean that primary students should *not* study an academic subject for its own sake? In the B.Ed course I was involved in planning and evaluating, we assumed that primary students, given a very flexible unit structure, would opt to do several academic subjects in medium doses rather than one or two in large doses on the grounds that this would give them a better background for the role of class-teacher of many subjects. But, in fact, they used this flexibility to construct for themselves course programmes very like the old 'main plus subsidiary'. When we interviewed them on this they tended to argue strongly for the study in depth of something that interested them as a right for all B.Ed students, whether primary or secondary (Alexander, 1978). So this remains a complex issue and perhaps casts some doubt on the wisdom of those few colleges which have abandoned the academic subject altogether for their primary students.

Theory and Practice: the Perennial Problem

According to conventional wisdom, while the academic subject provides the student's 'personal' education, education studies provide the theoretical stiffening for practice which, ever since B.Eds appeared, has been seen as essential on two counts — both of which are somewhat suspect. The first argument is that without education theory a professional degree might lose its respectability, its 'degreeworthiness'. The other relates to the deeper and more complex issue of professional status: a profession, it is asserted, draws on an 'essential body of knowledge' about the professional activity. Part of this is knowledge of the subject matter to be taught and the rest is knowledge of children and educational processes. However, in higher education institutions (which the colleges now securely are) knowledge has to be general, academic and public (rather than particular, common-sense and individual) in order to count as 'knowledge' at all. So the 'essential body of knowledge' takes the form of a massive dose of education theory, and practical, common-sense, intuitive knowledge tends to be downgraded or even discounted altogether.

This approach to professional knowledge generates the notorious 'theory-practice problem' which is, in essence, two problems or questions:

1 How can theory and practice be brought closer together? (The relationship question).
2 What sort of theory, if any, should primary/middle students encounter – what is the nature of a 'theory' for teaching? (The content question).

Too often, only the relationship question has been asked and the more fundamental issue of *what sort* of theory has been avoided. Too often the enormous and rapidly expanding corpus of educational theory, the holy trinity of psychology, sociology and philosophy with the also-ran of history, has been taken as given, self-justifying, and the problem has been seen as one of making this theory more 'meaningful' rather than establishing whether trainee teachers really need it. Colleges have, admittedly, worked very hard at the *relationship* question and one of the consequences is a certain amount of trimming of content together with a shift to the thematic treatment of theory coupled with attempts to demonstrate the application of theory to practice through related school experience activities of the investigatory/workshop variety described earlier. But the concern has been to demonstrate the application of theory to practice as if the theory was there already, inviolate. To my mind, this is putting the cart before the horse – the theory should grow from the practice which it should help to illuminate and to improve. Sometimes it does but, more frequently, its treatment in colleges suggests the opposite.

Without attempting to do justice to the complexity of argument in this area, a number of propositions can be offered before we move to the other component of B.Eds – professional studies:

1 Intelligent teaching requires that teachers theorize, that is, that they have a coherent view of what they are doing and why, a clear conceptual framework, and a basis for analyzing their actions.
2 Such theorizing can draw usefully on academic education theory, but the latter does not have a monopoly. Academic theorizing is just one sort of theorizing.
3 Much academic education theory is meaningless to student teachers in three ways:
   (a) conceptually it is totally unlike the everyday theorizing of practising teachers;
   (b) students lack the practical experience against which to test it;
   (c) many students lack the intellectual and personal experience and maturity to tackle the sorts of issues sometimes involved.
4 What is needed is the establishment of a theoretical framework which is as far as possible consistent with, and supportive of, the everyday conceptual framework used by teachers but which is capable over a period of time of assimilating the more sophisticated theoretical discussions. Instead students are frequently turned against theorizing *at any level*, their view of teaching polarized into one which is more narrowly 'practical' than it need be.

5 Especially needed is a basis for thinking about the curriculum. There has been the growth of curriculum theory, work on objectives, evaluation and the like, but for eighteen to twenty-one year olds this has the same problems as the disciplines approach to education theory. What seems clear is that for many serving teachers the apparatus just does not exist for a deep and systematic appraisal of their curriculum. I make this assertion in full consciousness of the recent growth in the number of 'curriculum review' and 'school self-evaluation' documents and checklists produced by LEAs and schools. Such devices are helpful, certainly, in indicating *foci* for appraisal, and they are systematic in as far as they use categories, but being geared to yes/no responses they are essentially crude tools for qualitative appraisal and in their lack of an explicit basis of educational principles they demonstrate point 4 above. Two related questions need to be asked here, in both schools and training institutions: *'What sort of curriculum knowledge does the primary teacher need?'* and *'What sort of intellectual tools, skills and resources does he need for analyzing curriculum, for appraising it and improving it, and for ensuring that it relates meaningfully to the child and the social context?'*

6 Two practical conclusions follow from the foregoing discussions: first, a great deal of valuable course time is wasted on meaningless academic education theory and, secondly, given the immense problems of curriculum knowledge facing the primary class teacher, especially the teacher of older primary children, some of this time could be better spent on a deeper exploration of the primary curriculum.

Professional Studies and Views of Teaching

The explicitly *professional* side of college courses (professional studies, curriculum studies etc.) exhibit some diversity. I recently analyzed the professional components of a number of CNAA B.Eds to see if any distinct patterns emerged, whether there were definite sorts of teacher implied by the emphasis of the 'professional' parts of the course. Five distinct professional 'emphases' or 'orientations' were discernible, each of them representing a different view of what the nature of primary teaching most requires from the young teacher.

1 The *'child-oriented'* professional course places its major emphasis upon developing the student's understanding of the child's development and learning processes. In a sense this might seem a superfluous category in that *all* courses have substantial elements on child development. But in a negative way it is a matter of emphasis. The curriculum courses are there, but represent a subsidiary concern and there may be major elements on children with special needs including the less able and the more able which the next category may ignore.

2 Designers of the *'curriculum-oriented'* professional course perceive mastery of curriculum knowledge and related teaching skills as the central professional 'need', and most 'professional' time is given to the various curriculum areas the student may teach. Here, too, there is likely to be substantial emphasis on curriculum theory. Within this 'curriculum-orientation' there are two main subdivisions. First, most middle school curriculum-oriented courses enable students to study at least one curriculum subject in greater depth than the others to produce a 'semi-specialist' teacher. Increasingly, since the primary survey and recent DES recommendations, the 'semi-specialist' approach is also offered for intending teachers of younger children, especially juniors. The second subdivision, at the other end of the continuum, is the 'generalist', curriculum-oriented professional course for the classteacher in which there are no options and all students study all the subjects they are to teach.

3 The third type of professional course is what I call the *'skill-oriented'* course, in which practical teaching skills of a curriculum non-specific variety are identified as a major basis for professional study – skills like questioning, small group teaching, the organization of individual learning, pastoral skills (the successors to the earlier emphasis on blackboard technique and work display); and where there is much emphasis on the analysis of pupil behaviour, and pupil-teacher interaction and classroom organization.

4 The fourth type is what I call the *'context-oriented'* course where the particular problems of a college's physical and social setting dictate the main thrust of the professional courses. Most notable are those courses focusing on the needs of the child and his teacher in inner-city and multi-ethnic schools. Here the curriculum may be seen not as generalized and universal but as needing to be locally tailored, *à la* Midwinter.

'Child-oriented', *'skill-oriented'* and *'context-oriented'* courses do not neglect the school curriculum – all B.Eds now include basic professional studies in language/reading and maths – but the rest of the curriculum can sometimes get pretty scant treatment. For what the course planners in these cases are arguing is that other aspects of the teacher's professional armoury are as important as his understanding of particular subject-matter and how it might be taught – on the one hand (*skill-orientation*) a broad range of general classroom skills without which no teacher can promote learning, however good his grasp of the principles of primary science or whatever and, on the other hand, (*context-orientation*) his understanding of the crucial part the child's social or physical environment or his ethnic or religious background plays in his predisposition and response to the educational process.

5 Some course planners attempt to secure maximum coverage of *curriculum, general skill* and *child/context* elements in order to help the student cope in any situation and this fifth approach is termed *'neutral-orientation'*.

This combination of dimensions gives up to thirty broad types of approach at a macro level of overall structure and professional emphasis and, implicitly, thirty 'professional profiles' (see figure 1).

Now, clearly, these are all only emphases – they are each in their way fundamental to the teaching task, not mutually exclusive. But the problem is that such is the pressure on the college professional curriculum that considerable emphasis on one or two of these can lead to very scant treatment or even the total omission of others.

But the choice which course planners exercise in this matter is not just the logistical one of 'fitting everything in'. There has to be an *educational* basis for deciding what goes in, what is left out, what is a priority, what is mandatory, what is optional, and in this respect the planners' final choice of emphasis reflects views of *what is important in primary education – of what really matters out there in the schools.* However, what is confirmed by a juxtaposition of these 'models' is the risk of introversion and circularity I identified earlier. For all but the 'context-oriented' courses suggest a curriculum which is hermetically-sealed from its cultural surroundings or at least is insufficiently explicit about the sorts of cultural values it represents. Even the 'context-oriented' approach may tend to be piecemeal and grafted-on rather than fundamental and coherent – a bit of multi-culturalism here, a bit of urban education there. The one professional emphasis which is frequently missing is one of the most basic and obvious – a coherent curricular response to culture and to social change.

Curriculum Coverage and Curriculum Knowledge

The problem of 'curriculum coverage' is summed up in the HMI B.Ed survey (DES, 1979). Colleges give, HMI say, 'in terms of time, reasonable coverage of language and number ... (but) ... leave other areas of the primary school curriculum to rather superficial compulsory courses ... The time available for these other areas was in general sensibly used, but it was inadequate'.

At first sight, the problem seems to be one of time: time, first, for professional studies as a proportion of the total B.Ed; and, secondly, time as distributed within professional studies to the various curriculum areas. In the first case, the HMI B.Ed survey shows how 'subject studies' (the 'personal' as opposed to 'professional' education) can be allocated from one quarter to one half of the student's time overall. It is not so easy to calculate how much time goes to professional studies because, as has

Figure 1. *Major dimensions in current B.Ed. courses for intending primary/middle school teachers*
(Based on an analysis of recent submissions to CNAA)

		PROFESSIONAL EMPHASIS					
		Child emphasis	Curriculum emphasis A (Semi-specialist)	Curriculum Emphasis B (Generalist)	General Pedagogy/skill emphasis	Context emphasis	Neutral emphasis
OVERALL STRUCTURE	Traditional* concurrent						
	Other** concurrent						
	Traditional consecutive						
	Other consecutive						
	Professional***						

* 'Traditional' here means one or two in-depth main/subsidiary subjects in the 'academic' part of the course.
** 'Other' here usually means a multiple-choice modular/unit approach to the 'academic' part of the course.
*** 'Professional' here means that the academic/professional distinction is avoided by there being no main/subsidiary subjects or other modular equivalents.

been seen, it may not be a discrete component but may be, to some extent, integrated or interrelated with school experience and, to a lesser extent, with education theory. The figures are also complicated by the differing professional emphases of courses, whereby some might devote more time to curriculum areas but at the expense, say, of general professional skills. However, taking the main curriculum areas a class teacher covers and using HMI's B.Ed survey figures, on average 'curriculum' is given about 15 per cent of the three year B.Ed. These figures need to be treated with caution (not least because of the small sample involved) but comparison of that 15 per cent with the 25 per cent average for education theory and the 22 per cent–50 per cent for subject studies gives considerable food for thought. Have the colleges really got their priorities right?

The second problem is how to divide up the professional studies time. In the time in which secondary students study the teaching of their one or two subjects, primary students have to cover the whole curriculum. In response to pressure from many sources and to documents like Bullock, colleges give the main share of primary professional studies time to language and reading (90 hours or 6 per cent of the B.Ed on average) and mathematics (60 hours or 4 per cent on average; HMI figures again – DES, 1979). For the rest of the curriculum beyond the basics, the allowance may be pitifully small – a twenty hour course on science here, a thirty hour course on physical education there (not even concentrated but spread out over a year or so.) – and so on. Sometimes the time is divided on the basis of a market-place haggle: departments bid and generally the strongest wins. This quantitative distribution of time to the different parts of the B.Ed and to the curriculum areas within professional studies reflects college politics, validating bodies' priorities (some universities do not consider professional studies to be sufficiently important even to merit scrutiny when courses are validated (Alexander and Wormald, 1981)), the generally lower status of professional studies work in colleges and various other institutional and historical problems. But, to outsiders, the way the cake is cut can only seem to reflect a view of what is of greater or lesser importance for the intending primary teacher (see Alexander, 1979).

However, the 'curriculum coverage' problem is only partly a matter of time; it is also a matter of treatment. For what tutors actually do with their modest allocation of 'curriculum' time lays the foundation for the teacher's approach in the classroom. Here, though I have no research evidence for it, I would hazard a guess that there is a clear causal connection between inadequate treatment of the 'beyond-the-basics' curriculum areas in college and the superficiality, lack of progression and match reported by HMI in the primary survey. What tends to happen is that, structurally, there are variations on the mandatory-plus-options theme and the beyond-the-basics areas are sometimes treated as separate subjects, sometimes as broad areas. In the latter case, it is common to find units in 'the expressive arts' or 'creative studies' and in 'social and enviromental studies' or even 'scientific and social and environmental studies'. As far as these categories go, the colleges are in a cleft stick: by and large the pressure against separate subject treatment apart from maths, language, science and music, is very strong, and tutors are only too aware of all the often emotive talk about the 'unity' of knowledge, 'compartmentalized' subjects and the rest. So the approach through broad curriculum areas seems more attractive. Moreover, by producing a smaller number of curriculum units, this approach gives the tutors greater scope and flexibility: imagine the problems of having compulsory units for all students in language, maths, science, religious education, history, geography, physical education, art, music, etc. all to be squeezed into the current average of 225 hours – say ninety for language, sixty for maths (as at present) and ten hours for each of the rest!

The other dilemma is whether or not students should have to take the complete range. The argument *for* is that they are to be class teachers; the argument *against* is the likelihood of superficial treatment. For middle school courses, matters are slightly easier – convention encourages semi-specialization. Similarly for infant courses the curriculum range is not so extensive, and there is no argument about the absolute primacy of basics. It is in the seven to eleven range where the problem is most acute, and it may be that teachers of older juniors are the least well equipped of all in these terms. However, as indicated previously, the 'semi-specialist' solution is emerging here too – but the question needs to be asked as to whether this 'solution' arises in response to clear professional needs or is merely a compromise in the face of internal political and organizational problems in the colleges.

Again, it is not just a quantitative matter – what is equally important is the view of curriculum expressed by the approach which offers a few broad 'integrated' curriculum areas. First, it seems to suggest that a class teacher needs no great depth of understanding in the various curriculum areas he is to teach – his task is something different. Secondly it can only provide the most rudimentary of bases for curriculum appraisal and development. Of course a teacher will be committed to integration or teaching on a thematic basis if his course has done this, but he will be unlikely to be able to defend this style of teaching or the view of knowledge it implies except in the most basic terms and slogans. To engage in curriculum development a teacher's understanding of the knowledge base of curriculum must reach far deeper than this. Thirdly, whether or not he teaches on an integrated or a separate subject basis, he needs sufficient depth of understanding of the areas of knowledge on which he draws, coupled with a keen appreciation of what it is appropriate and desirable to do at given stages, to identify the skills, concepts and attitudes he wishes children to acquire, with sufficient precision to engage in deliberate curriculum planning. This must demand a fairly detailed exploration of, for example, the nature of scientific enquiry, of aesthetic awareness and expression, of historical exploration and so on. If all the teacher has is a brief course in the teaching of the expressive arts which only offers him some tips about activities he might undertake, he will just not be able to identify these various skills, concepts and attitudes and there may be little real conceptual and skill progression in the children's work.

One of the most disturbing findings of the primary survey (HMI, 1978, para. 6.18) in this connection is that the work children did in music was consistently better matched to pupils' abilities than work in art, and that it achieved the best match across the whole curriculum for more able pupils. Is music a special case? I suggest that it is only special in a more *obvious* way than other subjects; namely, in respect of the performance skill element. If music requires the depth of competence achieved by the teacher with specialist training, what of the other areas of the curriculum which conventionally in teacher education get small amounts of time or no time at all – science, art, social and environmental education? All this raises two absolutely fundamental questions:

1 *What sort of curriculum knowledge does a competent primary school class teacher need?*
2 *How much of his total training should be devoted to the acquisition of this knowledge and the associated teaching skills?*

Here are some alternative answers based on familiar arguments:
(a) The teacher is teaching children, not subjects, in the primary school, so 'curriculum knowledge' is not really an issue: the most important *foci* for professional training should be child development and general teaching skills.
(b) The child's view of the world is not compartmentalized or subject-specific, so the teacher should enable him to explore it in his own terms rather than by imposing the culturally-evolved public paradigms of knowledge. Again this implies a concentration on child development, especially cognitive development, and general teaching skills.
(c) Process is more important than content: the teacher should teach generalized skills and enquiry processes not specific to individual subjects – especially study and communication skills.
(d) A teacher of any age-group, young primary or older secondary, needs himself to have mastered the underlying concepts and structures of the areas of knowledge to be taught in order to make a valid selection for teaching and in order to match the structure and sequence implied by an analysis of children's thinking, needs, interests and modes of learning.

I cannot commit myself to any *one* of these – all can be convincingly argued – but I know that if (d) is at all valid it has serious implications for teacher education, for the majority of B.Ed courses come nowhere near giving this sort of mastery, and one overriding consideration must surely be that a teacher needs sufficient curriculum knowledge not only so that he can develop a progression of curricular experiences matched to his pupils' abilities (the primary survey argument) but also so that he can justify his curriculum decisions, can appraise alternative possibilities, can avoid the myopia of curriculum dogma; in short, so that if challenged to identify the educational meaning and purpose of his curriculum he can do so. However, the analysis in detail of the primary teacher's curriculum knowledge needs is something which has not yet been undertaken, and is long overdue.

Implications of the Primary Survey for the Teacher Training Curriculum

The primary survey has a number of major implications for how training institutions might prepare teachers for their curriculum-related roles.

1 The first of these arises from what the survey fails to say rather than what it actually says. Being a survey of practice rather than a statement of aims it does not (and might not be expected to) contain much discussion about the ideal shape of the whole curriculum for the future. However, this omission ought to serve as the basis for identifying the first training need; namely, for *analysis in teacher training not only of what might be done within curriculum areas, but what those areas stand for educationally, what they add up to collectively in terms of expressing clear educational purposes.* Courses need to develop students' capacities both to analyze and appraise the purpose and meaning of existing curricula, and to consider alternatives. I submit that sometimes in primary education we are rather inward looking – the overall curricular framework is taken as given and work is done to improve it in its own terms rather than to question the framework itself. I do not consider that the primary survey's apparent complacency about the whole curriculum ('Taking primary schools as a whole, the curriculum is probably wide enough to serve current educational needs' (HMI, 1978, para. 8.67) can possibly be justified, and anyway we are not told what HMI consider 'current educational needs' to be. In the same way curriculum courses in college represent a view of the school curriculum which is unchallenged, inviolate: giving seventy-five hours to curriculum mathematics, fifteen hours to curriculum science and five hours to moral education adds up to a view of priorities in the primary curriculum which cries out to be sharply questioned. Most seriously, this virtually guarantees that the trainee teacher lacks the conceptual apparatus to reappraise the educational role of those areas dealt with so superficially, or any secure basis for hypothesising and justifying a radical shift in curriculum priorities at school level.

There are two further related arguments. First, that the curriculum has to have a meaningful relationship to its social context – education does not (child-centredness notwithstanding) exist in a cultural vacuum – and our society and world are changing at unprecedented speed. What is the relationship of the young child's curriculum to his likely adult life given this context of rapid change? Secondly, and more immediately, a particular form of the schooling within the three to thirteen range – the middle school – still suffers from a lack of clear identity, and middle school students in particular need to engage in this sort of analysis of the purposes and character of the whole curriculum.

2 The second teacher training priority *is for students to acquire principles for curriculum development*. The survey offers a number – most notably in relation to its discussion of match and the needs of the more able child. But it also offers four general principles which teacher trainers would do well to explore:

(i) breadth
(ii) balance
(iii) coherence
(iv) progression.

However, it needs to be noted that breadth and balance are different sorts of principles from coherence and progression, for the matters of how broad or narrow the primary curriculum should be, what should be included or omitted, what should be the relative weighting of the different sorts of knowledge, skills and attitudes, are *value* issues. They are decisions rooted in judgements about what constitutes the 'right' education for the young child and reinforce my first 'need' to engage in debate about the whole curriculum and its purposes. Coherence and progression, in contrast, are technical or pedagogical principles which are applied once the value issues of breadth and balance have been resolved. They relate to the how rather than the what of curriculum.

3 The survey adopts certain curriculum categories for its analysis – skills and attitudes, language and literacy, mathematics, aesthetic and physical education, social studies. In some quarters any curriculum categories raise professional hackles – despite HMI's careful disclaimers about not using these to prescribe a subject-based curriculum. 'Subjects' ought not to be such an emotive issue and far too much is made of the crude polarity between 'child-centred' and 'subject-centred' education. This suggests a conceptual deficiency in professional training – a third need concerned with the *examination of the distinctiveness of different sorts and areas of knowledge, both 'common-sense' and 'academic', the relationships between them and the appropriateness or otherwise of integration*. Quite obviously, the standard philosophical material, however challenging and insightful teacher educators might find it, is not producing the kind of professional appraisal which is needed at school level.

4 Few would dispute the view that literacy and numeracy are absolutely central to primary education. But the problem is that, negatively, talk of 'basics' implies a hierarchy of curriculum experiences, a few of which are essential and the rest which are not. In practical terms the consequence of a proper concern with linguistic and mathematical skills can be a relegation of the rest of the curriculum and thereby a possible stunting of children's development in these other areas. Again, the 'basics versus the rest' distinction is a far too taken-for-granted one and *the consideration of curriculum priorities needs to start at initial training in order to become intrinsic to the process of professional self- appraisal.*

5 The most obvious curriculum needs deriving from the survey relate *to distinct curriculum areas.* The implied weakness of professional training in science is being picked up by the colleges and, because the survey's analysis of supposed deficiencies in science, history, geography and art was so clear, they do not need underlining. But tackling such weaknesses throws into relief the practical problem of achieving depth of under-standing at the same time as breadth of curricular coverage. How is it to be done?

Another point on this issue. The message about science has gone home – certainly in terms of the expansion of inservice science courses and also at initial level, and is reinforced by statements from government and industry. However, there is, in my view, as yet far too little discussion at either INSET or initial level about what needs to be done to produce more satisfactory treatment of the areas other than science which were commented on: art, history and geography.

6 All the above needs are 'curriculum knowledge' needs. But there is the related organizational issue of staff deployment and in particular of the *role of teachers with specialist curriculum knowledge* – whether as specialist teachers or curriculum 'consultants'. This too must provoke debate in colleges on the whole question of generalist and semi-specialist routes, and there are signs that such debate is now well under way.

7 A most fundamental need is for colleges *to look at the implications of the findings on 'match'.* One part of the problem is the teacher's capacity to assess a child's abilities and potential – a general ability. But the other part is curriculum-specific, first, because these abilities and potentials are revealed in specific curricular contexts and, secondly, because to achieve 'match' a teacher also needs to have a precise awareness of the range of curriculum possibilities open to him – skills, concepts etc. – in order to make the right selection of learning experiences for the child. 'Match' is about evaluating children and this demands a range of *observational, appraisal* and *recording* skills; it demands the refinement of the intuitive appraisal which will always remain central to evaluation in the classroom; it demands an awareness of and ability to use (discriminatingly) formal assessment procedures; but match is also about the provision of

appropriate learning and this demands curriculum knowledge of a detailed kind so that the teacher knows the range of concepts and skills which need to be selected from in order that the child can move on, together with alternative routes — bypasses — for the brighter child, and horizontal alternatives for the less able child whose learning requires greater con- solidation at each stage. And for all children, that conceptual map of the curriculum needs to extend quite a long way backwards and forwards from where the child is now so that the teacher has a view of where it all leads. If this is required in not just one curriculum area (as by the secondary teacher) but right across the curriculum (by the primary class teacher), the demands on the teacher are enormous and clearly curriculum knowl- edge needs to feature far more prominently in initial training than it does at present.

A much simplified model of professional expertise might be taken to include:

(a) knowledge about the child;
(b) knowledge about teaching and learning processes;
(c) knowledge about the social context of schooling;
(d) knowledge about the curriculum;
(e) the skills needed to select from this knowledge in order to provide appropriate and valid learning experiences and
(f) a whole range of practical executive and interpersonal skills in order to apply these mainly intellectual capacities in the everyday, pres- sured context of the classroom.

I would suggest that current patterns of teacher training are quite strong on the first two aspects and on some of the related executive skills, though I have argued that the form in which this knowledge is sometimes presented (as predigested education theory) still needs urgent appraisal. But I would say that treatment of *curriculum* is just not adequate, either qualitatively or quantitatively, and I would hope that the primary survey, by focusing on the primary curriculum so strongly and fairly unprecedentedly, will encourage this shift in initial training.

But a shift to curriculum is on its own not enough. For if to achieve closer 'match' requires that the teacher brings together his appraisal of the child and his knowledge of curriculum possibilities, it follows that college course elements concerned with the students' understanding of children's development and learning, those concerned with his understanding of social context, and those concerned with curriculum areas, must operate in a close, complementary, reciprocal relationship. Organizationally they all too often do not: child development may be taught by the educational psychologists, the social context of education by sociologists and curriculum studies by subject department staff. Is it too simple to suggest that lack of 'match', and the failure to locate curriculum decisions in a cultural context which I referred to earlier, may stem partly from a lack of depth in curriculum treatment and partly from this sometimes deep institutional divide between study of the child, his social context and his curriculum?

Conclusion

The teacher education course represents a response to what colleges perceive to be the needs of the young teacher in his first appointment. But it also constitutes for most trainees the final stage of a process of full-time education which they have been engaged in since the age of five or earlier, and comes before direct continuous experience of children and classrooms – an education as intense and unremitting as anything experienced previously. The teacher education course thus has a relatively limited potential for achieving a lasting readjustment of the young adult's view of the educational process and its purposes. At the same time, by incorporating in its emphasis on certain sorts of knowledge and skill a particular view of the teaching role, the needs of young children, the nature of knowledge and the character and purposes of primary education, it tends to facilitate certain lines of subsequent professional development and to discourage others.

Teacher educators have engaged over the past few years in a process of course appraisal and renewal probably far more extensive than has taken place anywhere else in the education system and certainly this process has often been far more searching than the curriculum tinkering that passes for development in many schools. Yet at the end of it, at the point of appraisal prior to the second generation of post-James B.Eds and at a time when the B.Ed itself is apparently under threat, many of the basic structural divides and conceptual assumptions – academic versus professional, theory versus practice etc. – remain as entrenched as ever. But perhaps most serious, in the context of this paper's focus on curriculum, is the way the primary teacher's substantial need for depth and breadth of knowledge in and about curriculum is unlikely to be met for as long as this part of the college course remains so consistently under-emphasized in terms of time and so superficially and atheoretically conceived and treated.

The roots of this problem are complex and beyond the scope of this paper, though two obvious factors can be isolated. One is the low status and weak bargaining power of professional/curriculum studies when decisions are made in colleges and course validating bodies about the overall proportions of time to be given to the various components of the B.Ed. course: some have a major share by rarely-questioned right while others have to fight for the little they get. This is reinforced by the strength of the tradition in the teaching profession itself which has tended to regard curriculum knowledge – the teacher's and the child's – as of subsidiary importance until the secondary stage. The roots of this view have much to do, I suspect, with the historical evolution of present day primary education out of a combination of the narrowness and instrumentality of the elementary school tradition and the 'activity and experience' reactions against this tradition in Hadow and Plowden. Redressing the balance in favour of the child and reacting against the apparent dominance of narrowly-conceived 'subjects' produced, to some extent, a more generalized reaction against curriculum knowledge in any form. Similarly, the very proper concern with the child, as an individual located in a unique social context, has to some extent parochialized professional vision in relation to wider cultural and societal concerns and desensitized educational debate over the extent to which even the most individualized curriculum is culturally-located and conveys a message about curriculum priorities.

To some extent this situation is circular and self-perpetuating. Cursory treatment in colleges, particularly of 'beyond the basics' curriculum areas, must limit the extent of reconceptualization of these areas which is available in the school and will tend simply to confirm the sense that these areas are less 'useful' than the basics; that, indeed, the existing basic/non-basic division is a valid one. 'Usefulness' is conventionally set against 'worth-whileness' in college education theory courses; an unfortunate polarization for it implies mutual exclusion. It should not be necessary to be unhappy about 'usefulness' for of course education should be useful; what is at fault is not the criterion but its interpretation, confirmed when one sees the relatively restricted list of supposedly 'useful' curriculum activities set above others headed 'education for leisure' and 'education for social awareness and responsibility'. The inadequacy of conceptions of educational utility current in this period of recession and pessimism is matched by the failure to grasp just how deeply 'useful' in a more vital and profound sense are aesthetic, moral and social awareness and cultural and environmental understanding. The old curriculum hierarchy persists in part because the trainee teacher is not given the intellectual apparatus to question it or to postulate, justify and enact convincing alternative models of the whole curriculum; and, in part, because it stems from a philistine concept of education which most of us, including many who determine policy in teacher education and at school, LEA and national levels, have experienced and assimilated during our formative years. While the pervasiveness of the latter condition makes change at the level of national climate hard to achieve, change is, however, possible in teacher education courses, provided that teacher educators, validators and teachers are prepared to engage in debate of a sufficiently radical and disinterested character, and are prepared to concede, in the first instance, that curriculum might be problematic. Disinterestedness is significant here, because it is existing loyalties, prejudices, securities and interests – in schools as well as colleges and validating bodies – which, as much as conceptual limitations, prevent radical debate. Such debate needs to be concerned with the character of professional knowledge, thought and action and with the relationships between these and professional training; this way we might – to return to the borrowed concept with which this paper opened – achieve a more comprehensive sense of 'match' not merely between training and teaching but between primary education and the rapidly-changing world in which our children are growing up.

References

ALEXANDER, R.J. (1978) 'Unit choice in a B. Ed degree' *Evaluation Newsletter* 7.

ALEXANDER, R.J. (1979) 'The problematic nature of professional studies' in ALEXANDER, R.J. and WORMALD, E. (Eds) *Professional Studies for Teaching* Guildford, Society for Research in Higher Education.

ALEXANDER, R.J. and WORMALD, E. (1981) 'Watching the teacher education watchdogs' *Times Higher Education Supplement*, 27 February.

BENNETT, N. (1976) *Teaching Styles and Pupil Progress* London, Open Books.

BOARD OF EDUCATION (1944) *Teachers and Youth Leaders* (The McNair Report) London, HMSO.

CHAMBERS, P. (1979) 'The scope and direction of professional studies since James' in ALEXANDER, R.J. and WORMALD, E. *op cit.*

COMMITTEE ON HIGHER EDUCATION (1963) *Higher Education* (The Robbins Report) London, HMSO.

DEPARTMENT OF EDUCATION AND SCIENCE (1972) *Teacher Education and Training* (The James Report) London, HMSO.

DEPARTMENT OF EDUCATION AND SCIENCE (1979) *Developments in the B.Ed. Course* London, HMSO.

GALTON, M. and SIMON, B. (Eds) (1980) *Progress and Performance in the Primary Classroom* London, Routledge and Kegan Paul.

GALTON, M., SIMON, B. and CROLL, P. (1980) *Inside the Primary Classroom* London, Routledge and Kegan Paul.

HER MAJESTY'S INSPECTORATE (1978) *Primary Education in England* London, HMSO.

3
Evaluation and Accountability: The End of Intuition?

Introduction

As the introductory paper in this book suggests, evaluation and accountability are two allied notions which together have prompted a major new
direction in education: the trend towards increasing public appraisal
of the activities of primary and secondary schools. Both notions are
symptomatic of a major loss of public support for the teaching profession's
claim that curriculum, pedagogy and evaluation are solely professional
matters. In particular there have been public uncertainty and anxiety
about standards of achievement, often associated with the supposed
widespread incidence of 'informal' education. There have been moves
at a number of different levels to make explicit the criteria for judging the
adequacy of such 'standards' and for making public the results of applying
such criteria to schools' activities. In primary education professional
intuition about the appropriateness of curricula in meeting pupils' 'needs'
and the effectiveness of schools in fulfilling their generalized goals has
been challenged. Evidence – whether in the form of test scores, inspection
reports or more detailed explicit records – has been demanded both by
a hard-pressed administration feeling the sharp end of public anxiety and
by more local publics claiming the right to know what is going on in 'their'
schools. Together the three papers in this section document the rise of
demands for evaluation and accountability, appraise some current attempts
at meeting these demands and suggest ways in which primary schools
might move in the 'eighties if the demand for accountability is to be used
positively and helpfully for teachers, pupils and the general public alike.

Barry MacDonald's paper was originally written in 1976, the year when
the fortunes of primary education and the standing of the education
service in general reached a post-war nadir. He suggests that calls for closer
monitoring of schools arose out of a context of cultural fragmentation,
increasing consumerism and changes in the management of educational
resources: a context catalyzed by the deviance of the William Tyndale
Junior School which raised questions of accountability in an acute form.
He is very critical of the Assessment of Performance Unit which he believes

is operating an 'extremely rudimentary and simplistic' evaluation model based on the pre-specification of objectives. He is not arguing for an intuitive approach to judging educational activities and does believe that schools should become more accountable. He advocates a form of evaluation which attempts 'to portray for decision-makers and others the complexity of the relationship between action, circumstance and consequence in educational affairs' (p. !68–9), a complexity obscured by simple quantitative indices of educational performance. It remains to be seen how far the 'eighties will bear witness to his misgivings about central government initiatives, or how far schools will respond by providing alternative forms of accounting to those based on test results, whether administered by the APU, local authorities or anxious headteachers.

John Elliott's paper provides an illustration of how school evaluation might proceed and how those of a 'progressive' persuasion might be able to render an account in terms other than the results of tests of basic skills. After criticizing the APU he outlines a model of accountability which involves schools making clear what it is they are prepared to take responsibility for, publishing their own self-evaluation reports and creating contexts in which dialogue can take place about the nature and discharge of responsibility and about the formulation of policy in relation to issues raised by the accounting procedures. His article implies that no longer are 'intuition' and professional 'good sense' enough: clear, logical thinking concerning the range of schools' responsibilities, careful collection of data in relation to their discharge and sensitively conducted dialogue with various publics are all required. Though his paper does provide an interesting line of defence for progressive education, his concluding thoughts have a sting in their tail, especially his assertion that 'much of what passes for progressive education in our schools is only superficially so, and . . . more self-evaluation at the implementation level would reveal how far progressives have to go in translating their ideals into practice'. (p. 178).

Wynne Harlen's contribution, on the problem of matching, links the concerns of the second section of the book to the kinds of evaluation advocated by MacDonald and by Elliott. She conceives of matching as part of the process by which teachers and schools monitor their own performance and through which information is obtained for a dialogue with those outside schools. She defines matching as 'finding out what children can already do and what ideas they have as a basis for providing experiences which will develop these skills and concepts'. She reviews the primary survey's findings on match and argues that improvements will result not from reliance on definitive rules and prescriptions [or, for that matter, intuition: Ed] but from teachers developing conscious strategies. Such strategies require considerable curriculum knowledge of lines of development (with their constituent skills and concepts) and of methods, materials and activities. Here her views reinforce those of contributors to the first and second sections of the book.

Judging from the three papers, accountability and evaluation may not spell the end of teacher intuition as a way of dealing with the crowded ecology of the primary classroom but they do reinforce the view that intuition is no substitute for considered reflection which results in adequate evaluation and justification.

Who's Afraid of Evaluation?*

Barry MacDonald
University of East Anglia

Evaluation and Assessment

It may be helpful to begin by offering a distinction between 'evaluation' and 'assessment' in education. The distinction is a fairly conventional one, not intended to be definitive or provocative, but simply to avoid confusion within the compass of this article. The purpose of assessment is to make statements about the recipients of an educational service, statements about their actual and potential accomplishments in relation to the opportunities for learning provided by that service. Assessment is the basis for decisions about what students will get in the way of further provision, and for predictions of their future accomplishments. The purpose of evaluation, on the other hand, is not to make statements about the recipients, but to make statements about the educational service. Evaluation statements serve decisions about educational *provision*. It will be obvious that assessment can assist this purpose, and that some form of assessment is a likely component of any evaluation process. True enough, but the distinction by primary purpose is more significant than may at first sight appear to be the case.

The fact is that the instruments of assessment that we have laboriously cultivated and refined over the years, the examination procedures and the psychometric tests, are not much help to the educational evaluator. Such instruments are typically constructed so as to differentiate between the accomplishments of individual learners, that is, to achieve a distribution of scores. These instruments are known as norm-referenced, because they make it possible to rank the individual in relation to the performance of the group. This discrimination facilitates educational and vocational placement. But assessment for the purpose of evaluation calls for a different

*This is an edited version of the article published in *Education 3–13*, 4(2), (1976), pp. 87–91.

Eval'n

approach, because it is asking different questions. What did the students need to learn? Given the nature of the provision for learning, the circumstances of its implementation, and the intentions of the teachers, what could they reasonably have been expected to learn? What did they *all* learn and what did they all fail to learn? Instruments which set out to answer these kinds of questions require *criteria* rather than norms as their design basis. They are known as criterion-referenced, and they have an important function in the evaluation of educational programmes. The massive task of constructing such criterion-referenced tests which are reliable and valid is only now getting underway. Very few are readily available in this country at the present time, and this in part explains why during the last decade, evaluators have increasingly adopted and developed approaches to their task which place little emphasis on the measurement of student performance. I shall have more to say about this later: it is enough for the moment to have established that evaluation and assessment, as I have defined them, have different purposes and that, even though they share an interest in student learning, they require different instruments.

The Context of Evaluation – Values

But I don't want this article to be primarily a technological review of the province of evaluation. The rising demand for evaluation in education (and I think it wiser to talk of 'demand' rather than 'popularity') calls instead for a much broader consideration of the circumstances which surround this demand. Evaluation can so easily be an instrument of abuse that the context in which it's applied should always be carefully scrutinized. 'Who's Afraid of Evaluation?' the title of this article, is offered in a spirit of caution rather than contempt.

These are troubled times in education, are they not? The air is shrill with criticism, threats, challenges; war cries of one kind and another. Some of the rather sloganized exchanges that characterize the public debate have been with us for some time, and are familiar enough – formal versus informal teaching methods, comprehensivization versus selection, streaming versus mixed ability, and so on. They may have sharpened in tone of late, but we know them well, In a sense, many of us feel that much of this debate lies outside education, although it is about education. What actually happens within the schools is determined still by the values and preferences of those most intimately involved in educational provision *ugh!* – headmaster, teachers, and local administrators. This degree of autonomy in matters of curriculum provision, although a thorough analysis would no doubt qualify it in a number of ways, has been sufficiently substantial for us to feel that the affairs of the school are under professional control, and that this arrangement enjoys public confidence. Can we still say that today? I think not, and I have in mind not only the effects of the economic disaster which has overtaken educational expenditure and which I shall come to shortly, but of other trends and events whose effects are rather more difficult to calculate. Events like the William Tyndale saga, which culminated in an inconclusive three-month-long 'evaluation', and which raised a number of issues that are much less familiar than the 'chestnuts' referred to earlier. Tyndale was an event which compelled the confrontation of long dormant issues in education in the light of contemporary trends. For instance, who is accountable for educational provision, to whom, and by what means? And, if a pluralist society entails a pluralist teaching profession, what are the implications for the school as an agency of cultural transmission? To put this last question more baldly, can schools still be relied upon to reinforce the existing social order? The 'problem school' in this sense is a new phenomenon, one which many people link with the inner urban crisis of recent years, as well as with a general growth of political consciousness within the educational community. The extent to which Tyndale, and its successors, leads to an erosion of public confidence in the schools may well depend on the extent to which it is seen as an opportunity to change the existing distribution of power within the education system. The *Times Educational Supplement* saw in the actions of the parents of Tyndale the emergence of a new tide of educational 'consumerism'. The ILEA followed the inquiry by appointing a new group of inspectors to monitor school standards. The DES reinforced its recent call for a national monitoring system. There is, at least incipiently, a sense of crisis in the air, and a tendency to respond by seeking strong measures to re-establish control. Whereas Risinghill was seen by its critics as an aberration, Tyndale has been interpreted as an early warning signal.

The Context of Evaluation – Efficiency

If cultural fragmentation is one context which gives rise to calls for closer monitoring of the school system, inept management of resources is another. During the 'seventies we have seen, both at the national level and the local level, a significant change in the model of resource management applied to educational expenditure. Using techniques and procedures evolved primarily in industry and defence, the planners in Elizabeth House have designed, and are seeking ways to apply, a system of management which involves a shift from input to output budgeting, a system which calls for evaluation of the effects of alternative resource allocations in relation to objectives and costs. To put into operation such a system requires the co-operation of the planners at local level, and since 1971, there has been considerable exploration of the integration problems of local and national planning (see *Management in the Education Service: Challenge and Response* an SEO occasional paper published in 1974). The reorganization of local government in 1974 gave an immediate, and perhaps crucial, boost to the new model of management, introducing as it did the 'corporate management' structure. Corporate management involves the formation of cross-departmental executive committees, horizontal movement of staff at senior management level, and a strong emphasis on policy evaluation of a kind that is required if the aspirations of the Department planners are to be fulfilled. Now, at the local as well as the national level, we have a commitment to goal-setting and the evaluation of goal attainment. The new power structure of local authorities ensures that Education, the 'big spender', will come under pressure to justify its resources in terms of demonstrable outcomes. Game, set and match to the men from the Ministry.

The New Rhetoric

Add to the foregoing contexts the economic recession and we begin to understand why the mood of optimism which imbued public discussion about curriculum development in the 'sixties, and the rhetoric of constructive support and co-operation that went with it, are sadly frayed. Now we hear, suddenly it seems, a new vocabulary of relatively unfamiliar terms, a vocabulary more militant in tone than we are accustomed to, more strident in advocacy than many of us feel comfortable with. Top of the list is the word 'accountability', a concept we used to associate with financial audits, but which is now applied to the processes and outcomes of schooling, and to the obligations of those who have responsibility for those processes and outcomes. Many other 'new' words we are being asked to learn seem, like accountability, to belong to the world of production organizations, words like 'cost benefit' 'efficiency', 'management by objectives', 'programme budgeting', 'control systems' and the like. The tendency of language like this is to suggest that the production of educated people is much like the production of anything else, a technological problem of specification and manufacture. And, like the production of anything else, it can best be organized hierarchically, each part or sub-system dovetailing into a master plan which encompasses and orchestrates the whole organization.

In the case of education, specifying the product is the really tricky bit of the process. First of all, everyone in the organization must agree what the product is to be. To derive an analogy from car production, it's no use if some of the workers think it's a Mini while others think it's a Land Rover. Objectives must be pre-determined. Secondly there must be agreement about what the product will look like, how it will be identified. In education, this means that the objectives must be defined in terms of learner behaviour. And this is where another word enters the contemporary vocabulary, the word 'standards'. Not a new word of course, 'standards' is the traditional war cry of the educational 'right'. 'Standards' are what grammar schools stand for, what you get if you concentrate on the three Rs, what you lose when your hair touches the back of your neck or when you enter a comprehensive school. 'Standards' is the central construct of a familiar polemic at the political level of education policy disputes. But of late the concept has come more and more to be employed in its operational sense, as criteria of acceptable performance. When the Department of Education's newly fledged Assessment of Performance Unit talks of standards, it means levels of pupil achievement which can be used as the basis of a national monitoring system (Kay, 1974). In other words, specified behaviour objectives.

APU

While it would be going too far to suggest that what is taking place is a transformation in the way that schooling is viewed as resource investment, it would be wrong, and dangerous, to dismiss this trend as mere verbal fashion unlikely to impinge in any significant way upon the activities of the school. The changing rhetoric of educational management reflects in a very direct way the transformation of the economic circumstances of schooling that has been wrought in the past few years.

It would be difficult to resist the proposition that the British educational system, and particularly the school system, is about to launch itself into a new phase, perhaps a decade, of unprecedented concern with evaluation. Unprecedented that is, in modern times: some of the rhetoric of the platform speakers bears a chilling resemblance to the remark of Robert Lowe, Vice-President of the Education Department, when, in 1861, he recommended to the House of Commons the issue of a 'revised code' which introduced the notorious and ill-fated system of 'payment by results' – 'If the new system is not cheap, it shall be efficient, and if it is not efficient, it shall be cheap.' In one sense, current rhetoric goes one step further. The context of Lowe's promise was one of rapidly expanding expenditure on schooling, which payment by results failed to stem. The context today is one of a declining resource future. The new system, therefore, has no options. It shall be efficient, and it shall be cheap.

Thus baldly stated, the demand represents a transformation of the social and political circumstances of the school, one which has materialized with bewildering rapidity. The demand is backed by fiscal control and made legitimate by public concern about 'standards'; it cannot with impunity be ignored. Already there are some ominous signs. The ailing National Foundation for Educational Research is showing all the signs of revival as orders for new tests come in from the Department, itself gratified by Bullock's call for national monitoring of reading standards. A change of role is planned for the HMIs who want the local advisers to take over much of their individual school inspection function, and it is interesting to note a change of nomenclature at the local level, where some former advisers are now called evaluators. And here come the volunteers. I note in a recent issue of the *Times Educational Supplement* that the principal of a College of Further Education has welcomed accountability in the form of an external audit. Who's afraid of evaluation?

Accountability and Evaluation

Where does all this leave the school, and the evaluators, whoever they may be? The context which I have attempted to outline suggests that future evaluation efforts in the schools are likely to arise out of, and feed back into, a centralized system of performance monitoring based on pre-set targets. We should note several salient features of this system. In the first place, viewed as an accountability system, it is clear that some are more accountable than others. The Department of Education and Science for instance, though part of what Margaret Thatcher called the least accountable bureaucracy in Western Europe, and though it has led the crusade for accountability, is not offering to render its own operations and accomplishments more open to scrutiny. Of course the management model does in theory render the Department more accountable to its political masters but if one believes, with Professor Vaizey, that such accountability has 'vanished, even as a pretence' (Vaizey, 1974), and if one adds to this Tyrell Burgess's view that the effect of corporate management is to make 'it harder than ever for the representatives to control the officials' (in the *Guardian* May 7, 1974), then we face the possibility of an accountability system which only bites at the level of the schools. In the second place, the model of evaluation which is being advocated is extremely rudimentary and simplistic, one which no professional evaluator working in this country today would try to defend. Evaluation as the measurement of pupil attainment of pre-specified objectives is an excellent instrument for the purpose of central control of education, but a poor instrument of quality assurance, and an even poorer instrument for increasing understanding of the problems and potentials of educational provision. It is a bureaucratic concept of evaluation for a bureaucratic concept of accountability. Let the buyer beware. Ernest House has observed, in relation to the enactment of comparable accountability procedures in America, 'I believe such schemes are simplistic, unworkable, contrary to empirical findings, and ultimately immoral. They are likely to lead to suspicion, acrimony, inflexibility, cheating, and finally control – which I believe is their purpose (House, 1973).

However we do not need to postulate malign intentions in order to predict malign effects and indeed would be unjustified in doing so. Few would deny that schools should be accountable, more so than they have been in the past, and most of us would support the need for more systematic study of alternatives in educational provision – their values, their processes, their circumstances and their effects. But there are many ways to be accountable, many audiences with legitimate claims for information, and different notions of what constitutes educational excellence. Evaluators increasingly acknowledge these propositions in their designs, which have moved away from simple output measurement in an effort to portray for decision-makers and others the complexity of the relationships between actions, circumstance, and consequence in educational affairs. It is this complexity that is in danger of being ignored if we subscribe to a form of evaluation that places overmuch reliance on a single productivity index, an index which, as I pointed out at the beginning of this article, is underpinned by an undeveloped technology.

One final point: to judge schools by what we can measure in pupils is to judge them by our instruments, not by our heads or by our varying values. Ledger-book evaluation may lead us to assign false priorities, undue emphasis in our provision. These recent words of Robert Stake are worth bearing in mind; 'The world encourages a great variety of competences across persons and tolerates a great incompetence in persons. Poor achievement is not despicable (though failure to provide opportunity for better achievement is). Poor achievement is often the scapegoat focus-of-attention when a person is rejected really because of social class, race, personality, or appearance. The incompetences of the handsome rich are greatly tolerated. A successful life is possible for any person with any combination of talents. With a heavy accent on low competence in certain academic areas, the schools can help deny a person the ordinary opportunities of a successful life (Stake, 1976).

And what of those who hold that education is characterized by indeterminacy of ends, anyway? Who's afraid of evaluation? I am, are you?

References

HOUSE, E. (1973) 'The price of productivity: Who pays?' published in mimeo by the University of Illinois.

KAY, B. (1975) 'Monitoring pupils' performance' *Trends in Education* July.

STAKE, R. (1976) 'Measuring achievement in the schools' published in mimeo by the University of Illinois.

VAIZEY, J. (1974) 'Expansion and contraction' *Times Educational Supplement* 28, June.

Accountability, Progressive Education and School-based Evaluation*

1979.

John Elliott
Cambridge Institute of Education

In educational discussion, it is often claimed that standards are declining and that progressive methods of teaching are wholly or partly the cause. In this article I want to look first of all at the issues which surround these two claims and ask 'what are they really about?'. Secondly, I shall look at the development of monitoring and accountability systems as a political and administrative response to these issues. In particular I hope to show that the development of accounting procedures for teachers and schools based on the monitoring of pupil achievements is inconsistent with the ideals of progressive education. Finally, I want to outline an alternative model of public accountability which is school-rather than bureaucratically-based and likely to be more acceptable to progressive educators.

The Issues about Standards

Both the issue about declining standards and that about causal responsibility appear on an initial inspection to be about the facts. But, in asserting that standards are declining, people are not simply asserting a fact but making a value judgment. The factual component amounts to 'standards are changing'. The evaluative component amounts to 'the changes are undesirable'. Now those who disagree may not disagree with the fact that 'standards are changing' but with the evaluation that 'the changes are undesirable'. In which case the question at issue is 'What sort of things are worth learning?'.

In asserting that progressive methods are the, or partial, cause of declining standards the traditionalist is in part making a claim about the observable facts; namely, that the adoption of such methods is normally sufficient, or along with other factors sufficient, to bring about a change in educational

*This is an edited version of the article published in *Education 3–13*, 7(1), (1979), pp. 27–31.

standards. However, causal statements about social situations cannot simply be reduced to observational statements. There are usually a large number of factors operating which are sufficient to bring about the occurrence one is concerned about. Why then, does the traditionalist select progressive methods as the, or a partial, cause of declining standards rather than some other factor or factors whose presence would be sufficient to bring about a decline?

Robert Ennis (1973) has argued that we select a particular factor as the, or a partial, cause in order to ascribe blame for the occurrence we are interested in. Thus, to assert that progressive methods are causally responsible for a decline in standards is not merely to state a fact based on observation but to attribute blame for the decline to these methods and those who adopt them.

In answering the traditionalist, the progressive educator need not disagree about the observable facts. He may admit that a change from traditional to progressive methods has accompanied a change of standards and even agree that this latter change is undesirable. But without being at all inconsistent he can deny that progressive methods are the, or a partial, cause by claiming that some other factor or factors are operating causally, for example, large classes, inadequate resources, low pupil motivation, low socio-economic status of parents. In doing so, he attributes blame to these other factors and thereby attempts to exonerate progressive methods and teachers. He can keep on citing such factors; the factual evidence will never be conclusive.

Faced with continually inconclusive factual evidence, the traditionalist may try another line of argument. 'Do you admit that a return to traditional methods would prevent or help to prevent a decline in standards?', he asks the progressive. 'I have already admitted it', replies the progressive. 'Well, since teachers have a responsibility, a duty, to maintain standards, shouldn't they abandon progressive methods and return to traditional ones?', the traditionalist pleads. 'I disagree that teachers should accept responsibility for what their pupils learn. Their main responsibilities are for the way they make provision for learning; for the quality of the learning environment. As teachers we are under no obligation to sacrifice the quality of the learning environment for the sake of maintaining achievement levels. Quantity may have to be sacrificed for quality', the progressive argues.

This fabricated dialogue illustrates something which lies at the heart of the issue about the causal responsibility of progressive methods for declining standards; namely, the responsibilities which go with being a teacher. In my dialogue, the traditionalist selects progressive teaching methods as the, or a, cause for declining standards because he assumes that a teacher's primary responsibility is for what pupils learn. On the other hand, the progressive teacher denies that progressive methods are causally responsible because he assumes that a teacher's main responsibility is for the way he teaches. A teacher is accountable for the things he has respon-sibilities for, so there is no way of arriving at a rational consensus on the accountability question if there is no rational procedure for resolving disagreements about the nature of these responsibilities.

Achievement Testing and Accountability: The Official Response

As in the United States, so in the UK, the official response to public concern about standards has been an attempt to establish procedures for monitoring achievement levels in the form of an 'Assessment of Performance Unit' at the DES. This development appears at first sight to be rather more sophisticated in its approach than some of its counterparts in the USA, though like them it relies on the notion of consultative procedures to arrive at a consensus to guide the Unit's activities.

In an article about the APU in *Education 3–13* Brian Kay the APU's first director, returns repeatedly to the problem of consensus, and appears to be rather irritated by the lack of it. For example, he expresses the hope that the Unit and its working groups 'can escape the tendency to polarize which bedevils much of our educational thinking and, though to a lesser degree, educational practice' (1976). He argues that consensus is possible because 'there is a solid core of sound educational practice which follows a middle way' and adds, 'This seems to offer a serviceable starting point for our work'. What a quick way of reaching a consensus about standards. One simply excludes discussing those views which too radically conflict with one another. Such a neat political device may be a quick way of reaching a consensus; it could hardly fail. But it is hardly a good way of reaching a *rational consensus* based on a consideration of alternative views. The desire for consensus at any price tends to characterize politicians and officials who want to resolve social conflict primarily by technical means. Value-pluralism for them is just an embarrassment and the quicker it can be 'resolved' the better.

Dialogue is the method for trying to resolve rationally those fundamental issues which lie outside the realm of empirical proof. It proceeds by exploring alternative views and arguments; it does not push them to one side for the sake of a quick consensus. But it is dialogue which is threatened by the emergence of monitoring and accountability procedures at the bureaucratic level. The emergence of such procedures at the present time is evidence of increasing bureaucratic and political intrusion into life in our social institutions: a form of control which not only threatens dialogue within and between these institutions but the foundations of democracy itself. As I understand it, 'a democratic society' is a society in which social conflict is to be treated as a subject for dialogue among the people rather than an object of political and bureaucratic control. The bureaucratic development of 'consultative procedures' for determining standards is no real aid to democracy. Such procedures are inimical to dialogue because in the last resort a consensus on norms and values has to be reached for the sake of technical considerations.

In the USA, standardized achievement tests have been used as the basis for calling teachers and schools to account for declining standards. Such a use assumes that teachers have a responsibility to maintain and improve achievement levels. But judging from research such as that by Start (1974) and Jackson (1968), it appears that many teachers see themselves as having a responsibility for the quality of the classroom climate in which pupils learn rather than for what they learn. This doesn't mean such teachers are necessarily unconcerned about what pupils learn. It is not inconsistent for a teacher to have certain pupil achievements in mind as goals for his teaching but to deny at the same time that he can accept responsibility for their attainment. One reason why he may refuse to accept responsibility for pupil achievements is that the factors which influence achievement levels are difficult to control and it is not always within his power to prevent declining standards. Thus he will do his best to maintain and raise achievement levels but is not prepared to accept responsibility in these respects.

This sort of objection doesn't involve radical disagreement over values. The disagreement is primarily a factual one about the limits of teachers' powers to control achievement levels. In other words, can teaching reasonably be viewed as a sufficient condition for declining standards? Another more radical objection to teachers accepting responsibility for pupil achievements is that to do so would be an infringement of their pupils' capacity to accept responsibility for their own learning, and that it is the protection and fostering of this capacity for rational autonomy which teachers are primarily responsible for.

It is this sort of objection which underlies the consistent denial of my fictitious progressive educator that progressive methods are causally responsible for declining standards. They cannot be causally responsible because the progressive teacher's responsibility to protect and foster the rational autonomy of the pupil is inconsistent with his accepting responsibility for what pupils achieve. As I have argued, in holding this view the progressive educator need not be unconcerned about achievement levels. He can accept responsibility for deciding what is worth learning in his classroom, but since pupils have the right to evaluate this decision he cannot accept responsibility for whether they learn what he decides is worthwhile. I do not see any conflict in principle between the progressive teacher holding particular pupil achievements in mind as goals and his ideal of rational autonomy so long as he doesn't accept a responsibility to ensure that his goals are achieved at any price. I know that some progressive educators would disagree with me but this is because I think they confuse a responsibility for deciding what is worth learning with a responsibility for ensuring that pupils learn it.

Brian Kay has denied that the national monitoring procedures developed by the APU will be used to judge individual teachers or schools. In *Education 3–13*, he argues that the APU 'represents part of the response of the DES to demands for greater accountability by the educational service for the resources it consumes' (Kay, 1976). It appears, therefore, that its monitoring procedures will operate at the level of the 'educational service as a whole'. What exactly is meant by 'the educational service' is not clear. Does he mean the teaching profession as a collective body or would he include LEA administrators and advisers, not to mention the DES itself? If he means 'the teaching profession' as a whole then the procedures developed are intended as a basis for *making judgments about teachers,* irrespective of the extent to which individual schools and teachers are anonymized.

Although the unit's work is not intended to have any direct effects on individual teachers and schools it is intended to affect them indirectly. One of these indirect effects is that it will act as a normative influence in getting teachers to assess their practice against 'the best standards'; these being defined in terms of pupil achievements. Kay puts it like this:

> If the educational process is monitored according to criteria which reflect the best current practices in encouraging pupils' development in language, mathematics, science, moral and aesthetic sensibility and physical expression and dexterity, then the general level of these may rise towards that of the best. This is why it is so vital that the criteria used should both reflect the best practice and be reasonably comprehensive.

Thus self-evaluation by individual teachers and schools is an anticipated indirect effect of the work of the unit. But notice that it is only to be encouraged on the basis of 'the best criteria' which will presumably be determined by the unit and reinforced by government policy. Earlier in his article, Kay expresses reservations about the *Times Educational Supplement's* suggestion that teachers and schools should develop their own methods of self-evaluation. He argues that 'at a time of change and experiment there is a need for a general debate to help in defining criteria of assessment. Many people would also ask that self-assessment should be complemented by some form of objective monitoring, based on a sampling process, if only as a moderating device'.

It seems that self-evaluation is only desirable when the following conditions obtain:

1 the criteria of evaluation are achievement criteria
2 the criteria represent a consensus view of the responsibilities of teachers and schools
3 it is moderated externally.

The first condition would rule out self-evaluation based on alternative conceptions of the responsibilities of teachers to that of 'responsibility for pupil achievement levels'. The second begs a whole lot of questions about how the consensus is reached; questions I raised earlier. The third condition ascribes authority to the results of external monitoring over self-monitoring and thereby preempts the use of self-monitoring as a means of questioning the former.

Inasmuch as the APU aspires to impose these kinds of limits on the development of self-evaluation methods in schools it can only be considered to be a constraint both on the professional autonomy of teachers with respect to the question of their responsibilities towards pupils and on the emergence of genuine dialogue between teachers, schools and the general public about the nature of those responsibilities.

Accountability: an Alternative Model

However, it is possible to produce a form of public accountability which both respects the professional autonomy of teachers and their right to dialogue with the public about their responsibilities. Its main features would be as follows:

1 A school and its teachers would acknowledge accountability to their public by producing their own self-evaluation reports for public scrutiny and discussion. As a check against bias they could incorporate discussion with external evaluation consultants who had free access to classrooms and the school.

2 A school and its teachers would self-evaluate in the light of their own conceptions of the sort of things they are accountable for, but the evaluation reports should make these criteria clear and indicate a willingness to enter into dialogue with their public about them. Such an indication might involve incorporating into reports, questions and issues about the criteria which are raised by the external evaluation consultants.

3 A school and its teachers would accept responsibility for establishing contexts in which genuine discussion and dialogue could take place and procedures for formulating and adapting policy as a result.

Such procedures would ground public accountability in dialogue, and in doing so reconcile the obligation of schools and teachers to be responsive to public opinion with their professional autonomy. They define quite a different conception of accountability to the one now emerging at the political/administrative level, which are basically methods of bureaucratic control. It is too much to expect central and local administrative systems to encourage the growth of what Ernie House has called 'responsible accountability' which is grounded in dialogue and based on the development of the self-monitoring capacity of schools and teachers. The initiative for developing and sustaining this alternative model must come from the teaching profession and the schools. If the challenge is neglected then teachers will deserve to be treated as technicians and social engineers whose sphere of action is restricted to means rather than ends, rather than as professionals who are allowed to self-determine their own ends. It will also, of course, mean 'the demise of dialogue' amongst teachers about fundamental educational issues.

Self-evaluation for Progressive Education

Finally, I want to explore the sort of self-evaluation it is appropriate for progressive teachers to engage in, if their major aim is to promote rational autonomy on the part of their pupils. I believe their aim of rational auton-omy is better conceived in terms of promoting particular educational processes than in producing particular measurable results. It is possible through logical analysis of the aim to specify what teachers have to do to provide pupils with opportunities for autonomous learning.

Work with teachers on the Ford T project produced the following pro-cedural principles:

Negative principles

The teacher should:

1 Refrain from preventing pupils from identifying and initiating their own problems for investigation.
2 Refrain from preventing pupils from expressing their own ideas and hypotheses.
3 Refrain from restricting students' access to relevant evidence and drawing their own conclusions from it.
4 Refrain from restricting students' access to discussion.

Positive principles

The teacher should:

5 Help students to develop the capacity to identify and initiate their own problems.
6 Help students to develop their own ideas into testable hypotheses.
7 Help students to evaluate evidence in the light of its relevance, truth and sufficiency.
8 Help students to learn how to discuss.

Conformity to such procedural criteria as those listed above does not so much ensure that pupils will learn autonomously as ensure the conditions in their learning environment which give them adequate opportunity to do so. It is important to stress that one cannot make pupils learn autono-mously as one can often make them learn to believe or do certain things.

I would suggest that however intuitive progressive teachers' conceptions of their responsibilities are, the kinds of procedural criteria I have cited come nearer to reflecting them than the achievement criteria specified by bureaucratically-controlled monitoring systems. They specify the sort of things progressive teachers and schools would use, albeit intuitively, as a basis for self-evaluation. Self-evaluation against such process criteria requires teachers and schools to assess the extent to which the means specified by their aim have been implemented rather than to assess the causal relationship between means and intended learning out-comes. In my view, much of what passes for progressive education in our schools is only superficially so, and I believe that more self-evaluation at the im-plementation level would reveal how far progressives have to go in translating their ideals into practice.

Some will argue that public accounting procedures based on self-conducted case studies of the quality of the intellectual climate in class-rooms is hardly going to appeal to a public which evaluates education in terms of its results. But it is a mistake to equate what the public thinks is in its interest and what is in fact in its interest. In the context of dialogue I believe it possible for progressive teachers to put forward good reasons why making provision for the development of rational autonomy in schools is in the public interest. I haven't space to clarify these reasons in depth but they would be related to the fact that a society cannot survive as a democracy without citizens who have developed the capacity to self-determine their own beliefs and conduct.

References

ENNIS, R. (1973) 'On causality' *Educational Researcher* 2(6).

KAY, B. (1976) 'The assessment of performance unit: Its task and rationale' *Education 3–13*, 4(2).

JACKSON, P. (1968) *Life in Classrooms* New York, Holt, Rinehart and Winston.

START, K. (1974) 'Establishing children's learning as the criterion for teacher effectiveness' *Educational Research* 16(3).

Matching*

Wynne Harlen
Chelsea College, University of London

Survey Findings

The Plowden Report contained many thought-provoking passages, but one stands out as capturing most succinctly what is of import and challenge to all concerned with children's learning:

> Learning is a continuous process from birth. The teacher's task is to provide an environment and opportunities which are sufficiently challenging for children and yet not so difficult as to be outside their reach. There has to be the right mixture of the familiar and the novel, the right <u>match</u> to the stage of learning the child has reached. If the material is too familiar or the learning skills too easy, children will become inattentive and bored. If too great maturity is demanded of them, they fall back on half remembered formulae and become concerned only to give the reply the teacher wants. Children can think and form concepts, so long as they work at their own level, and are not made to feel that they are failures.'   Para. 533 (CACE, 1967)

1967

The concept of 'match' was taken as one important theme in the HMI survey of primary schools, where an attempt was made to quantify the 'degree of match' for children in different ability groups within their class in various subject areas. These data provide, at last, some measure (however crude) of how well matching is carried out in schools. For some areas of the curriculum, notably science and the humanities, the findings are not happy ones. But they are not surprising to anyone who is closely involved in primary education, and they cannot be easily dismissed. Arguments have been advanced that matching is not important, indeed that learning can

1978

*This is an edited version of the chapter first published in RICHARDS, C. (Ed) (1980) *Primary Education: Issues for the Eighties* London, A.C. Black, pp. 53–70.

Table 1. Classes achieving reasonably satisfactory match for less able groups

Less able groups			
Percentage of classes	7 year old classes	9 year old classes	11 year old classes
94–85	Reading	Reading	Reading
84–75	Mathematics Writing Spoken language Physical education	Mathematics Writing	Mathematics Writing
74–65	Music	Spoken language Physical education Music	Spoken language Physical education History
64–55	Art and craft	History	Music Geography
54–45	History Geography	Geography	Art and craft
44–35	Science (observational) Science (experimental)	Art and craft Science (observational)	Science (observational) Science (experimental)
34–25	–	Science (experimental)	–

Table 2. Classes achieving reasonably satisfactory match for the average groups

Average groups			
Percentage of classes	7 year old classes	9 year old classes	11 year old classes
94–85	Reading	Reading	–
84–75	Mathematics	Mathematics	Reading Mathematics
74–65	Physical education Writing Spoken language Music	Physical education Writing	Physical education Writing Spoken language
64–55	–	Spoken language Music	Music History
54–45	History Art and craft	History	Geography
44–35	Geography Science (observational)	Geography Art and craft	Art and craft Science (observational)
34–25	Science (experimental)	Science (observational)	Science (experimental)
24–20	–	Science (experimental)	–

Table 3. Classes achieving reasonably satisfactory match for more able groups

	More able groups		
Percentage of classes	7 year old classes	9 year old classes	11 year old classes
64–55	Reading Physical education Spoken language	Reading Physical education	Reading Physical education
54–45	Mathematics Music Writing	Mathematics Music	Mathematics Music Spoken language
44–35	Art and craft	Writing Spoken language	Writing
34–25	History Geography	–	Art and craft History
24–15	Science (observational) Science (experimental)	Art and craft History Geography Science (observational)	Geography Science (observational) Science (experimental)
14–10	–	Science (experimental)	–

take place better when there is 'mismatching' (Bennett, 1978), but I believe such arguments suggest a difference of interpretation of matching rather than a serious disclaimer of matching as proposed here. It is clearly important to discuss just what we do mean by matching and the part it plays in helping learning. Firstly, however, we take a more detailed look at the findings in the HMI survey about matching.

To appreciate the full weight of the survey results about matching it is necessary to look at all the three tables for less able, average and more able groups, each at three age levels (Tables 1–3). The judgment as to ability level was made by the teachers and this part of the method of gathering the data has been criticized. These criticisms do not, however, weaken the force of these results, for what happens in a classroom that affects matching depends on the teacher's views of the ability of individual pupils, not on a more objective measure of ability not known to the teacher. The striking patterns in these results hardly need to be pointed out. It is clear that the order of success in matching among different subjects varies little, with reading, mathematics, writing and physical education being consistently near the top of the scale. At the bottom, with heavy constancy, is science, with geography and history, art and craft not far ahead. It is also clear that the proportion of good match improves from the more able to the average to the less able and, to a smaller extent, from older to younger pupils.

Interpretations

How can we interpret these findings? As a concerned science educationist

I might put the question more pointedly: why is science always at the bottom of the pile, not only in matching, but also, as is clear elsewhere in the report (chapter 5 iv) in the provision of adequate time and equipment? There is something more important at stake here, though, than just the interest of one subject area and the question has to be discussed in more general terms. The survey itself confirmed what many teachers would like to believe, that 'the range of work and the standards achieved are related, sometimes in ways that are not immediately obvious; for example, a narrow concentration on teaching a skill is not always the best way of achieving high standards in it' (6.1). The inclusion of a range of subjects beyond the 'basics' is thus seen to be not only worthwhile for development in these subjects but also for the 'basics' themselves. However, it is in the subjects 'beyond the basics', the art, the humanities, the sciences, that 'matching' is least apparent. Thus we return to the question of how this comes about.

There are several possible factors which might well be associated, though no one could be described as *the* cause. First, the order of descending success in matching is also the order of descending 'importance' of subjects, as seen in most people's eyes. This is a fact which is largely common knowledge, but also has the support of research. The project on 'The Aims of Primary Education' reported that the results of teachers' ratings of different aims were that 'conspicuous by their complete absence among the priority aims were any references to the arts, music, physical education, religious education, sex education, science or a second language. Aims in all of these areas were congregated in the lower half of the rank order and most of them failed to reach even an average rank of "important"' (Ashton *et al*, 1975, p. 62). We may regret that the notion of what is basic, and therefore important, in primary education does not extend to the concepts which help children understand the physical, human and social world around them, but it cannot be denied that this is the case at present. Also, it will take a great deal of time for any change in the established priorities. Putting this together with the 'matching' findings might suggest that what teachers do not consider important they do not teach very well. But it is too early to draw such conclusions, for there are other factors to be considered.

The second factor which may be associated with success in matching is a reflection of what is important in initial training programmes. Teachers cannot be expected to teach subjects well if their preparation in these subjects has been insufficient. Again it does not need any suspension of credibility to accept that the order of success in matching correlates with the order of time spent in training in the various subject areas. The peculiar difference which exists in some cases between what teachers are expected to do when in service and what their training covers is hard to understand. For example, the primary survey, whilst endorsing the use of posts of responsibility to provide a teacher with knowledge and ability to give leadership in planning and guiding work, did not advocate specialist teaching. In schools, each teacher is expected, with some help, to be able to deal with science, history, geography, and so on, yet there is a significant proportion of teachers leaving initial training courses without any training in teaching science and in at least one of the humanities.

A third factor might well be teachers' own background knowledge. In science this must certainly be very significant and could be no less important for history, geography, art and craft. At the primary level it is not important for pupils to learn about particular periods in history, particular facts in science, and so on, but rather to begin to develop concepts and study skills which can be applied to a range of subject matter. However, to do this it is necessary for there to be *some* content to study, one does not learn to observe without observing *something*, or to reason logically without reasoning about *something*, or about how living things behave without studying some particular living things. A lack of knowledge of relevant facts, even though these do not have to be transmitted to the children, is undoubtedly inhibiting to a teacher. In science, particularly, we then have a situation leading to a vicious circle – of pupils having no adequate science experiences in the primary school, being deterred by academic science courses in the secondary school and leaving with a dislike of the subject, some to become teachers who perpetuate these conditions.

A fourth factor relates to the kind of materials which teachers have to help them. At the top end of the matching ratings we find reading and mathematics, for which ready worked out teaching schemes and materials abound. If he or she so wishes a teacher can use sets of books, for pupils and teacher, and associated aids which, on account of their structure, ensure a fair basis for matching. Such materials can never replace the sensitive interaction of teachers with pupils which is necessary for matching, but they at least provide the essential resources. As we go down the matching scale the degree of structure in materials recently produced for teachers declines. This is inevitable since these are subjects where complex concepts and sophisticated study skills are the aim, rather than mastery of a well-defined set of facts and procedures. Structure of the same kind as in reading schemes is thus not appropriate, but structure of a different kind *is* appropriate. It could be such as to indicate the development of various concepts in children and exemplify subject matter which would foster it. Instead of this, much material for teachers tends to suggest isolated activities or topics which are not obviously related to the systematic development of underlying concepts and skills.

There may well be other factors which could be postulated as correlating with success in matching; it is likely to be a combination of factors, those mentioned and others, which accounts for differential success in matching. We can come a little nearer to finding the most likely causes by looking now at what is the meaning of matching, what it entails and why it is important. Support for its importance comes not only from the opinions of experienced educationists, as represented in the paragraph quoted above from the Plowden Report, but also from the findings of those who have studied children's mental development, for example Bruner (1960) and Piaget (1970), who may disagree on other matters but are of one voice in regard to matching. From a different angle again Bloom (1971) has pointed out the damaging consequences of mismatching.

The Meaning of Matching

Perhaps the first point to make about matching is that it does *not* mean giving children more of what they can already do. It is this misuse of the term which I believe is responsible for claims that learning is better when there is mismatching. What matching does mean, in simple terms, is finding out what children can already do and what ideas they have, as a basis for providing experiences which will develop these skills and concepts. The keynote of matching is thus finding the right challenge for a child, the size of step that he can take by using but also extending existing ideas. There is as much a mismatch if this step is too small, leading to boredom, as there is if it is too large, leading to failure.

The second point is to recognize that while this may seem reasonable and indeed obvious in theory, it is extremely difficult to translate into practice. The process of learning is dynamic, not static, and 'what children can do' is changing constantly. Furthermore, even if the difficulty of matching could be overcome for one child, the teacher has the problem of attempting this for thirty or more individuals, all varying in past experience, background and existing ideas. A child who can work at a more advanced level will be underoccupied by activities which provide a worthwhile challenge for another. The teacher has thus not only to attempt to cater for a multitude of differences between pupils but also to distinguish easy success, accompanied by signs of boredom and lack of interest, from success which results from a challenge which has made a pupil try hard and has resulted in some development in his thinking.

As if these complexities were not enough, we have further to acknowledge that it is not just the intellectual demand of an activity which has to be matched to the level from which the pupils can operate, but that there are other features of learners and learning experiences which have to be matched as well as possible. Past experiences and knowledge gained out of school interact with school activities, so that children will react differently to them. We find an obvious example of this in children's reactions to swimming classes at school; generally, reactions range from over-enthusiasm to cowering resistance. These reactions are physical and thus clearly observable, but there must be the same range of less observable reactions to the sight of the maths book or the sound of the word 'project'. In addition there are, of course, individual differences in interests, attitudes, preferred modes of learning and time required for particular activities.

All this might seem to suggest that hope has to be abandoned of putting into practice the idea of matching. But what it points to is that a solution in terms of a prescription or a set of guidelines cannot be expected. There is, however, strategy which can be adopted for improving the degree of matching, whilst it has to be admitted that the theoretical ideal of complete matching for every pupil all the time is unattainable. In teaching, decisions are all the time being made, to adapt or adjust materials, methods, organization pupil–pupil and pupil–teacher interactions. The aim of these decisions is to help the children's learning and it is through examining how these decisions are made that we can see how matching can be improved.

Figure 1 (after Harlen, 1978) looks at the decisions the teacher makes and the influences on such decision-making. Here the teacher, subject to external constraints and other influences, including his or her own ability, which limit the range of options, makes decisions about the learning environment and the intended outcomes. The phrase 'learning environment' is used here to convey the whole set of conditions arising from decisions about materials, methods, the teacher's rôle, etc., which affect the pupils' learning. The interaction of pupils and learning environment changes them both; the changes in the pupils may be both intended and unintended. There would be nothing wrong with this scheme of decision-making if we knew exactly how to bring about intended learning. But this is not the case for, as already mentioned, there are many factors influencing learning which make each situation unique. To take them into account the teacher needs more information as a basis for decisions than is suggested in the diagram. Since there are no prescriptions to be found for matching to every different set of circumstances, it is necessary to do this by a series of adjustments made in response to information about what is happening. Information is needed about pupils' ideas and about interactions of pupils with the learning environment so that the moment-to-moment decisions can respond to what is taking place. Instead of suggesting the teacher makes decisions independently of the response of the pupils, the model of decision-making for matching must show feedback being gathered and used, as illustrated in Fig. 2.

Here the dotted lines represent information gathered about the interaction of pupils and learning environment, about the pupils and about the outcomes, both intended and unintended. What cannot be easily represented in a diagram is that this process is a cyclic one. Information on its own does not solve the crucial problem of matching which concerns deciding the next step which each pupil can and should take. But if the process of making a decision and gathering information about its effect is a cyclic one, then the optimum conditions can be approached through a series of approximations. The effect of gathering information in this way is also cumulative, helping not only the present situation but building up a store of knowledge about pupils and activities which can inform future decisions. Thus this concept of matching is as a dynamic process in which feedback plays an essential rôle.

Figure 1. Influences and Feedback on Teacher Decision-Making

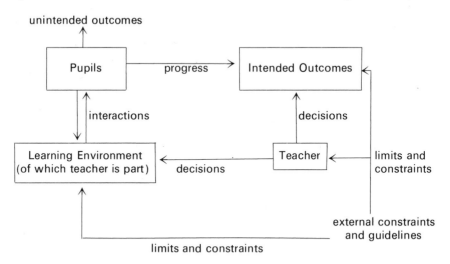

Most teachers will, hopefully, recognize this as something they already do, or attempt to do, but would not have found it necessary to analyze in this way. Analysis is necessary, however, if we wish to identify what kind of help teachers may need for matching to be improved. Teachers are required to make decisions about intended outcomes and so must be able to find help as to what lines of development are appropriate and what the points of this development are. This includes knowing, for example, that some ideas children will form would be described as 'wrong' by adult specialists, but are unavoidable steps in development because of children's limited experience and their ways of thinking. Having some idea of lines of progress which can be expected has to be supported by knowing how to foster progress; what methods, materials, activities are likely to be appropriate at each stage.

It has been stressed all along in this chapter that decisions about content are only part of the matter; methods and organizations are also important in providing learning opportunities. For too long the impression has been given that a single method and one type of organization is the answer to all teaching problems. 'Discovery learning' and 'informal' organization have been mistakenly advocated in this way at one time or another, as if they were panaceae for teaching all parts of every subject. What teachers need to have is a repertoire of methods and organizations, but most important, to know how to select the appropriate ones for particular circumstances.

Opportunities to Improve the Gathering of Relevant Information

Basic to the attempt at matching is the gathering of feedback for the evaluation of what is happening and how pupils are responding. The word 'evaluation' is used advisedly here, instead of 'assessment' and it is relevant to explain the reason. Evaluation is a broad term which describes the collection of information and the clarification of criteria used in judging and using the information. Assessment describes a range of methods which can be used for collecting information. Assessment implies some attempt to measure or to compare with a standard, but this need not be a fixed and widely used standard. Thus a remark made to a child such as 'good', either spoken or written, implies an assessment, often in terms of a standard which applies only to that child. A similar response by another child might bring forth a different remark, since the assessment might be against a different set of expectations for that pupil. The word assessment covers a range of methods, from the use of standardized tests to informal observation using child-based standards, as just mentioned. But there are other methods of gathering information than assessment. These others do not imply an attempt to summarize or measure; they can be best described as 'collection' or 'description'.

Figure 2. Influences and Feedback on Teacher Decision-Making

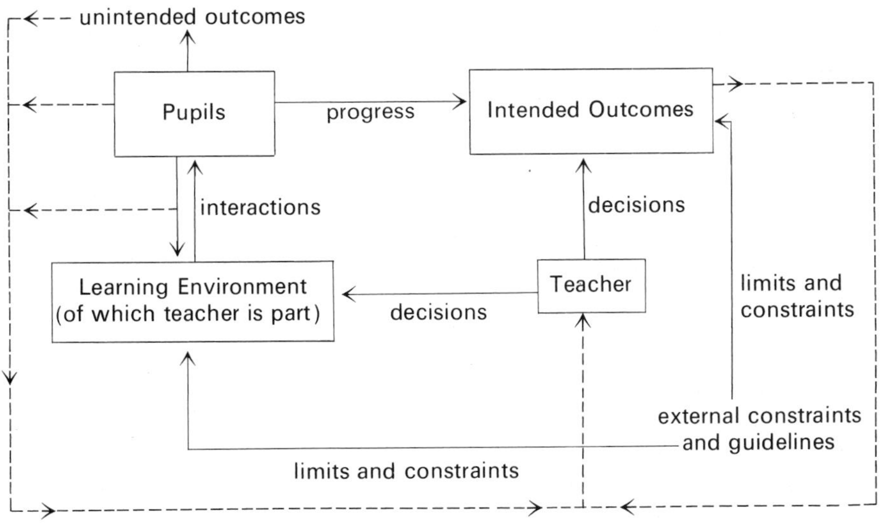

Taking samples of work, making notes describing behaviour, using recording techniques, are examples of these ways of gathering information. They do, of course, imply some selection on the part of the teacher and are often criticized as being too subjective for this reason. But it has to be remembered that all information is subjective to some degree. Even in objectively-marked standardized tests someone has decided what questions to ask, which abilities and facts will be covered and which left out. Subjectivity is inherent in all data gathering; it can be minimized if this is necessary, but there is a price to pay for it. It is very important for teachers to know when different methods are acceptable and when they are not. For just as in the case of selecting materials and methods for teaching, methods of evaluating have to be chosen to suit their purpose.

Although gathering information for matching serves quite a different purpose than assessment of pupils for determining local or national performance levels, it may be that the current interest in national or local assessment can be turned to advantage for helping the teaching-learning process. It is essential, however, to distinguish between the kinds of information required for these different purposes and to identify methods which are most suitable for each. The feedback which a teacher requires to help matching has to be gathered frequently and repeatedly, and must cover the whole range of teaching intentions – skills, attitudes, concepts. Methods used therefore have to be unobtrusive and flexible, so that information can be gathered about individual pupils at different times as required. Clearly they must not be time-consuming or demand special equipment or preparation, they must not interfere with learning activities, not disturb pupils or make them anxious; but they must still be as valid and reliable as possible. It is evident that testing of any kind does not meet these specifications. Tests have a rôle where comparisons are being made between pupils and it is important to control the kind of behaviour which is assessed. But what is required for matching is information about how the pupils are coping with their normal learning activities, not how they perform in specially contrived test situations.

Observation of pupils during their normal work is a method of gathering feedback which suits the requirements very well. Pupils are unaware of it taking place, it can be used as often as necessary, does not interfere with on-going work and will give information about all those aspects of development for which learning opportunities are provided. There are, of course, some disadvantages and hidden demands on the teacher. For whilst observation may not require preparation of materials, as testing does, it does require mental preparation in thinking out what to look for, in deciding criteria to be applied and in interpreting what is found. Moreover, since observation means more than looking, but involves a greater emphasis on listening and giving attention to certain of children's responses, it may well affect teaching style, so that more time can be spent in receiving signals and giving pupils more chance to explain their ideas and ways of thinking about things. Further discussion and examples of methods based on observation and of other methods for gathering information from pupils can be found in Harlen (1978).

It is also possible to turn the growing demands for accountability in education to advantage providing, that is, that schools maintain the initiative in this matter. The absence of pressure from outside for teachers to account for what they do has led, in some cases, to an absence of effort inside to evaluate what is done. A teacher has to be able to account to himself before he can account to others and this means extending the gathering of information beyond the bounds of the classroom to the functioning of the whole school. The feedback needed for matching can then be seen as part of a programme in which teachers and schools monitor themselves and constantly assess their success in providing a truly educational environment suited to their pupils. Accountability can be a positive and helpful force where it starts in the school, involves teachers in the clarification of their intentions and the evaluation of how well these are implemented and leads to a dialogue with those outside the school who have the right to know what is happening. The negative effect on schools of accountability schemes comes when these are imposed from outside the schools, applying criteria which may not be shared by those inside. The 'back to basics' move had many contributing factors but one was certainly that schools were caught unable to give good answers to why a broad curriculum was better than a narrow one.

Responding to New Demands – Some Issues

These are only some of the directions from which there appear to be forces combining to emphasize the importance in teachers' work of evaluation and self-appraisal. The possibility of teachers being able to respond to more demands depends, however, on two crucial conditions; that time is made available and that teachers receive the help to acquire or sharpen the necessary skills. It is no use disguising that evaluation is time-consuming, particularly when first undertaken. Evaluation can also save time by enabling better informed decisions, but there has to be an initial outlay of effort before there is compensation for it. Similarly, there can be no denying that changes of attitude may well be needed; there is little point in gathering information unless there is the willingness to take note of it, to accept the criticism of existing practice which it often entails and to make changes.

What can be done to ease the problem of making time for the in-service courses that will be needed by some to acquire skills of evaluation, time for gathering information and, most important, time to reflect on it? The frustrating situation at present is that opportunities potentially exist, in falling rolls, to re-allocate a teacher's time. For economic reasons these opportunities are being missed and teachers have no chance to spend less of their working time in pupil contact. There seems little practical alternative at the moment to teachers spending some of their own time in reflection and discussion with colleagues. The educational reasons for this are put in strong words by Elliott (1979): 'A school that is reluctant to engage in an honest self-appraisal reveals a lack of genuine concern about the extent to which its policies are socially and educationally worthwhile.' Elliott also points out what the alternative is, that if schools do not evaluate themselves then others will do so from outside with the consequent loss of autonomy: 'Externally imposed evaluation systems are essentially the means of getting schools to comply with policies decided elsewhere.'

For all decisions, from the moment-to-moment ones aimed at matching activities to pupils to the ones at the level of policy which decide the broad framework of pupils' experiences, information is required. The techniques for collecting data are not complex nor do they require the services of experts, but teachers do need to know about them and especially how to choose relevant and efficient ones for particular purposes. The question then arises as to what kind of in-service education can provide the necessary help? We have learned much that is relevant in answering this question from the attempts to introduce new curriculum materials. When teachers have been presented with new *products* and told how to use them, the result has often been little or no real change of the kind intended. When involved in the *process* of examining what is lacking in existing practice and developing ways of improving it, then the innovation has been more likely to be implemented. It is through involvement that the process of dissemination of new skills or materials reaches the point that Rudduck and Kelly (1976) described as 're-education'. When dissemination falls short of this point it fails to bring about real changes. Similarly, in disseminating the new skills necessary for evaluation it is not sufficient to communicate what techniques exist or to provide new ones, but rather to involve teachers in disscussing the need for evaluation, analyzing real problems and seeing for themselves where certain techniques are appropriate. It was the experience of the 'Progress in Learning Science' project which attempted to help with the process of matching, that solutions produced by others were not seen as helpful by teachers unless the thinking which had gone into them was experienced at first hand (Harlen, 1977).

Finally, returning to the problem of helping with matching, it may be that there is help which is required in those curriculum areas where matching is less satisfactory over and above making time and in-service courses available. It may be that some of the other possible associated factors mentioned at the beginning of this chapter should be examined. Pre-service courses could themselves be evaluated to see if they provide an adequate preparation for the demands on teachers, including the skills required for self-appraisal and for decision-making at various levels. Not everything can be done at the pre-service stage, however, and the whole professional preparation and continued development of teachers would benefit from a thorough examination of what is best attempted in pre-service and what in in-service. The lack of co-ordination between these is a waste of scarce time at both stages.

Further, we might re-examine the kind of help given to teachers in the areas where their own knowledge is likely to be patchy at best. Curriculum developers have frowned upon the notion of 'structured' materials, preferring, for good theoretical reasons, to leave the decision about selecting and sequencing activities to teachers. But there are different kinds of structure and not all lead to poor teaching. It is perhaps time to be more open-minded about the value of different kinds of materials. A degree of structure is helpful, both to teachers and pupils, but what this degree is varies between individuals. More work is necessary to discover how best to give the amount of support which some teachers must have to function with confidence and yet at the same time also provide the flexibility for adaptation to the needs of individual pupils. All this is to acknowledge that teachers are individuals, as are pupils, and vary in their need of support. Matching is as relevant in helping teachers as it is in helping children.

References

ASHTON, P., KNEEN, P., DAVIES, F. and HOLLY, B.J. (1975) *The Aims of Primary Education: A Study of Teachers' Opinions* Schools Council Research Series, London, Macmillan Education.

BENNETT, N. (1978) 'Surveyed from a shaky base' *Times Educational Supplement* 3 November.

BLOOM, B.S. (1971) 'Affective consequence of school achievement' in BLOCK, J.H. (Ed) *Mastery Learning* New York, Holt, Rinehart and Winston.

BRUNER, J.S. (1960) *The Process of Education* New York; Vintage.

CENTRAL ADVISORY COUNCIL FOR EDUCATION (1967) *Children and their Primary Schools* London, HMSO.

ELLIOTT, J. (1979) 'The case for school self-evaluation' *Forum* Autumn.

HARLEN, W. (1977) 'A stronger teacher role in curriculum development' *Journal of Curriculum Studies* 9(1), May.

HARLEN, W. (1978) 'Evaluation and individual pupils' in HARLEN, W. (Ed) *Evaluation and the Teacher's Role* Schools Council Research Series, London, Macmillan Education.

PIAGET, J. (1970) *Science of Education and the Psychology of the Child* London, Longman.

RUDDUCK, J. and KELLY, P.J. (1976) *The Dissemination of Curriculum Development* Slough, NFER (European trend reports in educational research).

4
Policy, Organization and Management: The End of Teacher Autonomy?

Introduction

The conclusion to the introductory paper argues that the issue of control is fundamental to understanding recent developments affecting education. Intimately bound up with this issue is the question of school and teacher autonomy – its status (myth, wishful thinking, fantasy or reality?), its range and its legitimacy. Each of the three papers in this section contribute directly or indirectly to a reappraisal of autonomy, but each also features one or more new developments within primary education which merit attention in this book.

John White's essay explores some of the consequences for teacher autonomy and professionalism of moves towards establishing a national framework for the education service along the lines discussed in the fourth paper in this book. He starts from the position which he argued for in *Towards a Compulsory Curriculum*, that the aims of education and the broad framework of school curricula should no longer be determined by the teaching profession alone, as they have been *de facto*, but should be decided democratically by politicians. He contends that, under this new dispensation, teachers would not simply become mindless, obedient executors of policy and practice determined elsewhere but would exercise a great deal of autonomy as they translated general policies into practical courses of action in particular circumstances. Heightened political awareness, deeper reflection about aims and their realization and greater willingness to dovetail their curricula with those of others would all be required of teachers. They would retain their discretion as to what particular teaching methods and detailed content they would use in specific situations. The image of the teacher as autonomous craftsman would be replaced by the teacher as 'broad-visioned' practitioner, capable of interpreting and justifying policies in particular circumstances and, where necessary, of criticizing such policies from practical, moral and logical viewpoints. There would be obvious implications for teacher education at both initial and inservice levels.

The contraction in the numbers of children attending primary schools which has been proceeding since 1974 and will continue into the mid-'eighties is the focus of Eric Briault's contribution. He outlines how pervasive are the effects of contraction – on schools, on staffing and on the maintenance of the primary and middle school curriculum. He discusses the major factors, forces and decision-making processes (most out of the schools' control) which affect the resolution of such issues. His article illustrates the constraining circumstances in which primary schools are having to work – constraints which are heightened at a time of contraction, though many were also operating, though less oppressively, when pupil numbers were expanding. The ideal of the autonomous school operating in virtual isolation was never fully realizable within the state system but can now be seen as even more impossible of realization during a period of contraction. Greater power inevitably devolves on local education authorities – elected members and professional administrators – as they seek to manage the diverse, only partially predictable consequences of contraction; problems compounded by economic constraints, parental consumerism and calls for greater accountability. His paper is aptly titled 'The politics of primary contraction'.

The third paper in this section reflects another new direction in primary education – the development of increasing interest in management ideas applied to schools, perhaps prompted by the need to react to some of the issues raised in the papers by Briault, MacDonald, Garland and Richards. Institutions of higher education and many local education authorities have mounted courses in education management, many of which have been concerned with what Harry Gray terms 'technical and material aspects of management'. This collection could not include articles covering the range of approaches and issues in this area; instead it focuses on one of the less well-known, and possibly more fruitful, approaches – OD or Organization Development. This views organizations as 'complexities of inter-personal relationships' and conceives of organizational problems not as mechanical or technical but as problems of 'inter-personal relationships'. Its key notions include mutual interaction, common responsibility, consensus, accountability and interdependence. OD seeks to replace the isolation and distrust which characterize so many institutions with greater openness and collegiality. Through OD, Harry Gray believes that schools can be more appropriately responsive both to the demands of their clients and to the aspirations of their own members. Though he does not discuss teacher autonomy in detail, his position implies a restructuring of conventional notions – the individual teacher has to surrender something of his freedom of action (with its concomitant anxiety and vulnerability) in return for greater involvement and satisfaction in the school as an institution.

This section was sub-titled 'the end of teacher autonomy?'. Each of the three papers (and others in different sections of the book) suggest ways in which schools' and teachers' freedom of action is, or could be, circumscribed, but none implies the withdrawal of teacher autonomy. In particular, all accept that control over teaching methodology is essentially a professional matter. The famous passage from the 1918 Handbook of Suggestions is nowhere challenged:

> The only uniformity of practice that the Board of Education desire to see in the teaching of Public Elementary Schools is that each teacher shall think for himself, and work out for himself such methods of teaching as may use his powers to the best advantage and be best suited to the particular needs and conditions of the school. Uniformity in details of practice (except in the mere routine of school management), is not desirable even if it were attainable. But freedom implies a corresponding responsibility in its use.

The Primary Teacher as Servant of the State*

John White
Institute of Education, University of London

Teachers as Professionals

A problem facing many primary teachers is the indefiniteness of their job – its lack of clear aims and methodology, as well as its increasingly uncertain 'professional' nature at a time when external bodies are claiming a larger say in determining curriculum content. Until recently things were more clear-cut, at least for teachers leaving their colleges of education with a belief in 'progressive' education. On a 'progressive' view, as I am using the term, educational aims are not things to be imposed on a child from without, but implicit in his own nature: the teacher's job is to create the conditions which best enable each child's individuality to unfold harmoniously. This picture of the 'progressive' teacher is very familiar and I need not elaborate it. What I do wish to emphasize is that progressivism gives the primary teacher *status*, indeed a remarkably high status. It makes her the unquestioned expert on how children should develop. How could external bodies, whether in the shape of the state, LEAs, Taylor Committee governors or whatever, decide on aims and content? The only person who knows what these should be must be both an authority on the laws of child development, and an expert on applying these sensitively to particular cases, that is, the teacher-psychologist of the progressive tradition. How, too, could a teacher have doubts about her basic aims and methodology? Once again, the theory leaves no room for worries like these. It sees the teacher as a confident professional, the supreme authority on all classroom matters.

This model of professionalism has received some hard knocks in recent years and in my view rightly so. One cannot find out what the aims of education should be from any amount of child observation or psychological theory. Empirical facts do not embody ethical values. The teacher-psy-

*From *Education 3–13*, 7(2), (1979), pp. 18–23.

J. White

chologist of the progressives' model is not and could never be an authority on the broad content and aims of primary education.

The assumption that teachers should have the right to determine aims is unsound. Whatever aims teachers adopt must surely be intended to have *some* influence on the kind of person a pupil grows up to be, and thereby, however minimally, on the kind of society in which he grows up. Since decisions about the kind of society we should have are political decisions, the choice of this set of educational aims rather than that rests basically on a political judgment. The crucial question is: why should teachers be empowered to make such judgments? If they had some special expertise, which the rest of us lack, on the nature of the Good Society, things might be different. But they have not. There are *no* experts on this topic. It is because there are none that democrats believe that political decisions cannot be imposed on people in the name of authority: each man is potentially in as good a position as any other to contribute to political decisions.

For reasons like this many have been advocating recently that the aims of education and the broad framework of school curricula should no longer be determined by teachers, as they have been *de facto*, but democratically, whether at local or at national level. This demand seems to hold within it another threat to the notion of the primary teacher as a professional. She has already lost her credentials as an autonomous teacher-psychologist; and now, if the broad framework within which she is working is to be determined by the electorate, she is apparently to be reduced to no more than a functionary, an obedient executive of political decisions taken elsewhere.

Many non-teachers would welcome such a large circumscription of her role, as has become evident in public reactions to Tyndale and in the Great Debate. I myself have argued elsewhere against the excessive freedom given to teachers in the British system and in favour of greater public control over aims and content. But I have never made it clear, either publicly or to myself, how far I would wish this reversal of policy to be taken. *Is* the primary teacher to become a 'mere functionary' or is there still a place for professional autonomy?

I shall take it as read, as I have in the past, that the teacher should be indeed an authority on what teaching methods and detailed content she should use in specific situations; only she is in a position to know how publicly prescribed content is to be accommodated to the particular abilities, motivations etc. of each of her pupils. The difficulty arises not so much here but over the general framework in which she is working.

Teachers as Civil Servants

Supporters of teacher autonomy sometimes speak disparagingly of teachers' 'being turned into civil servants' under a régime of public control, pointing to continental experience to show the very little scope teachers there have to make independent decisions on curricular matters. But perhaps we need to explore the concept of teacher as civil servant a little further. Civil servants in Britain operate at various levels of autonomy, from the tightly circumscribed work of a clerical officer to the very broad scope which, say, a Permanent Secretary has in interpreting government policy. I see no reason why, if teachers in Britain are to become a kind of civil servant, they will have to operate at the more restricted, rather than the less restricted, end of this continuum. Why cannot we reconceptualize the teacher (in our context the primary teacher) as a senior rather than a junior civil servant?

Now I do not want to get into disputes about the proper organization of the civil service, about whether we should have the kinds of grades we do have, and so on. Perhaps present hierarchies should be scrapped, I don't know. I am only interested in the senior civil servant – national or local – as providing a possible model of what the primary teacher might be under a system of democratic control. First, both jobs would presuppose an acceptance, at least for professional purposes, of a democratically-decided policy forming a framework for all they did. One has, of course, to write in the qualification 'at least for professional purposes' since senior civil servants might *not* accept government policy as private citizens. Perhaps the same could be true of teachers. Problems of conscience will arise, of course. I say rather more about these below. Secondly, for all their subjugation to political authority, senior civil servants do not tend to complain about their lack of freedom. On the contrary: as we have seen, they have considerable room for autonomous interpretation of whatever guidelines are laid down. Teachers could be in a similar position. One might imagine it being publicly laid down, for instance, that such and such areas of science be normally prescribed as minimum achievements for children of such and such an age: this could well leave individual teachers of science considerable scope in deciding the best routes, given their particular constraints and opportunities, to lead to this destination. (This is only, of course, an illustration, not a prescription).

It may strike some as bizarre to compare, say, the teachers of reception classes to senior civil servants. These teachers themselves may be the first to ridicule this idea: the gap between the two sorts of work, the status gap, if you like, is just too enormous. But how far do we think like this because we have conditioned ourselves over the years to do so? Other cultures, other thinkers have had a more exalted picture of the teacher than the British (or, rather, the English and Welsh, since the Scots have tended in another direction). It is true that there is one significant difference between teachers and senior civil servants, but this should not obscure the way in which they are alike. They are alike in that there need be no one between them and their political masters who 'interprets', as I have put it, political policy, that is, translates it into practical courses of action.

In this way, teachers are different from, say, *clerical* civil servants, since the latter *do* have others above them who do this interpreting. The significant difference between teachers and senior civil servants is this: individual civil servants help to forge plans of action applying to the country (or county or borough etc.) as a whole, while individual teachers' translations of public policy apply only to the pupils they teach. No doubt this is one, and one well-founded, source of the ridicule which would meet the attempt to put the infant teacher and the senior civil servant under the same umbrella. But the difference here is only quantitative: *qualitatively* the two kinds of job may still be similar, in that they can both embody the 'interpreting' role described above.

Many would want to argue, even so, that the civil servant's job is immeasurably more *complex* than the primary teacher's and so cannot be fruitfully compared with it. But *is* it more complex? Think for a moment of the difficult judgments parents constantly have to make about just *one* child's moral development. This problem is compounded many times over for the teacher, even if she has a small class. Add to this the many-sided judgments she has to make about the selection and presentation of material across the whole curriculum, as well as the fact (quite alien to the civil servant's situation) that while making many of these decisions she is at the same time functioning as a model for the children of how they should behave and think – and it should be abundantly clear just how very complex her job is.

In some ways, of course, the jobs of teacher and civil servant are very different. For one thing, teachers do not have hierarchies of subordinates working beneath them. But this will not be seen as a disadvantage by any but the more megalomaniac of teachers. At least teachers need not be tempted into any of the various types of authoritarianism which may entice those at the top of bureaucratic trees. Some of them *can* be so tempted, if they choose to organize their school in a rigidly hierarchical way, but the smallness of scale of the institutions in which they work makes democratic régimes, perhaps even without heads, a possibility. For this reason, primary teachers often have better opportunities to create such régimes than their secondary colleagues. In general, horizontal relationships between equals could become the dominant kind of bonding in the teaching profession, without the vertical, superior-inferior relationships found in the civil service. The need for such horizontal links among teachers, as I am now conceiving them, should be obvious. Teachers of children of different ages cannot be left to interpret officially laid down guidelines completely independently: the teacher of six year olds has some responsibility to see that what she teaches meshes in with what the teachers of the same children at ten, twelve or fourteen do with them. It is sometimes urged against the comparison between teachers and senior civil servants that the latter are small, close-knit bodies and that teachers can never hope to emulate them in their cohesiveness since they are so numerous and so scattered. But there is no reason why the teachers in different schools in the same local area should not dovetail their curricula and syllabuses, working as a single unit in much the same way as senior civil servants, with, for instance, far more mobility between different institutions in the system. There is, in fact, every reason why they should cooperate in this way; otherwise the education which any particular pupil will receive in the whole course of his schooling is likely to be the hit-and-miss, hotchpotch affair it too often is today.

I hope these various points are enough to show where I am laying the emphasis in the comparison between the primary teacher and the senior civil servant. Despite the several ways in which they are different, both of them are in the unique position of being the direct translators of political policy into more determinate courses of action.

Teachers as Reflective Thinkers

The new role I have been sketching for the primary teacher is very different from that in the progressive tradition. She will above all be a person of wide horizons. She will need, first, to understand the aims of the whole education system as democratically laid down; she will need to reflect on how to fit her own teaching into this framework ensuring at the same time that it meshes in with what her colleagues are doing in other institutions. Her horizons can no longer be bounded by her school, let alone, as with some of our most autonomous primary teachers today, by her classroom. She must see her day-to-day activity ultimately against the political framework which is to give it its *raison d'être*.

I am aware that this conception of the primary teacher runs quite against everything that we have come to expect of her. Of all members of the teaching profession, she has traditionally been the least politically aware. Her typical milieu has been the world of art and crafts, of movement and drama, of learning to read and count. It has typically been a cosy, inward-looking world, quite cut off from the complexities of politics. The new primary teacher will need to be more knowledgeable, more reflective about society and its values than her present-day counterpart. It is difficult to draw a line round the kinds of knowledge one would ideally require of her. A deeper understanding of political realities necessitates some knowledge of economics, sociology, applied science, social and political history . . . one could go on and on. A deeper reflectiveness about aims and their realization depends among other things on something of a philosophical understanding. All this imposes great intellectual demands on her, demands which her initial training can never hope to meet on its own, if at all. I shall come back to this point later.

Meanwhile let me take up in more detail the point just made about reflection on aims. Ideally one would hope that public prescriptions about aims and content were also backed by a public rationale, which discussed in full such matters as the justification of different proposals and the relative priority to be given to each. Teachers will have to be able to argue their way around such rationalia.

If this kind of educational ideal is ever to be realised, it is clear that primary teachers will have to be far more adequately trained than hitherto to reflect on the larger purposes of their job. Their current lack of sophistication in this field, which emerges, as we shall see in a moment, from the Schools Council's *Aims into Practice in the Primary School* (Ashton *et al*, 1975), is not to be blamed on them. It is the product of a system in which discussion of aims has been, wittingly or unwittingly, discouraged, for fear of opening rifts between ideological positions and endangering a 'consensus' thought necessary for the system to operate.

A brief look at *Aims into Practice* will show more clearly the kind of reflectiveness required. The book is based on a survey of primary teachers' objectives. It discovered that their views on aims (I am using 'aim' and 'objective' interchangeably) tend to lie in a continuum. At one extreme teachers believe that 'education is the means used by society . . . to ensure that new generations will maintain it both practically and ideologically' (p. 11). Such teachers 'rate as most important aims dealing the basic skills and with conventionally acceptable social behaviour' (p. 12). At the other extreme 'is the view that education is a personal service to the individual' (p. 11). Here the aims thought most important are 'concerned with developing independence, both emotional and intellectual, and with a much broader educational front, including art, music, movement, drama, and so on' (p. 12). Few teachers, we are told, are exclusively attached to one of these extreme positions: 'the great majority hold both to some extent' (p. 11), but with differing emphases.

The tension described is immediately recognizable. So, too, is the compromise which many teachers seem to settle for, that is, to pay a certain amount of attention to basic skills and in the rest of the time to foster the child's personal development by allowing him plenty of choice among *activities*, especially creative activities; a régime, for instance, of reading and sums in the morning, 'choosing time' in the afternoon.

The question now is: have those teachers – that is, most teachers – who adhere to both ends of the continuum really thought things through in depth? I am sceptical. For if one looks at all closely at either of the competitors, one sees obvious deficiencies. Why should the society-centred view, for example, put such emphasis on basic skills and conventionally acceptable social behaviour? Why not on the arts, on science, on political understanding? If we are concerned with the well-being of society, why should this broader understanding be thought less important? Presumably it is because the society-centred aim is dominated, as in the 'Great Debate', by economic demands: we will not survive as an industrial nation without a work force that is literate and numerate and also industrious, punctual and cooperative. But why should economic considerations be overriding? Citizens of a society are more than workers, and there is no reason why their education should be restricted in this way. Why, too, should the *status quo* be taken as a baseline? Perhaps 'conventionally acceptable social behaviour' is *un*acceptable from another, namely a moral, point of view. Just because conventional ways of doing things do exist or have existed, this is no reason for claiming that they *should exist*.

Narrowness of vision also affects the pupil-centred point of view. Why should creative activities in art, movement, music and drama etc. be especially highlighted? There are historical reasons for this, I believe, to do especially with Percy Nunn's aesthetically-inclined theory of 'individuality'. If we are concerned with the well-being of the individual, why are science or political understanding (again) to be played down? Won't the pupil need *all sorts of* intellectual equipment, and not just the aesthetic, properly to fulfil himself?

But now we are getting into difficult waters. What is to count as 'self-fulfilment' or as the 'well-being of the individual' is a philosophical problem of some depth. So, too, is the meaning of the 'well-being of society'. Whatever one finally says about both these matters, two things should be clear at the outset. First, there is no good reason to narrow them down in the way proposed. The compromise curriculum, of basic skills, social training and plenty of creative activities is too thin a diet. Second, the opposition of pupil to society is misconceived, simply because the pupil is a member of society. Of course, if 'social needs' are to be limited to the requirements of the industrial establishment, then the pupil may indeed have no part in this, except as a means to others' ends; and it is as a reaction to this that many teachers have taken up the cause of individual self-development. But if 'society' is to be understood in any less restrictive sense, which includes the pupil himself as one of its members, the whole continuum of aims on which *Aims into Practice* located so many of its teachers, simply collapses.

We would do well to abandon the continuum. It is rooted in conflicting attitudes to modern industrial society. Against those who see education as the handmaiden of industry are those unwilling to sacrifice individuals' potentialities to capital's demands. But their reaction is often too negative. It leads too readily to a fruitless escapism: if the 'real world' of industry is too inhuman to contemplate, let us turn our backs on it and paint and sing and do collages. Teachers who hold both attitudes – that is, the majority discovered by the survey – must be riven by conflict, half chained to necessity and half desiring to be free of it. It would not be surprising if this conflict were transmitted gradually to their pupils. And is this not indeed precisely what we find in a large part of our adult population today: on the one side a resignation to industrial semi-serfdom, and on the other the vain hope that one may one day strike it rich?

The continuum merely mirrors the social *status quo*. It allows little or no place to any critical challenge to it. This comes out very clearly in the recent HMI survey of *Primary Education in England*. (HMI, 1978) This draws attention to the schools' general failure to teach pupils to argue a case, to reason things out. Social studies and science, both areas in which critical skills may be developed, are particularly ill provided for. (Political education is presumably so little in evidence in any of the schools surveyed that it is not mentioned even once).

This is not the place to go in detail into what should replace the continuum, assuming it is abandoned. But I have at least hinted at the need to see individual pupils as members of society, not as standing over against it; to reconsider how the 'good of society' and the 'good of the individual' are really to be opposed; to broaden the primary curriculum, whether approached from 'society' or from the 'individual'; to create a new kind of industrial society in which there is less escapism because there is less sense of servitude. This last remark, I believe, strikes at the heart of things. We need somehow to construct a society in which men can work without the thought that they are sacrificing their one, unique life for nothing; in which their work is freely and willingly undertaken as a condition of their own and others' self-fulfilment. How this will be possible without a wide-scale democratization of industry and a political education to prepare one for it, I do not know (see White, 1979).

Teachers as Political Activists

I have argued that *Aims into Practice* reveals that if the primary teacher's role is to be remodelled in the way described, she will have to reflect more deeply than at present on aims. She should not take for granted what passes as the conventional wisdom, but should follow through the logic of an argument to its underlying assumptions, challenge these assumptions, put forward less inadequate alternatives if the latter prove wanting. This will lead her inevitably to frame her own picture of the kind of society we should be working to create. If my intuition is correct, reason will guide her towards the vision of a participatory democracy in both industry and in local and national politics. Obviously more would need to be said in support of this view. But, if correct, it brings out the point that the kind of reflectiveness one may expect in a teacher about her aims is all of a piece with the reflectiveness one would look for in her as a citizen of a democracy: each role demands a sophisticated political awareness.

This comes out also in another way. As the person directly responsible for translating politically-determined aims into practice, she has some obligation to try to ensure that these official aims *are* so translatable. They may fail to be realizable in several ways: there may be practical difficulties in doing so; they may be impossibly vague or inconsistent; if one follows through their implications, they may be seen to be at odds with certain basic moral principles, and so on. Of these three kinds of defect specified, the first might make the aims *practically* unrealizable, the second *logically* unrealizable and the third *morally* unrealizable, that is, unrealizable by one whose basic moral principles they offended. So there is some obligation on the teacher, arising not only from her role as executant, but also from her being an autonomous moral agent, to bring pressure to bear to ensure that the official aims are aims that she can – practically, logically and morally – teach to. She is not to be a passive recipient of aims from above, but must play an active part in helping to improve them. This means political involvement – of two kinds. She has a duty to draw the attention of policy-makers to any practical or logical defects in actual guidelines. There must be *official* channels enabling her to do this. As for the moral obstacles, she can attempt to influence the political community – by pressure group activity, work within a political party, journalism or whatever – to change the guidelines themselves.

All this is implicit, I think, in the new model of the primary teacher. Not that every teacher will live up to all the expectations in the model in every particular. Not all, for instance, despite what I seemed to say in the last paragraph, will be political activists. There is certainly, as I indicated, *some moral obligation* on them to be, if official aims are morally inadequate, in their view. But whether this obligation is to be overridden by other more important moral obligations is something that each individual teacher must be left to work out for herself. Certainly I do not mean to imply that the gifted teacher of music, who would be not nearly so good a teacher if she had to attend to political matters, should necessarily sacrifice her teaching. Whether she does so is a matter for own conscience. But at the very least, in *seeing* this as a matter for her own conscience, she must be aware of the conflicting obligations on her, the pedagogical and the political. And this means that she must possess the breadth of vision, the wide intellectual and moral horizons which I have been advocating.

Similar considerations apply to the teacher who has conscientious objections to official aims so great that she cannot teach to them. For her it is not a matter of accepting imperfect aims *pro tem*, trying meanwhile to improve them by political action: she just cannot in all conscience agree to them. For her, too, there will be a conflict of obligations, between accepting, on the one hand, that she is not arbitrarily to lay down her own aims, and being morally unable, on the other, to accept an actual democratically-arrived-at decision. For her, too, how she resolves the conflict – whether by bending the rules, by resignation, or however – must be left to her.

The Greatest Challenge

The new portrait of the primary teacher is so far from present actualities that many will dismiss it as impossibly utopian: it is too intellectually, perhaps even too spiritually, demanding for the average teacher; theoretically, it may form a pretty whole, but from a practical point of view it is a non-starter.

I disagree. What I hope to have done is set up some kind of signpost, indicating a new direction in which to move. How far we can get along the road I don't know. The greatest challenge is to find practical ways of getting the primary teacher to accept this grander conception of her role. Something, no doubt, may be attempted in her initial induction into the job of teaching during her pre-service training. But horizons cannot be widened at a stroke. Years of deepening understanding and reflectiveness are necessary, acquired in intimate association with practical classroom experience. How the teacher achieves this deepened understanding – by in-service courses, by informal discussion with colleagues, by solitary reflection – is another matter. It is a pity that our status-oriented society opens few paths before the ambitious young teacher beyong the climb up to headships, the inspectorate, LEA work or similar better-paid jobs. *No* work in education could be so responsible as the classroom teacher's and no work potentially so intellectually challenging. If we could once get the conditions of work right – manageable classes, adequate time to think out what one is doing, and so on – what more 'successful' persons in the educational system could there be than the broad-visioned, practically competent classroom teacher?

References

ASHTON, P., KEEN, P., DAVIES, F. and HOLLY, B. (1975) *Aims into Practice in the Primary School* London, University of London Press.
HER MAJESTY'S INSPECTORATE (1978) *Primary Education in England* London, HMSO.
WHITE, P.A. (1979) 'Work-place democracy and political education' *Journal of Philosophy of Education* XIII.

The Politics of Primary Contraction*

Eric Briault
University of Sussex

The number of live births in England and Wales in 1964 was 876,000. Since that date the number in each successive year has declined and the number of live births in 1977 was 569,000. Even if the slight upturn in the number of live births, which had occurred in the first three quarters of 1978, is maintained, the contraction of the primary school system, which has already been experienced for several years, is bound to continue, at least until the middle 1980s. This article looks at the implications of these facts for the education of children up to the age of thirteen under three broad headings. The first section deals with the major issues which arise, the second considers the factors affecting these issues and the third attempts to examine the decision-making processes through which those involved with the education service will deal with the issues.

Issues

The first set of issues concerns the organization of educational provision for children between the ages of three and thirteen. Clearly the decline in rolls, which is very unevenly distributed in different parts of England and Wales, is equally unevenly distributed as between different areas within an individual authority. The contraction of an individual primary school may eventually give rise to the question as to whether the school is still viable and whether, and if so at what stage, it should be closed. This is a highly politically sensitive issue and one which operates differently in urban areas where alternative primary schools are readily accessible as compared with rural areas where distances are different and where the relationship between a primary school and the area it serves is of a quite different character.

*From *Education 3–13*, 7(1), (1979).

Over and above the critical issue of sheer survival, questions of organization and reorganization arise in a contracting situation. The most common of these are where there has been, during a period of expansion, an infants' and a junior school on the same site or at least serving the same immediate area. Decisions have to be made as to how long a separate infants' department in particular should remain a separate school in terms of the Burnham report and, in particular, in terms of separate headship. Educational arguments for and against the all-through five to eleven or five to twelve school ought to be considered more frequently and more radically in a contracting situation. There has, indeed, been a fairly general tendency to reorganize separate infants' and junior departments, roughly at the stage when there is no more than a single form of entry in each year. Other organizational changes have already affected the upper end of the primary school, with various authorities restructuring their provision on a pattern of first schools from five to eight, middle schools from eight to twelve and secondary schools taking in their pupils at twelve instead of eleven. The variant of the reconstruction of the secondary system to provide for middle schools, of course, directly affects the size and, therefore, the viability of the primary school. There have been areas where the reconstruction has given nine to thirteen schools, others ten to thirteen, still others eleven to fourteen. Policy changes by individual authorities to modify the former five to eleven, eleven to sixteen or eleven to eighteen pattern for educational or other reasons have been, in a number of cases, overtaken by falling rolls which have introduced a new factor into consideration of the individual changes, so that many authorities find themselves at the present time with a heterogeneous pattern. The formation of the new local education authorities in 1974 has led, in many cases, to the amalgamation under one education committee of areas where different patterns had already been established. The extent to which the authorities have sought to bring about uniformity in the ages of transfer within the system across the whole of the area which they now cover has varied considerably and the stage reached in such further changes has varied even more widely.

A special aspect of the organization of education for young children has been the growth of nursery schools and nursery classes in the development introduced in 1972. The growth of pre-school education has again been extremely uneven, being most rapid in the inner city areas with the additional financial support provided for such development through a number of means and has been least in the rural areas of counties. Contraction in the primary schools has made accommodation available, so that much of the provision for children below the age of five has been in individual classes attached to and using accommodation in existing primary schools. Alongside this, however, and particularly in the first few years after the introduction of growth of nursery educational provision, there has been some development of separate nursery schools in the larger cities.

A political educational issue at the present time, therefore, is the extent to which nursery education should continue to be expanded and whether or not this should be by the development of nursery classes in more and more individual primary schools, or by the establishment of further nursery schools.

The second major issue is that of staffing. Is the existing pupil/teacher ratio to be adhered to in a period of contraction or are the schools to be allowed to benefit from the retention of existing staff and to have a gradually improving pupil/teacher ratio? Behind that broad policy issue lie a number of more detailed questions which very directly affect the individual school which is experiencing a fall in roll. Many authorities provide for a small pool of resources, often held at area or divisional level, which can be allocated at the discretion of officers or advisers to meet the particular circumstances of individual schools. Such circumstances are, of course, of a very varied nature— the proportion of immigrant or non-English speaking pupils, the degree of exceptional deprivation in the neighbourhood, all the factors which led to the setting up of the SP allowances with the recognition of the special problems of deprived areas. It is arguable that one of the circumstances to be taken into account in the allocation of a margin of additional help should be the difficulties which would be caused to the individual school by the strict application of the pupil/teacher ratio in a contracting situation. It is, in fact, in the 'small print' of the way in which an authority's overall ratio is applied to the individual school that the effect in the circumstances of contraction is generally felt. Let us take an oversimplified example. Suppose that the authority operates an overall pupil/teacher ratio for assistant staff (that is, excluding the head) of one to thirty. Then a six-class school with 180 pupils will neatly qualify for six teachers. At what point in the fall of the roll from 180 down to 150 is one of the six teachers withdrawn? Does the school have to reach 180 to get six teachers and to retain them? Or does the crunch line come at, say, 165? Or are the six teachers retained so long as the roll is over 150? There is all the difference in the way in which the school operates and in the average size of its classes according to the way in which the formula is applied. If the authority has taken a policy decision that no class need exceed thirty, then presumably at 151 on roll the school will retain its six teachers. This, however, is an unlikely situation and a more common one would be an intention that no class should exceed, say, thirty-five, the strict application of which would make it possible for the authority to withdraw one of the six teachers as soon as the roll fell to 175. This, however, would be unlikely and to a greater or lesser extent the issue then becomes one of judgment, presumably to be made by officers or advisers and to have a relationship to the use of the small pool of extra resources, if such exists, as to a statisfactory or at least not too unsatisfactory distribution of the children between the individual classes. The problem is one which is at its most acute in the summer term as the admissions of five plus children build up in January and again after Easter. In practice, most authorities make *ad hoc* and temporary arrangements if an extra class has to be created in the summer term but there is bound to be an annual, sometimes rather fraught discussion between heads and managers on the one side and the authority's administration on the other as to the number of classes to be established in the succeeding year in a contracting situation.

A further minor issue relating to staffing is whether the authority allows some of the pupils over and above the exact multiple of thirty, or whatever the basic ratio is, to be counted in such a way as to allow for the employment of part-time staff. Where the margins of extra resources are small, these are frequently distributed in terms of part-timers but, of course, the authority to employ such a teacher over and above, say, five teachers for one-hundred-and-sixty-five pupils against a ratio of 1:30 would not be considered anything like as worthwhile as the ability to organize the school into six classes.

The other issue relating to staffing is the matter of redeployment, where the contracting school has to lose a teacher and where there is no resignation or retirement. Most authorities now have agreements with their teachers' associations at local level about redeployment arrangements and it seems as if these are working reasonably smoothly. For the individual teacher, redeployment may, on the one hand, be a moderately welcome opportunity for a change of scene or, on the other hand, an interruption of a desire for a continuity of teaching, often linked with a less acceptable journey. It seems as if the arrangements for the redeployment of individual teachers are being carried out with full consultation and with considerable care and many authorities show an acceptable degree of flexibility, in so far as they prove themselves prepared, if redeployment has not been satisfactorily arranged by the end of the school year, to leave the teacher at the existing school for a further period of time, till a satisfactory change can be arranged. The problem of longer journeys, particularly in county areas, is one which may or may not be met by the payment of additional travelling costs, which are in any case subject to income tax.

Two other matters relating to redeployment may be briefly mentioned: the first is that authorities have generally agreed with the teachers' asso-ciations that a teacher who has been redeployed should not be moved again for an agreed period. The length of that period seems to vary quite con-siderably from one authority to another. The second issue which arises occasionally is where it proves necessary to redeploy a teacher who is holding a post above the basic scale. This gives rise to a difficulty of the acceptability in the receiving school of a fresh teacher who will take up a scale 2 post which conceivably might have been allocated to an existing member of staff. Such an arrangement is likely to bring the managers into a greater or lesser degree of conflict with the administration and conceivably with the authority at political level. As far as the SP allowance is concerned, authorities will obviously seek to place a redeployed teacher from an

SPA school in another SPA school, but where they have been unable to do this they appear to be overcoming the problem by a notional secondment of the teacher, retaining the SP allowance, to the non-SPA school, or by the offer to the teacher of a peripatetic scale 2 post as a recompense for the loss of the SP allowance.

The third issue and the one which, as far as the writer is aware, has been little investigated, is that of the curriculum. In the primary school, as distinct from the middle school, the almost universal arrangement for class teaching leads to the expectation that the curriculum in subject matter terms will be covered by each individual class teacher and the reduction in the number of classes, therefore, should not affect this matter. It is probably, however, not quite so simple as that. A particular example may well be that of music, where the school may enjoy the help of some visiting teachers or, more likely, will have a class teacher who is something of a music specialist and who will contribute to the musical education within the school as a whole. Should that teacher be the one who, for other reasons, has to be redeployed, then there may indeed be a significant effect on that particular aspect of the curriculum of the school. While music may be the simplest example, it would appear that some other subjects, such as science, possibly art or physical education, can suffer similarly by the loss of a particularly gifted teacher or one with some special contribution. It would be a matter of considerable interest if there could be carried out a series of studies of these rather hidden curricular changes in contracting primary schools.

At the level of the middle school, particularly where this is one that runs to thirteen or fourteen, some of the problems which are already being observed in the limited number of secondary schools which are experiencing falling rolls, may be expected to occur. The degree to which there is subject specialization in the middle school varies very widely and, of course, particularly with the differences in the upper age limit of such schools. In many cases, however, staff are appointed as specialists or semi-specialists and, given the relatively small size of most middle schools, some of the subjects have to be covered by no more than one specialist teacher. The contraction of such a school can lead to the situation where the staff must be reduced, and the most convenient way of such reduction is, of course, by natural wastage. This, however, may often operate in such a way as to remove from the school a teacher carrying, at any rate, some specialist teaching role and if there is to be no replacement, then that teaching must be spread among the remaining staff. Again, as far as one knows there is no specific information about this problem at this level, but it is undoubtedly an issue which will have to be considered in areas where the numbers in middle schools are already falling.

Finally, some reference may be made to the in-school organization of classes. In the primary sector, children are usually placed in classes according to age; there appears to be little streaming even in the junior sections of primary schools although it occurs, no doubt, in the middle schools. With the smaller primary schools, there has always been the need to have children of more than one year group in a particular class, and as the school contracts then this problem becomes more severe. The particular application of the staffing arrangements to the summer term roll will very much affect the need to move children from one class to another in the course of a school year, a practice which has always taken place but which is generally considered to be undesirable. It is unfortunately a practice which will probably be adopted increasingly in a period of contraction. There has in recent years, however, been a growth of family grouping arrangements as an approach to the organization of younger children into classes. Clearly a family grouping policy applied to the whole or a greater part of a primary school will tend to overcome difficulties of class grouping which arise where the intention is to place children in their year groups. It is important to recognize that family grouping has not been introduced to meet the problems of contraction, but equally important to observe that it is an arrangement which, in fact, does minimize those problems as far as class organization is concerned.

Major Factors

Let us consider now, and more briefly, the major factors affecting the issues which have been identified. The first of these is clearly finance. The education service within a local authority has to compete with the other local authority services for its share of the total resources and, of course, rate support grant is not ear-marked to individual services. Moreover the way in which rate support grant is distributed among the different authorities and notably between the urban areas on the one hand and the counties on the other means that the financial pressures upon the individual local education authority vary widely from one area to another. Be that as it may, there is always a ceiling on the amount of expenditure which the local authority is prepared to undertake from the rate support grant plus the rates themselves and thus upon the total expenditure on the education service. Such pressures tend to lead to an expectation that the real costs of the education service will be held at an existing level or not allowed to grow beyond a certain margin. They also tend to lead those who deal with finance to assume that the savings arising from a contraction of this or that part of the education service will, in fact, materialize – that is to say, an expectation that costs per head will remain similar. In a period of contraction, in fact, unit costs are bound to go up, since the fixed cost of maintaining an individual school is unchanged even though there are fewer pupils within it. Correspondingly, however, those concerned primarily with finance tend to expect that the other running costs, of which by far the largest is teaching staff, followed by non-teaching staff and including also capitation, will fall *pro rata* to the contraction in the roll.

The second factor is the judgment that has to be made about the viability of a particular school. Put bluntly, this means the judgment as to how small a school is allowed to become before it is closed. From the financial point of view, the smaller the school, the higher the cost per head, and the greater, therefore, the pressure at some stage to consider its closure, since that is a means by which the costs of the premises which cannot be changed can be taken out of the budget and, indeed, perhaps an opportunity to make other use of the building or even to realize its capital value. We are observing, at the present time, a mounting campaign to save village schools and any proposal to close a particular school, as we have observed earlier, raises a wide variety of issues and gives rise to many pressures. There is, however, a legitimate educational factor which is the professional judgment as to how small a school can be and still be regarded as educationally satisfactory. The answers given vary widely as does the judgment of successive Secretaries of State.

The third factor has been touched upon already, namely, that of the premises. This needs spelling out a little, however, if only to remark that the age and condition of the premises must be a fact to be taken into account, since these will affect the costs of maintenance quite significantly. The actual site of the school in question is also of very considerable importance, for in certain circumstances this may represent a very considerable capital asset, whereas in others its value either for other uses within the education service or for sale will be minimal.

The fourth factor to be taken into account is the broader social issue of the role of the particular school in the community it serves. This is especially the issue of the saving or closing of the village school, but the role of the school within the community, of whatever kind, is a factor of significance which ought to be taken into account as the roll contracts. A particular aspect of this factor is that the reduction of roll releases, or can release, accommodation which can be put to educational, or indeed other social purposes, within the community which the school continues to serve.

The final factor worth a reference is that of the operation of parental choice. In the urban circumstances of the great majority of the primary schools in this country, parents have some choice of school, in some cases a very considerable choice of school. Under conditions of pressure on accommodation, many authorities have operated fairly rigid catchment area arrangements for primary schools. As contraction takes place, these become less and less necessary and gradually fall out of use. In these circumstances, parents have a real choice of school and may well make this choice in response to their limited knowledge of this or that school and may well be affected by rumour, by influences of various kinds, including their attitude towards the proportion of non-white pupils in the school. The tale of the West Indian parent who refused to send his child to a particular school because there were too many black children there is by no means apocryphal. Given free parental choice, then, in a contracting situation, individual primary schools will undoubtedly contract at differing rates and the spectre of possible closure will approach more rapidly one school compared with another. If an authority intends to plan systematically the reduction in the number of its primary schools in an urban area, then it will at some stage presumably have to place limitations, once again, upon the operation of parental choice.

Decision-making

The last section of this article is concerned with decision-making about the issues in the light of the factors that have been identified. The general position is well-known, namely that powers of decision-making in the education service in this country are widely distributed and not, as in so many other countries, concentrated in a hierarchical pattern of authority. Those who have decision-making powers may be briefly listed: the Secretary of State and the Department of Education and Science; the local education authority acting at the level of the Council, the Education Committee, the sub-committees of the Education Committee, the Chairman of the committee or sub-committees or small sections set up *ad hoc* for particular purposes; the officers of the Authority; the advisers at the local authority level; the managers of the individual school; heads of schools; and the individual teachers themselves. A number of decisions are, in fact, reached as a result of the interplay of the powers and responsibilities of more than one of those listed.

In respect of organization and closure, some effective decision-making powers are exercised by parents themselves, in so far as by choosing one school and rejecting another, they are bringing about the contraction of a school to the point where reorganization from two departments to one department, or actual closure may eventually result. Decisions by the Education Committee or by officers as to the opening of nursery classes in one school rather than in another are likely to affect admissions to the primary school and competition to be allowed a nursery class may be a significant factor where the surplus of primary school places is inevitably going to lead to eventual closures. Admissions policy and, in particular, the detailed arrangements for catchment areas or for free parental choice are matters where decisions lie chiefly in the hands of administration. Heads, managers, teachers and parents all play a subtle part, however, in the whole process of admissions to one school rather than another, and press publicity at local or even at national level can, as experience has shown, affect the popularity or unpopularity of a particular school and, therefore, be influential (if not decisive) in matters of organization and closure.

The main decision-making power in respect of reorganization and of closure clearly lies with the local education authority and particularly with its schools' sub-committee. These bodies, however, act only upon the reports of officers who, in turn, will have been influenced, to a greater or lesser extent, by their professional advisers. The case for and against closure must be set out by the Chief Education Officer and his advice is clearly a major influence in the decision taken by the authority. If closure is proposed, that decision is, of course, a decision to issue Section 13 notices expressing an intention to close and the final power of approval lies with the Secretary of State. While at the primary school level party political factors are not of great importance in respect of individual decisions, there are factors of a political nature involved in the way in which the various people able to influence closure or not, in fact behave in particular circumstances. The key to the understanding of these matters is probably a recognition of the relative sensitiveness of the elected member to pressures brought to bear upon him by those who will have the opportunity of voting for or against him at a subsequent election. Indeed the timing of controversial proposals can be observed to have a significant relationship in many cases to the imminence or otherwise of local authority elections. The individually elected member is clearly more sensitive to pressures against the closure of a school in the area which he represents than he is to pressures from parents in other areas and probably the Chairman of the Education Committee and the Chairmen of the sub-committees are in a specially vulnerable position in this respect, though one is bound to say that it does not often appear to influence their own broad approach to their responsibilities for the service as a whole.

The factors affecting staffing have been referred to and the major one of these is cost. There is clearly likely to be continuing, very understandable pressure from the teachers' unions to improve staffing during a time of contraction, both on the educational grounds of the expected improvements from smaller classes and on the grounds that, with fewer children to educate, an authority can afford to retain teachers in such a way as to improve the pupil/teacher ratio. Critical decisions probably originate in the corporate management structure of the local authority and are taken, certainly as to overall staffing levels, in the group meeting of the controlling party of the authority in relation to the preparation of the budget. At this level of decision, the education service is very dependent upon the power and influence of the Chairman of the Education Committee and of other key members of what in many authorities is called a policy or a resources committee. Given that the local authority is one where there is a clear majority of one political party or the other, the influence of the party in opposition on this key matter of staffing numbers is probably minimal.

On the issue of redeployment, the broad policy is one where the teachers' unions have an important part to play and have clearly influenced the overall arrangements. The particular arrangements for the redeployment of the individual teacher seem to relate to decision-making powers by heads of schools and advisers or administrators at area or education office level. The identification of the teacher who is to be redeployed is a highly sensitive matter and seems to depend upon the interplay of the powers and advice of heads and advisers and administrators, with the teacher union representatives on the whole holding watching briefs rather than playing decisive parts.

Curriculum matters remain almost wholly within the hands of the heads and the teachers, but the impact of decisions about staffing, both as to overall numbers and as to redeployment, can be significant upon the details of the curricular provision. Managers, too, play a significant decision-making part in relation to employment of replacement teachers, though generally they follow the advice of the head of the school. It may be that managers will play some role in relation to the proposed loss of staff, not only as to numbers but in respect of the needs of the school. There probably are cases where the curriculum needs of the school would best be met by the retention of the most recently appointed teacher with some specialist ability to offer, and the redeployment of one who had been at the school rather longer. Where this is not readily acceptable to the teacher concerned, it may well be that managers might play a part in bringing pressure to bear in the interests of the maintenance of the curriculum. At primary level this is probably of very small importance but it is an aspect that may well become significant in individual cases at the middle school level where specialist teaching is more common.

Opportunity

Most of what has been said in this paper is about the problems of the primary school contraction. It is important to recognize the opportunities which that same contraction will give rise to. Fewer children in premises which, in the past, may well have been overcrowded will make it possible to provide more specialist areas, whether parts of larger rooms or whole rooms set aside for specialist purposes. It will release accommodation which can be used by other members of the community for educational activities and conceivably, therefore, can open up greater involvement between the school and its neighbourhood. Contraction ought, at any rate in the long term, to lead to staffing improvements and these should enhance the whole quality of primary education. The purpose of the whole provision of the education service, after all, is to provide the best possible learning experiences for the children concerned. It is probably not too optimistic to believe that, for the most part, those many people who have greater or less power of decision-making, in respect of the issues arising from contraction, will tend to consider the effect of this or that decision upon the quality of the education provided for the individual child. Judgments, however, upon many of the issues as to which decision is more likely to enhance the quality of education will continue to vary. The most critical, probably, is whether a very small school close at hand provides overall better educational opportunities than a considerably larger one some distance away. It is an issue which will be argued in many individual cases for a number of years yet.

Organization Development (OD) and the Primary School

Harry Gray
Huddersfield Polytechnic

Approaches

In recent years there has been an increasing interest in management ideas in education and quite a blossoming of courses of varying kinds and length. Many of these are concerned with technical and material aspects of management: the management of resources, educational planning and quantifiable aspects of education. Many teachers look first of all for practical and technical solutions but are usually disappointed when they come to apply the theories and techniques to their own schools. This is especially the situation for teachers and heads in small schools which do not seem to require 'heavy' management. Even in large schools it is quickly perceived that problems do not go away once a management technique has been applied; on the contrary, many management techniques only seem to make things more difficult and the pupils more remote.

In fact, the same problem has occurred in industry and commerce. Even when technological approaches to management have appeared to be relevant and to work, there has still been something important missing. The technical solutions have missed out on something organizationally essential – the sense of wholeness is the organization. People and the dynamics of people working together have been much more complex and much less open to 'managing' than has too often been presumed and, as a consequence, management theorists have begun to look harder at the nature of 'organization' and the ways organizations develop.

The term that has come into use to describe this organizational approach is Organization Development or 'OD'. Managers and consultants using OD approaches are concerned with the complexity of human dynamics in organizations and with helping people, managers and managed, to work out what is going on in the organization and to find out how to do things better. OD concentrates on the importance of mutual interaction, common responsibility, consensus, accountability and interdependence. A key feature in OD-based management is the use of consultants, both internal to the organization and brought in from outside, to help members sort out their problems and work through to new and mutually acceptable solutions.

OD is different from most other management approaches in that it is not confined to improving the quality of top and senior managers alone but is concerned to involve everyone in the organization in the management process. In practice, senior managers are often among the first to be trained in OD approaches but OD is not about teaching 'bosses' how to 'boss' but rather to help them to share management with their colleagues. Of late, an increasing number of heads have become interested in OD because of its concern with sharing and its helpfulness in understanding the dynamics of interpersonal relationships.

OD is not a familiar term in primary education management but, since its purpose is to interpret the things that have to be done to further the needs of the organization in terms of the needs of the people who have to do them, such an approach ought to appeal very much to teachers in primary schools. It is because primary school teachers have been concerned professionally with individual children as persons in their own right to be nurtured and encouraged creatively to explore their skills and talents and not as objects to be moulded and trained like artefacts, that so much that is worthwhile has happened in English education. And this is also a reason why humanistic approaches to management such as OD should have considerable appeal in primary education.

Organization Development: Some Assumptions and Concepts

The basic assumption in OD theory is that organizations are in their essential characteristics 'human' organizations and institutions. That is, they function in terms of people over and above any mechanical or technical considerations. Problems in organizations are seen not as mechanical problems but rather as problems of relationships among people. So unless problem-solving occurs in terms of people, the problems remain unsolved, however nicely mechanical and 'ideal' solutions may have been advanced. Schools are of particular interest as forms of organization because, like churches, they have no essential technology or mechanical quality that can obscure the ways people inter-relate. Schools are almost pure organizations in that they consist of people and nothing else of essential importance. A school may exist in a home, a palace, a field, a theatre, a church, or anywhere people can gather together and learn. But more than this, schools exist only because the activity of education exists, albeit in a formalized form. It is really the process of education that is organized, not the school; that is, the 'school' is an institutionalized form of education.

From the point of view of management theory (or, more correctly, organization theory, since theories of management derive from theories of organization) the essential factor in developing management strategies and skills is an understanding of the basic task (or mission) of the organization, and the critical relationship people have in the performance of that task. A common complaint about 'management theory' applied to education is that it ignores the child (or student). In fact, of course, this is only true of some mechanistic approaches to management. Proper theories of management such as OD acknowledge the true place of the child as central because the essential task of the school is the education of the child. Unless the school is organized around this basic task, the education of the child cannot properly take place.

But this is not to say that only the interests of the child are the concern of management. Organized education also involves teachers, parents and a variety of other people. All of these have legitimate needs and demands and they must be appropriately balanced against one another. It is usual for organization theorists to be concerned with the conflict of needs among children, teachers and others in the school. Clearly schools do not exist only for the children or only for the teachers, or the administrators, or the parents. Schools exist for all of them and their needs are by no means always compatible. There is considerable evidence, for instance, that the expressed wishes and needs of each group are in some measure incompatible with the wishes (and needs) of others. Schools 'work' only in so far as these incompatible needs can be accommodated – not reconciled, not coalesced but allowed to exist alongside one another, a creative coexistence.

It must also be true that if there are significant differences between each major user group, there are also differences of a like order among each member of a group. It is quite nonsensical – as primary teachers know – to posit a complete identity of interest among all members of a group (be it a class of children, the whole child population or parents at large). Given that the school has no *essential* technology to influence behaviour, the inter-relationships among all the individuals who go to make up a school are exceedingly complex. The practical purpose of 'management' in its most usual manifestation is to reduce this complexity to simple and 'manageable' forms. Some people would argue that organization of such a complexity is so demanding that, in fact, essential purposes are overlooked and alternative, more manageable activities take place, so that the activities of the school become a kind of game, a pattern of ritualistic behaviour. This does happen, at least from time to time, and is one of the practical concerns management must deal with at some point, for it cannot be ignored for ever.

Because of the complexity of interests in the school, it is difficult to speak of goals and objectives as if there were an easy collective aggregation. By definition, organizational 'goals' cannot be individual goals also, so it is more appropriate in organization theory to talk of organizations as serving purposes; that is, they allow individual goals to be achieved through the group processes that occur within them. Some educationists write about institutional goal setting but a moment's thought will lead to the conclusion that this may well be no more than evasion of the issue of personalized needs. Though some American OD has concerned itself with collective goal setting, in the UK attention has been directed to helping people to understand just how individuals often use collectivity as a way of *avoiding* the personal dimensions of organizational activity.

Many people new to management ideas find the idea of 'structure' confusing. Older management texts talked of structure as if it were pre-existent, as if schools had inherent material structure. In fact, they have an exceedingly complex structure but it is not pre-existent. Structure is what actually occurs, not what one would like to occur. The structure of an organization derives from the activities the members choose to engage in, and these activities in turn are determined by the tasks members set themselves (albeit for a multiplicity of reasons). Functions derive from the performance of tasks and do not follow from positions with institutional tasks.

This is a difficult idea to explain. Organization theory describes behaviour as a 'function of the organization', hence any specific function (for example, learning, leadership) is primarily a function of the organization not the individual. Leadership behaviour is any behaviour that helps people to do their work: it may be performed by anyone in the group or organization and not necessarily the appointed leader. In this view, the heads of schools are not leaders by virtue of their position (that is, head) but only when doing whatever helps other members to perform the tasks, do their work. It is crucial to OD views of management to understand this; initiatives may come from anyone and are valid only in terms of their effectiveness, not the status of the person taking them.

This is a truly democratic view of organizations that is not acceptable to some people. Not only does it mean that all members of a school – teachers and children – are of equal functional status but it also means that they are equally responsible for what happens. It would appear that the concept of collective responsibility is often not well understood, particularly in large institutions. For example, collective responsibility does not mean that everyone should do everyone else's job, or that specialization is illegitimate. It does mean that no individual can say the responsibility for any action, decision or solution is not in some way their own, too. In a way, this is well understood in the infant school where the right of the children to make decisions and for the individual to choose what they want/need to do is accepted. A teacher cannot 'make' a child learn to read. They can only create conditions in which a child will exercise choices. Learning to make proper choices is at the core of education – learning rights and responsibilities. In the infant school, the pupil often has rights that are denied students in later stages of schooling, because infant schools are more child-centred.

Of course, in practice, educational institutions are run on a simplified pattern of predetermined role behaviour. But that does not mean that the underlying psychological conditions are changed. It cannot be said that when a head makes decisions which colleagues disagree with and the consequence is catastrophic that colleagues are therefore blameless if they did not attempt to influence the head otherwise. By and large people within organizations tend to leave decision-making to others and then complain when they do not like the consequences; they do not resist the original decision-making. Equally, heads who make bad decisions often complain that colleagues were not interested enough in the first place to offer advice and guidance. And some arrogant individuals take all the credit for good decisions but blame their colleagues for the bad ones.

Because organizations are complex psychological entities with a host of conflicting needs, interests and dispositions, all of which have in some way to co-exist, they are arenas of active conflict. Some managers try to ignore this dynamic conflict, other refuse to admit its existence but the most effective managers use it to increase member involvement and commitment and so improve creativity and problem solving. In the past, OD has sometimes been accused of playing down conflict and stressing consensus-seeking but this is unfair, certainly within the English tradition. If conflict is inherent in all organizations, it would seem most sensible to use it rather than banish it. Because organization by its very nature is a limiting factor, members who are restrained from achieving their needs in some way or another become frustrated and alienated. But, if the reasons for alienation and frustration can be discovered, the creative forces in individuals can be channelled into positive organizational activity. OD is concerned to open up the dynamics of personal involvement in organizations and it does this by using skills of group facilitation and providing individual support, by helping members to accept and understand individual differences and the causes of conflict.

In summary, the theory of organizations that undergirds OD practice is that organizations are complexities of interpersonal relationships where individuals are motivated to participate only in so far as they see some personal advantage in so doing. Managing organizations by using OD skills means harnessing individual drives and the need for personal satisfactions so that the maximum number of members will feel their membership to be worthwhile and so put their effort into improving the quality of life in the organization. In this way the organization continues to provide necessary stimulus and reward until the members no longer have any use for that particular form of organization.

Change and Stress

It is important to grasp the idea that organizations, as means to ends, must necessarily be temporary. There is nothing in organization theory to suggest that organizations should continue for ever and certainly nothing to suggest that they should maintain the same form. Indeed, quite the contrary. It is a normal and reasonable expectation for organizations to be continually changing their form (structure) as needs, tasks, purposes and resources change – as they do continuously. It is remarkable how conservative people are about organizations though that is one of their characteristic dynamics. Good management holds the right relationship between change and conservation while nevertheless steering the organization through gentle and continuous change. And sometimes guiding it through cataclysmic and terrifying change, when circumstances so determine events. From the perspective of OD, change is of the essence of organizations but change must be made as benign as is humanly possible.

The degree of anxiety that organization itself creates, whether or not it is changing rapidly, is too often overlooked. Although organization can be supportive, especially when it is self-determined, organization imposed from elsewhere is always a restraint and often a hurtful one. Because living in an organization means that one must overtly fulfil other people's expectation of oneself, organizations are stressful. Generally speaking, we understand this for children – and the good primary school attempts strenuously to mitigate the effect of expectations on individual children – but attention to staff is less forthcoming especially to senior staff such as heads.

OD is concerned to create a particular supportive and stimulating climate in the organization, a climate which is all pervasive. It is characterized by openness towards colleagues and a willingness to share, a preparedness to confront others when a concern is felt, a willingness to work through problems however difficult and uncomfortable, a readiness to accept responsibility and be committed to others, and a disposition towards being supportive and encouraging of colleagues. Because of the traditional role behaviour of heads, it is almost always essential for the head himself to be committed to OD and to be the first to be 'trained'. In this way, the person most vulnerable when the organizational changes consequent to OD occur is protected and he can support others through some of the crises that exploration of personal positions produces.

Much OD, at least in the early stages, is therapy of one sort or another. Organizations are themselves stressful situations but most people bring from outside anxieties and concerns that affect their performance. Until these personal matters can be dealt with, no attention to the organization is of much consequence. Indeed, since organizations are only made up of individuals, ultimately the individual is the basic unit of concern. In my experience, OD without professional, personal help for members cannot achieve very much and may indeed only uncover deep-seated problems which are then incapable of resolution.

OD theory and practice have no room for cosmetic changes, because it is little more than cosmetic change that management conventionally attempts. It is no use attempting to change the structure without changing dispositions and attitudes and, of course, attitudes are dispositions most firmly held. The more entrenched attitudes have become, the more defensive they are and the more threatening appears the 'promise' to change them. By and large, OD practitioners prefer to work at the affective or emotional level of an individual or organization, believing that most attitudes are not susceptible to rational argument especially when there are critical problems in a conflict situation. That is not to say that people do not change attitudes and opinions rationally; they do. But, in the confusion of organizational situations, crisis or otherwise, people defend their beliefs because they feel the need to protect the public level of relationships.

An OD consultant does not, therefore, attempt to change attitudes head on but instead he creates situations in which attitudes can be examined and tested. He does this by creating experiential situations where trust can be tested and experienced, confidence can be built up and experiments in new relationships and behaviour successfully carried through. He is concerned to listen. He does not come with prepared answers or even packaged techniques. Any method can be used to share ideas – flip charts, pictures, montages, groups exercises and games. His objective is to help all members of the organization to listen and share before making decisions and then to work towards some agreement or acceptance of disagreement. Small groups meeting alone and then together, finding common ground and facing up to anxieties, fears and disagreements, are characteristic of the time spent in OD exercises. Formal meetings are conducted with openness and in a variety of modes rather than with tight authoritarian direction. This is not to say that OD, through a consultant, is undisciplined; the essential discipline comes from his deep understanding of group and organizational dynamics.

A consultant working in this way with a staff of a primary school will provide opportunities for individuals to present and discuss their feelings about the school, their hopes, concerns and misgivings. They will look at what they believe to be the needs of the children, the needs of the staff, their expectations of the head and how they would like to involve the parents and people from the education office. They will plan together and build a climate of common acceptance and mutual regard. An attempt will be made to help them to share what are the common problems and possible solutions will be discussed. At the end plans for action will be considered and some lines of action decided upon. The objective is to open up discussion and increase the level of participation and sense of involvement.

For OD to move on from this stage, training for the staff (or at least some of them) is essential. This training may take a variety of forms: counselling training, T-groups, encounter groups, workshops, problem-solving sessions. Particularly important is an understanding of group dynamics to facilitate the handling of meetings, committees and workshops. Once staff have been introduced to the skills involved, they can employ these in the normal working activities of the school. Such skills include listening, paraphrasing, sharing interpretations, suspending judgment, being supportive, confronting, levelling and so on. It is important that they occur in an open, supportive climate and are used in normal situations rather than being reserved for crises.

Consequences

Once under way, OD managerial approaches should increasingly result in improved skill in handling meetings, a willingness to confront one another over difficulties, a preparedness to resolve conflict, more use of personal counselling, third parties used as facilitators in problem areas, newer techniques for setting targets and an increased commitment to innovation, experiment and trying things out. Generally, the climate of the school should be easier, happier and there should be a greater readiness to take risks. People should really feel themselves to be partners and there should be a readiness to share problems and anxieties as well as hopes and dreams.

Perhaps it all sounds a little idealistic and that would be true. But the other side of OD is that it is often more realistic than other approaches to management just because there is less fear and a greater willingness to risk and explore because individuals better understand what really happens to people in organizations. Most organizations avoid upset and the deep issues: OD helps us to face them and resolve them.

One of the consequences of OD is that it demystifies management, making participants aware of the true place of technicalities and helping them to see that much of what goes on for management and administration is a cover for deeper failures and inadequacies. Once they begin to understand the true nature of organizations the latter begin to fall into their place and cease to be the giant, overpowering constructs we make them. My experience seems to confirm just how few people actually understand, let alone handle, what is going on in organizations, especially schools and colleges. The reason seems to have something to do with fear of intimacy, of closeness. To manage with people successfully you have to give something of yourself, to offer yourself, to expose yourself. You do not get close to people by parading your strengths, only by acknowledging publicly your vulnerabilities, your humanity. Too few managers can do this; they are afraid of their image slipping, their mask cracking, and that fear is what incapacitates them in their managerial behaviour.

I believe OD is more concerned to recognize the importance of learning, of coping with failure, and of recognizing our common humanity, than most other approaches to management. Organizations as we know them seem to want supermen, or even gods, to run them and so senior people try to exhibit these qualities. That is where they go wrong and why when they fall, they fall so far. Fear of failure is perhaps the most incapacitating mental condition that any person can experience yet organizations are so constructed that we dare not fail. It is not just that we create unrealistic levels of achievement but we pressure individuals to go well beyond what many can cope with. Yet we should learn the lesson of the good school where there is no such thing as failure but rather the acknowledgement that there are critical points of growth for individuals. The good primary school does not label children as failures, only as successes. Managers need to learn this, too.

But the practical consequence is that there is much deceit, pretence, and huffing and puffing in organizations, especially among senior members. OD can help them to come to terms with their true selves, show them that they are acceptable and good as they really are, if they will accept what they really are. Yet, strangely, to ask people to accept reality is often to receive the rebuff that it is unrealistic, impractical in the 'real' world. But the real world of most people is a desperate protective fantasy and it is the fantasy that is being protected. How can heads who fantasize about their schools be realistic about the pupils and teachers? As I hope I have shown, OD can help the shift to 'true reality' by its understanding of what organizations are and how people behave in them.

I hope I have shown that good management is a consequence of a clear understanding of what the organization is about. For the school that purpose is education, itself a process, not a content. An educated person is one who is continually growing up, maturing and learning, who can face the world with a disposition that will enable his experiences to work for him, an individual who grows in realistic confidence and personal awareness, who is unafraid of his inner self and fearless of others. It is a tall idealistic, philosophical order – a sense of continuity and searching but also of achievement and fulfilment. Schools exist to help people to be like this because they value and respect them. If these values are clear, then the kind of organization we develop for schools will facilitate their realization, not prevent this from happening.

In many ways the English primary school has been developing along lines that are sympathetic to OD values. The core consideration for the continuance of that development is how such schools deal with freedom – whether they help children to be free or whether they repress them. I do not mean this in a glib way for I know that freedom and responsibility go hand in hand. But the question is, if we do not allow freedom for all, who is free to decide for others? OD is about the discovery of this freedom in its organizational manifestation. Once teachers accept the organizational implications, they still have to work on the personal and philosophical implications. Can it be that the consequence of liberal education is to frighten us and make us fearful of the freedom that we and others have begun to discover?

The Future

There is some evidence that OD will prove attractive to an increasingly large number of heads, particularly as they find traditional approaches to management wanting. Though most of the literature originates in the United States and is concerned with a somewhat different approach (a more highly structured technology) there is an increasing amount of writing about OD scattered throughout the various educational journals, some of it concerned with counselling approaches and innovative schemes in curriculum development. The journal *Educational Change and Development* is largely devoted to OD type approaches and the Network for Organization Development in Education (NODE) organizes an annual conference each Easter where educationists and others gather together to share ideas and experiences. In universities and polytechnics OD is familiar in programmes offered by departments of management.

While the term OD itself may not convey a full idea of what OD is about, many heads and senior teachers find that they have been working on OD values, and in an OD way when they talk together with OD 'professionals'. We can confidently predict that not only will OD change and develop itself but that many more people will come to understand what an OD view of organization means. In a period of considerable managerial crisis some of us believe that OD has the best answer yet. Certainly it is worth finding out more about it.

Further reading

Readers who would like to find out more about OD, particularly in its application to education, may care to read the following:

GRAY, H.L. (1980) *Management in Education* Driffield, Nafferton; includes some accounts of OD interventions and underlying theory.

MILES, M.B. (1971) *Learning to Work in Groups* Teachers College Press; New York. One of the earliest handbooks for group work training, containing useful ideas for organizing training programmes and conducting meetings in school.

SCHMUCK, R., RUNKEL, P., ARENDS, J. and ARENDS, R. (1977) *The Second Handbook of Organization Development in Schools* Mayfield Publishing Co.; the classic American handbook. Well worth reading for a flavour of OD as it has developed. British readers may find some of the assumptions problematical.

There is also a journal *Educational Change and Development* that provides a running commentary on the scene with a strong UK bias. It is issued once a term. Further information from the Business Manager, Educational Change and Development, Department of Education Management, Sheffield City Polytechnic, 36 Collegiate Crescent, Sheffield, S10 3BP.

5
Studying
Primary Classrooms:
The End of
The Black Box?

Introduction

In the 'seventies the classroom was 'discovered' as an important arena for educational research. Classroom interactions were studied by increasing numbers of social scientists; a wide range of theoretical and methodological approaches were employed; practising teachers themselves were urged to take a research stance towards their own teaching. Instead of remaining 'a black box' opaque and virtually ignored by researchers, the classroom became the focus of activity, a focus which seems likely to be retained by many of the educational researchers of the 'eighties. Research into classroom studies can be categorized into a number of groupings, three of which are represented in this section: ethnographic research, systematic classroom observation and teacher-based research. Primary classrooms have been, and are likely to be, studied by researchers from all three 'traditions'.

Ethnography, the traditional research methodology of cultural and social anthropology, views classroom interactions not as familiar phenomena but as though they were part of a strange culture. The methodology is grounded in participant or non-participant observation and relies heavily on qualitative data deriving from that observation and also from interviews and sometimes analysis of documents. Ronald King's paper is part of a study in which, over a three year period, he attempted to make sense of infant education through understanding the subjective meanings which class teachers attached to their activities and which they transmitted directly or indirectly to pupils in their day-to-day interactions. His book, *All Things Bright and Beautiful?* (1978), examines how infant teachers create the everyday world of the classroom and his paper reproduced here explores how teachers present other worlds to children: the story worlds of reading, the writing worlds of news and story, the world of number and mathematics and the world of conventional pictorial representation. He illustrates how children come to share teachers' definitions of these 'multiple realities' and how they learn what is appropriate and inappropriate in each. His contribution illustrates the value and the insights to be gained from regarding classroom activities as phenomena to be explained rather than procedures to be taken-for-granted.

The second research tradition attempts to provide 'objective' data about classrooms through observing classroom activities systematically. Compared with the ethnographic tradition it places greater emphasis on quantification, though qualitative data are also often drawn upon to provide the context in which the quantified findings can be placed. Maurice Galton's paper discusses the observation schedules (or 'sets of rules') used by the ORACLE research team to focus on those aspects of classroom life which they hypothesized to be significant in determining teaching styles. The paper defines the concept of 'teaching style' and contrasts the use of systematic classroom observation with the use of questionaires as a way of providing descriptions of various styles. Galton exemplifies points by referring to the ORACLE research into styles employed in fifty-eight classes containing children of junior school age. As discussed in the introductory paper to this collection, these styles and the attempt to relate them to measures of pupils' progress are an important contribution to the study of primary pedagogy. They are likely to be refined, extended or replaced by the systematic observational researchers of the 'eighties.

The third paper in this section represents two new directions in primary education. First, it is part of the attempt being made to reformulate 'progressive education' on a more adequate intellectual basis after the powerful attacks of its critics. Secondly, it represents a small but important research tradition which involves teachers examining their practice critically and systematically. This approach aims at what Lawrence Stenhouse has described as the 'development of a sensitive and self-critical subjective perspective and not an aspiration towards an unobtainable objectivity'. As a result of his experience of collaborative work with Michael Armstrong and others, Stephen Rowland advocates classroom-based research with pairs of teachers working together – one taking major responsibility for the management of the curriculum, the other responsible for the research, but both sharing in these activities. The thrust of the research effort being pursued by the Leicestershire Classroom Research Inservice Training Scheme is close observation and analysis to gain insight into what Armstrong terms 'the character and quality of children's intellectual understanding: the insights which they display and the problems which they encounter, their inventiveness and originality and their intellectual dependence'. The results of such investigations are descriptions, interpretations and evaluations in case-study form, as exemplified by Armstrong's book *Closely Observed Children*. Rowland's paper concentrates on two issues concerned with understanding classroom life: the nature of the relationship between teacher and pupil and the question of pupil autonomy within this relationship. By reference to painstaking analysis of field-notes he argues that 'formal/informal' dichotomies (or, for that matter, ORACLE's four 'teaching styles') are not helpful in describing the learning relationships between teachers and pupils. He believes more fundamental dimensions to be the extent to which the pupil exerts a control over his work, the nature of the teacher's collaboration in this and the ways in which the pupil influences this collaboration. Such teacher- and classroom-based research promises to throw more light on the 'black box' of the primary classroom, but, unlike the other two research traditions featured here, promises insights into how children's minds operate in teaching-learning situations, a fascinating and hitherto neglected 'inner black box'.

Multiple Realities and their Reproduction in Infants' Classrooms*

Ronald King
University of Exeter

A number of studies in the sociology of education have drawn upon the social phenomenology of Alfred Schutz, which stresses the primacy of everyday life as the immediate and most important social reality. The purpose of this paper is to report the application of a relatively neglected aspect of Schutz's work, the concept of multiple realities, in relation to some of the teaching–learning processes in infants' classrooms, and to consider its general usefulness in the analysis of the curriculum.

The Research

The research reported here was part of a study of three large infants' schools (King, 1978) which used an action approach derived from Weber (one of the starting points for Schutz's theories), who defined social action as, 'all human behaviour when and insofar as the acting individual attaches subjective meaning to it' (Weber, trans. 1947). My primary task was to interpret the meanings teachers assigned to their actions in the classroom. This was attempted by long-term observations and follow-up interviews.

My basic interpretation, which, following Schutz's postulate of adequacy (Schutz, 1953) was broadly confirmed by the teachers, was that their actions in the classroom were related to their definitions of the nature of young children and their education. These took the form of what Berger and Luckmann (1971) call recipes, that is, accepted ways of doing things. In Weberian terms they were institutionalized ideologies, taken for granted and given the status of the truth (Eldridge, 1971). The principal elements were: developmentalism, individualism, play as learning and childhood innocence, all familiar as the child-centred progressive ideology, as propagated by the Plowden Report (1967).

*This is an edited version of the article which appeared in *Journal of Curriculum Studies* 10(2), (1978) pp. 159–167.

The concept of innocence was the most important in relation to the report that follows. There were two aspects to this. First, young children although capable of being naughty, were not necessarily judged as being naughty in intention. This was shown very clearly in the oblique methods of social control used by the teachers, who would say, 'Someone's being silly', rather than make a direct rebuke, and in their professional equanimity when children, for example, split paints for the fourth time or wet their pants.

Innocence also refers to the way children were protected from what their teachers defined as harmful or upsetting aspects of the outside world. This was shown very clearly in their management of the knowledge of death. When guinea pigs became old they were taken away from school by the teachers, partly because they tended to get snappy, but also to prevent their deaths being witnessed by the children. A gerbil in a cage outside a classroom died just as afternoon school was finishing. A girl noticed its death throes and asked, 'What's wrong with it?' He teacher replied, 'Oh nothing to worry about, you can go home now'. Later she said to me, 'Thank goodness they didn't see it'.

The Multiple Realities of Story Worlds

The main emphasis in the research was the teacher's creation of the every-day world of the classroom, but other worlds were also presented to the children. When they read the books provided or had books read to them by their teachers they were given access to a number of story worlds. The teachers had not written these books but in many cases they had chosen them, and so implicitly, and sometimes explicitly, approved of their contents. This is confirmed in their disapproving certain other kinds of books. When children brought annuals they had received as Christmas presents to school their teachers showed a polite but unenthusiastic interest and never read from them at story time. Some expressed a rather inchoate abhorrence of these books which was often extended to comics.

The most obvious of the approved story worlds were those in the intro-ductory reading books. At one school the *Ladybird* series was in use. A content analysis, including the illustrations, shows why they were approved, since the story world created by the author is in many ways similar to the classroom world that the teachers attempted to create.

The principal characters of the first nine books are Peter and Jane. They are described and illustrated as infants' teachers ideally defined young children to be. They are invariably happy, having 'fun' and 'liking' everything. Of the 429 scenes identifiable in these books twenty-nine per cent show active or imaginative play. Peter and Jane play happily together with their friends, taking turns, sharing sweets and cakes, and are never naughty. They are moderately adventurous but are careful to do nothing dangerous. They are kind and caring towards animals and other children, taking presents to a friend in hospital and even their own toys for some less fortunate patients. At home they are keen to help, and are always careful to tidy up their toys before going to bed.

Peter and Jane go to school and are seen with their teachers who are talking to or supervising small groups of children, giving them interesting things to do or showing them something in a *Ladybird* book. However, Peter and Jane are more often seen outside school, but engaged in teacher-approved activities in contexts similar to those provided in the classroom. They have their own dressing-up box and a cupboard full of toys. They have no sandpit or water tray but they splash and play in the nearby stream and are taken on trips to the seaside. They have no playground or climbing frame but they play in the grassy garden and build Indian camps and tree houses. The house they live in is their Wendy house and Jane does 'real' cooking in her mother's kitchen. Shopping is done in 'real' shops not the toy shops of the classroom.

The adults in Peter and Jane's world are smiling, kind and helpful. Mother is the more prominent parent who, like the infants' teacher, talks and plays with them. The bedtime story is parallelled by story time at the end of the school day, followed by teacher tucking the children into their coats instead of their beds until tomorrow morning.

The reading scheme used in another of the three schools was the *Gay Way* series. The books of this series, colour coded from red to orange, present three fairly distinct story worlds; a 'real' world of human beings, an animal-humanoid world, and the traditional story world, each, in the terms of Alfred Schutz (1967) 'a finite province of meaning'. Schutz pointed out that human beings have the capacity for living in quite different worlds of meaning. We assign different significances to an accident in the street outside our house, to a similar event on the television news, or reported in a newspaper, or part of the events in a play or novel. Schutz called these worlds of meaning multiple-realities, the most intense, the paramount reality being that of everyday life. In school this is the everyday life of the classroom. The realities of the three story worlds of the *Gay Way* series corresponded in different degrees to the teachers' definition of the classroom situation, but in ways that were consistent with their child-centred ideologies.

The *'real' world of human beings* is very similar to Peter and Jane's world. Ken, Pat and Pipkin (a girl) also live in the country and own pets they care for. They are happy, kind, co-operative and affectionate children, playing and having fun with games similar to those of Peter and Jane. The adults, too, are kindly and helpful. There is no evil in this world, and when things go wrong, as when Pipkin's doll falls out of the train window, someone puts it right, as, without a reproach, her mother recovers the doll.

The animals in the 'real' world of human beings do not talk to one another or to people, as they do in the *animal–humanoid world*. Although not dressed as humans they are drawn in an anthropomorphic way. The dominant theme of the stories is the need for security. The animals are constantly looking for, and making homes, sometimes needing to co-operate to accomplish this. Many stories of lost kittens, chicks and baby rabbits end in their finding their mothers (fathers are conspicuously absent). Animals can be naughty. In the first book the pig excluded from the tin-pot house squashes it by sitting on it. But, usually naughtiness and carelessness have their consequences; unlatched gates and unlocked doors lead to unpleasant experiences. Some animals are quite malevolent, especially the fox. Death occurs in this world. The black beetle drowns in the stew, a consequence of his foolishness in stirring it with a small spoon. His companion, the ant, briefly grieves for him, but is soon consoled by the appearance of another beetle. In the *Mouse and the Flea*, jokes get out of hand leading to the mouse jumping out of his skin and losing his back legs and tail.

The presentation of the animal–humanoid world as a reality distanced from that of the 'real' world, mitigates the presumed effects that descriptions of macabre mutilations, evil and death may have upon the vulnerable innocence of children. Such things are presumed less 'real', and therefore less upsetting than they would be in the world of Pipkin.

In the 'real' world of humans, conventional reality is largely preserved. In the animal–humanoid world it is modified by the replacement of humans by animals. Human beings, when they rarely appear, do not communicate with animals. In the *traditional story world* humans, animals, plants and objects speak to one another. Magic transformations are possible. Events are unpredictable. They are not always the logical consequences of actions but are due to luck, spells or bad fortune.

The 'real' world of Pipkin is wholly good, and, apart from the bad foxes and trolls, the animal–humanoid is also good; misfortune only follows foolishness. In the traditional story world all reality is rather slippery, and morality is less clearly defined. A common theme, as in *The Animals' Winter Hut*, is the necessity to stick together in a wicked and unpredictable world. The child-reader is protected from harm by the distancing of this story world away from the everyday life idealized in the 'real' world stories. The 'unreality' of magic, of talking animals and objects are part of this, and the humans are not dressed in contemporary styles but in the usual middle-European medieval peasant-dress of the traditional story world. In addition, these stories only occur in the later books of the series, to be read by older children.

This analysis and speculative interpretation of the multiple realities of the story world concerns only the meanings of the teachers. No imputations are made of the orientation of the authors, although W. Murray, author of the *Ladybird* series, is described as a lecturer and headmaster, and E.R. Boyce, author of the *Gay Way* series has also written several books on infant education, so that both have the status of 'experts' in this field.

Nor is any imputation made about the meanings that children assign to the experiences of reading these stories or of having others read to them. Sometimes it appeared to teachers that some children had not properly defined the story world as a different order of reality. A boy's mother reported he had nightmares after hearing his teacher read the story of Daedelus and Icarus. In telling me about it the teacher said, 'And I did tell them it was only a story'.

Writing – the reproduction of realities

From a study of the children's writing it was clear that they were able to reproduce these story worlds.

> Once upon a time there was a cat and it had five kittens one was called ping one was pong and the other three were called Dong Wong and Song one day mother cat took Dong and Wong to the shops and she bought some toys and they lived happily ever after.

> Once upon a time there was a princess and she was called Jane and one day she went out to meet her father and a witch peeped round the corer and got her and her mother saw it and Janes father came home and he saw the witch killing her and the king killed the witch and then he got Jane and he toke her home with him and put her in bed and made her better.

The teachers managed the children's writing of news so that they ordered its reality separately from that of a story.

> If it were your story-book you could tell me you've been in a Red Arrow, but you've not actually been in a Red Arrow – this is your newsbook. [N.B. Red Arrows are an aircraft display team.]

News was supposed to relate to the 'real' world and to orthodox reality, similar to that of the 'real' life stories in their reading books.

Creativity and Conventional Reality

Every day, every child did a drawing or painting, which, to begin with, they were allowed to define in their own way. (Teacher, looking at girl's drawing, 'I like it, what is it?')

In the following example the boy had defined painting as covering a surface with paint.

> Teacher introduces the new boy (his second day in school) to painting. He is shown the easel, the paints, the brushes and the apron he must wear, but he is not told how or what to paint. He

uses one colour to cover most of the paper. Another boy says to him, 'What are you painting?' He replies, 'A colour'. The other boy, 'A colour, just blue!' He changes brushes and completes the painting in green.

In the absence of the teacher defining a drawing or painting, young children learnt from one another; a whole table frequently did the same basic drawing by copying. The familiar images were those of houses, trees and flowers. These were seen by some teachers as expressions of the children's needs for security and as a therapeutic introduction to school. A few of the younger ones drew on the authority of 'what they told us at college' to support this.

The representations of houses, trees, flowers and people were versions of cultural images of these things. Although not directly presented to children by the teachers, these were displayed in the classroom, other than in other children's paintings and drawings. Lollypop trees and houses based on a rectangle and a triangle were found on lotto cards, teacher-prepared and commercial word and number cards, mathematics work books and in some story books.

Left to define paintings for themselves the children drew on the limited resources around them but to the teacher their limited images were an indication of the limited resources within them; their relative immaturity. I tried a simple, ethically acceptable, experiment one day. A boy was about to paint. I asked him what he was going to do. 'I don't know.' I suggested, 'Why don't you paint a boat?' The teacher was quite excited when she asked him her usual question, 'Tell me about your picture', and he replied, 'It's a boat'. 'He's never done anything like that before', she said to me later. At least three other children, following his example, 'progressed' to painting boats that day.

These early drawings and paintings were defined by the teachers as expressions of childish innocence. (Teacher, looking at boy's painting, 'Cubist. I suppose he'll lost all that soon'.)

Children were emancipated from their innocence by the actions of their teachers. After a period in which they could paint or draw what they wished, older children's images were monitored by the teacher's comments so as to introduce more elements of conventional reality. (Teacher, 'Where's the door on your house?'. Girl, 'Hasn't got one'. Teacher, 'How do you get in?'.)

The conventional reality that the children were required to represent was often more a conventional picture reality.

A group are making collage trees from squares of sticky paper. Teacher, 'Have you ever seen a black tree trunk?' 'You're not doing a green tree trunk are you?' No trees outside the window have the chocolate brown trunks that she requires. Some are shades of green, others almost black and even white.

This conventional picture reality was used in the learning of colours.

> There is a 'blue' display of pictures prepared by the teacher, including ones labelled, 'The sea is blue'. 'The sky is blue'. Outside the sky is grey. It can be red, purple, orange, yellow, or white.

Children learnt to reproduce these picture realities

> Girl of another's painting, 'Sky don't go that colour'. (Green).

Teachers also constrained children into the reproduction of conventional reality by their provision of materials.

> Children are making collage fruits and vegetables from sticky paper. 'Cabbage people, here are yours'. (Two shades of green). 'Tomato people, these are yours'. (Red).

Mathematics – the Suspension of Conventional Reality

Teachers defined mathematics as including the kinds of activities associated with the series of work books *Mathematics for Schools*, known after their senior author as *Fletcher books*. The teachers did not regard themselves as possessing a specialized body of knowledge to be transmitted to the children. They were experts in arranging for children to learn. Writing and reading and basic number work were regarded as skills that most adults possessed in some degree. Mathematics was not defined in this way, but was regarded as being slightly esoteric. This was the only classroom activity that some teachers confessed to not quite fully understanding themselves. Their acceptance of the *Fletcher* books was partly an acknowledgment of the authority of the headmistress in deciding this part of the curriculum, but also their implicit acceptance of the expert authority of the authors.

The expert tone of the series is set in the foreword by Professor W.H. Cockcroft, endorsing 'guides to good mathematics teaching', and the senior author Harold Fletcher, a senior inspector in mathematics. The introduction to the series neatly fuses the expert authority on the nature of mathematics and expert authority on the nature of the child. The methods used are posed as congruent with the child-centred ideologies of infant education.

> It aim is to inspire children by giving them a lively sense of *interest* and *pleasure* in mathematics and its *creative* use in everyday living.
> ... we have given careful consideration to the courses of all mathematical *experiences* and the logical and *psychological* processes involved, from the reception class upward ...
> ... the study of mathematics is to *free* children rather than inhibit them.

> ... help you plan a *happy*, modern, *progressive* and integrated
> mathematics course ...
> Given time and an opportunity to respond in accordance with
> *maturity*, the vast majority of children can succeed. [From, Under-
> stand the Series and Using the Series.]

I have italicized the key words in this fusion of external expert authority
and the teachers' professional ideologies.

The Fletcher world of mathematics has a superficial resemblance to
the 'real' life world presented to children in some of the stories they
read and which they reproduced in their writing. The illustrations are
similar showing children, animals, food, tools, toys, aeroplanes and cars.
A few of these even hint of the animal–humanoid world, such as an
anthropomorphized smiling snail and a cat with a bow tie. However, in
the world of mathematics conventional reality could be suspended.

> Sharon does maths workbook. She follows the instructions to
> colour some dolls blue and some red. 'I've never seen people with
> blue or red faces', she says, mainly to herself.
> A boy sorts sets using plastic shapes including yellow scottie
> dogs, orange pigs, yellow horses and purple elephants.

Such aberrations would have been commented on by teachers if they
had occurred in a non-mathematical context.

Mathematics was 'done' in work books and also as practical exercises,
defined as part of the concept-building process and also as part of the
purposeful nature of mathematics, 'in that it deals with people and life'.
However, practical mathematics transmuted the 'real' life world into the
reality of mathematics. A class exercise on measuring height became a
histogram. Marbles, acorns, shells, fingers and other counters become
figures on a page, objects become numbers.

In following the Fletcher scheme children were presented with phrases
such as, 'Partition the set in different ways'. Most teachers were aware
that some children could not read such instructions properly, but suggested
they 'know how to do it (the mathematics) without it.' When reading as a
part of 'reading' or when writing as a part of 'writing', children were
expected to recognize each word real or written. Only in mathematics could
words be left meaningless.

Curriculum as the Reproduction of Multiple Realities

Most educational studies using a phenomenological perspective have been
concerned with the social construction of the everyday reality of the
classroom (see Hargreaves *et al*, 1975). In this they have followed Schutz's
injunction that sociologists must try to interpret the assumptions and

rules that make everyday life possible. However, Nell Keddie, in her justly well-known study, whilst following this precept, also used the concept of multiple-realities, in contrasting the 'expert' knowledge of the teacher with the 'commonsense' knowledge of the pupils (Keddie, 1971). Her observations were that working-class children, generally defined by their teachers as less able, were less likely to suspend their commonsense knowledge based upon everyday life in favour of that of the teachers' expert knowledge. In an inversion of the usual educational interpretation she suggests that it was the pupils defined as 'able' (more commonly middle class) who lacked the ability to preserve their own commonsense knowledge.

Two important points should be made about this. First, the knowledge in question concerned the family as part of a social science course. This is one of the few examples where it is possible to pose the existence of commonsense knowledge based upon everyday life directly related to an element in the school curriculum. Where is the commonsense version of history, chemistry or Latin? Secondly, in following the Schutzian emphasis on the primacy of everyday life for people and for their sociological study, the same primacy is placed upon the commonsense knowledge of everyday life as an educational value judgement. The worlds of meaning that form the core of the curriculum are multiple-realities distanced from everyday life (Berger and Berger, 1976). An education based upon commonsense knowledge would be no education at all, although this is not to argue against a curriculum that starts with everyday life, or is relevant to it.

In this study teachers defined the reality of everyday life in their classrooms. Within this they also created other orders of reality: the story worlds of reading, the writing worlds of news and story, the world of number of mathematics, and the world of conventional pictorial representation. Children learnt to share their teacher's definitions of the nature of these provinces of meaning by reproducing them in their reading aloud, in their writing, in doing sums or problems and in painting and drawing. They also learnt which of these worlds they inhabited at a given time. Pink elephants may exist in one of the story worlds or the world of mathematics, but never in the 'real' life world of news or of Peter and Jane, or in a 'proper' painting. A task for sociologist, which has been attempted here, is to study the nature of the curriculum as a set of multiple-realities, and to explain how children gain access to their worlds of meaning.

References

BERGER, P.L. and BERGER, B. (1976) *Sociology: A Biographical Introduction* Harmondsworth, Penguin.

BERGER, P.L. and LUCKMANN, T. (1971) *The Social Construction of Reality* Harmondsworth, Penguin.

R. King

ELDRIDGE, J.E.T. (1971) 'Editor's introduction' in *Max Weber: The Interpretation of Social Reality* London, Nelson.

HARGREAVES, D.H. *et al* (1975) *Deviance in Classrooms* London, Routledge and Kegan Paul.

KEDDIE, N. (1971) 'Classroom knowledge' in YOUNG, M.F.D. *Knowledge and Control* London, Collier-Macmillan.

KING, R.A. (1978) *All Things Bright and Beautiful? A Sociological Study of Infant Classrooms* Chichester, Wiley.

SCHUTZ, A. (1953) 'A concept and theory formation in the social sciences' *Journal Philosophy* p. 51.

SCHUTZ, A. (1967) *Collected Papers Vol. 1. The Problem of Social Reality* The Hague, Nijhoff.

WEBER, M. (trans. 1947) in PARSONS, T. (Ed) *The Theory of Social and Economic Organizations* New York, Oxford University Press, Reprinted (1964) Chicago, Free Press.

Strategies and Tactics in Junior School Classrooms*

Maurice Galton
University of Leicester

During the 1970s there has been a rapid growth in the use of systematic observation to study teaching. Whereas the 1970 edition of *Mirrors for Behaviour* (Simon and Boyer, 1970) listed only two British instruments, a recently published anthology now shows that the number of home produced ones stands at 40 of which a sizeable number are designed for use at primary school level (Galton, 1978).

One use of these techniques has been to describe styles of teaching (Eggleston, Galton and Jones, 1976; Galton, Simon and Croll, 1980). Teachers are sorted into groups whose characteristics are defined in terms of the relative frequency with which their members use the categories of the observation schedule. Used in this way the definition of teaching style differs from that used by other authors, notably in the report of the findings of the Lancaster study (Bennett, 1976). The purpose of this article is therefore to attempt a more precise definition of the term and to contrast the use of interaction analysis and questionnaires in providing descriptions of various teaching styles.

To illustrate points in the discussion, data from the ORACLE study (Simon and Galton, 1975) will be used, particularly data from the Teacher Record, an observation instrument developed in an earlier study (Boydell, 1974). [Observational Research and Classroom Learning Evaluation, (ORACLE) is a five-year programme of research funded by the SSRC. Although this paper reflects the author's views, these have been developed over long periods of discussion with other members of the project team and their help, particularly that of Mr P. Croll, who undertook the data analysis, is most gratefully acknowledged.] This instrument clearly bears certain similarities to the Science Teacher Observation Schedule (STOS) which was developed to provide information about the range of teaching

*From British Educational Research Journal 5(2), (1979), pp. 197–210.

styles used in the new secondary science curricula (Eggleston, Galton and Jones, 1975). In developing their notion of teaching style these researchers laid stress on the distinction between teaching *strategy* and teaching *tactics* first put forward by Taba and Elzey (1964) and subsequently elaborated by Strasser (1967) in advancing a conceptual model of instruction. For Taba a strategy consists of a teacher's attempt to translate her aims into practice while tactics according to Strasser are the 'minute by minute exchanges' between a teacher and her pupils through which such strategies are implemented. The use of systematic observation with its precisely defined categories of teacher-pupil interaction provides an ideal means of examining such tactical exchanges. If these twin concepts are put into a practical context there appears to be three key strategic decisions that any teacher has to make when confronted with a new situation such as starting a fresh year with a new class. The first concerns the *organizational strategy*, how to manage the learning environment, the second the *curriculum strategy*, what to teach and the third the *instructional strategy*, how to teach it.

The organizational strategy is largely directed towards seeing that each pupil is allowed the maximum opportunity for learning. It will concern decision such as whether to teach the class as a whole or whether to organize group work or to provide for individualized instruction. When groups are used then there are decisions involving their composition (their size, balance between sexes, mixed ability, etc.). Such strategies are largely directed towards maintaining control and to producing an efficient working atmosphere. The curriculum strategy is concerned with the content and balance of the curriculum. At junior school stage, when separate subject teaching is preferred to an integrated approach, then the different degree of emphasis given to different subject areas will be reflected by the time-table. Within any subject area, however, there will be considerable room for each teacher to emphasize different aspects in her teaching. For example, a study by Ashton of primary teachers' aims showed that many teachers wished to give equal emphasis to applying basic skills to every-day practical situations as to using the four rules (Ashton *et al*, 1975). Such teachers would presumably give as much time to such activities as measuring and shopping games as they would to learning tables and doing formal sums.

The instructional strategy corresponds to what is often loosely called teaching methods and may include a combination of lecturing, demonstrating, class discussion, using work cards or project activity. For Taba the instructional strategy is the most important and she argues that the main function of teaching is to develop the pupils' capacity for thinking. Her instructional strategies are aimed at developing correct thinking in pupils and emphasise a questioning rather than a telling approach during class discussion. The ultimate aim is to allow pupils to manage their own learning so that they will make use of these questioning techniques even when the teacher is not present. It is clear that all three elements in the overall teaching strategy must be linked. A decision to engage in, for example, a discussion strategy would also involve decisions about organizational and curricular ones such as the nature of the groups and the selection and structuring of appropriate content in order to promote discussion among the pupils.

Teaching Tactics and Teaching Style

Once the lesson has begun the strategies have to be worked out by means of the exchanges between the teacher and her pupils – the teaching tactics. It is here suggested that each tactical exchange will seek to emphasise either an aspect of class *control,* the development of *social* and personal skills in the pupils or the pupils' *cognitive* development. Thus when a teacher asks a pupil a question 'two times two?' and receives the reply 'four' she is mainly concerned with a cognitive outcome but if she tells pupils, in a normal tone of voice, to 'carry on working and wait until I come to you' she is primarily exercising a management function designed to keep control of the teaching situation. The third type of tactic relating to social and personal development is not directly monitored by the observation schedules used in the ORACLE research, although it is reflected in some exchanges which give rise to teacher praise or criticism. However, because teachers who responded to the Ashton survey rated this a very important area it is being examined in a separate study as part of the ORACLE programme.

After a settling down period with the class a state of equilibrium is established where the teacher begins to make use of *a consistent set of tactics* and it is this which is here defined as her *teaching style.* According to Strasser the use of a set of tactics evolves mainly as a result of careful observation of pupil behaviour and less immediately because of previous knowledge about the pupils' attainment, but as the teacher and her pupils adjust to one another the latter's performance becomes an increasingly important factor in determining the relative success of the overall aims and strategy. Typically, however, researchers interested in teacher effectiveness have sought to define good and bad teaching mainly in terms of test results and to ignore pupil activity in the classroom. The ORACLE research programme is designed around the principle that a complete evaluation should concern itself with five elements in the teaching process listed in figure 1.

For simplicity only the outer links are joined although some elements of teaching strategy may have a direct effect on pupil behaviour so that inner links may be appropriate in certain cases. The arrows are double headed because there is as yet little research evidence clarifying in which direction these links should operate. ORACLE is one of the few studies to investigate

Figure 1. A Description of the Teaching Process

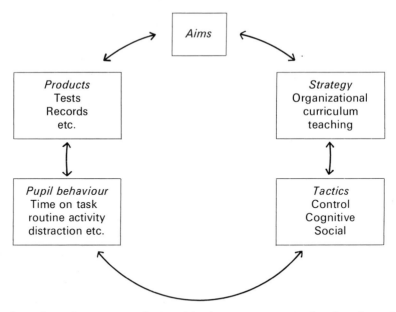

whether there is even a relationship between certain kinds of teaching tactics and different types of pupil behaviour. Studies using naturalistic rather than experimental designs must introduce an element of replication if evidence is to be obtained about the direction of such relationships. Pupils in the ORACLE study will have been observed, in some cases, over three years. This will enable behaviour of pupils who move from one teacher to another of different style to be investigated.

The Use of Questionnaires to Study Teaching

Both Barker-Lunn (1970) and Bennett (1976) used questionnaires to obtain the information from which to derive their profiles of teachers. Bennett is highly critical of Barker-Lunn, arguing that her categories were too gross. He is also highly critical of the use of observation systems for observing 'the narrow range of behaviours of a small and unrepresentative sample of teachers drawn from a population of unknown parameters' which has led to their being categorized 'according to some global, ill-defined dichotomy, unrelated to any theoretical perspective' (Bennett, 1976, p. 32). It thus seems strange that he should end up using what one reviewer termed 'emotionally laden catch-all terms such as formal and informal' for which he must be criticized in 'ignoring his own advice in the earlier part of the book' (Wragg, 1976, p. 285). The critics seemed much more concerned with the defects of the research design and the question of whether the results might validly be applied to other pupils besides those in the schools where the research was carried out (Gray and Satterley, 1976). They tended to ignore the more important issue, raised by Wragg's reservations about the typology, that such description gave little help to teachers who wished to examine their practice in the aftermath of the Lancaster study.

It could be argued, however, that this weakness derives directly from the use of questionnaires which require an individual to answer each item by selecting one response from a limited number of mutually exclusive categories. This means, for example, that on the Bennett's questionnaire teachers who gave tests every fortnight and who answered the question 'Do you give pupils an arithmetic test at least once a week?' would be classified as not giving regular tests alongside those teachers who never tested at all.

More importantly, certain results appear illogical in that some individuals were classified both as separate subject teachers and also as favouring an integrated subject approach. This comes about because of the way in which the data were collected and subsequently analyzed. Teachers were asked to estimate how much of a 25 hour working week they devoted to academic subjects taught separately, integrated subjects and aesthetic subjects, the latter including PE and games. The means on each of the categories were calculated and teachers were classified either as above or below the mean on each of the three dimensions. Because the amount of time given to aesthetics was dependent on that allocated to single subject and integrated subject teaching it was ommitted from the analysis, but teachers who gave little attention to such things as art, music and drama could easily find themselves 'above average' on both single subject and integrated subject teaching.

Even if teachers could recognize themselves within these formal – informal labels the descriptions provided give little guidance about what they might do or say to pupils during lessons. It was left to Wragg (1978) to try to identify, through observation, such practices in the most successful of all Bennett's teachers, who used the informal style. In so doing he gives support to the view that descriptions based on observation are likely to make better sense to teachers since they highlight the activities on which those who differ in their effectiveness, differ in their treatment of pupils. Such descriptions are at the tactical rather than the strategic level.

Only observational studies can supply such information. At their best questionnaires tell us about a teacher's aims and offer global descriptions of teaching in terms of its strategies. Both Barker-Lunn's and Bennett's descriptions of teaching style, based as they were on questionnaire data, provide for the most part information about organizational and curricular strategies. In placing such emphasis on the teacher's management function Bennett would appear to reject the model of teaching proposed here and to support the views advanced by Harnischfeger and Wiley (1975, 1978) who dispute the notion that teaching behaviour directly influences pupils achievement. They argue instead that 'active learning time', the use a pupil makes of opportunities to study a given content, is the most important indicator of his progress. In the Lancaster study a certain amount of observation took place but it was only directed at the pupils and not at the teachers. The success of the formal style was attributed to the organizational strategies that these teachers adopted (working in silence, class teaching, giving rewards, etc.) which resulted in their pupils spending more time on their work (Bennett, 1978).

Instruments Used and Method of Analysis

To examine the relationship between strategy and tactics the process data from the 58 teachers observed during the first year of the ORACLE study were supplemented by additional sources of information. These are shown in Table 1A session summary sheet (S1) and a daily summary sheet (S2) were completed at the end of each observation session and at the end of the day respectively. They concern the physical layout of the classroom, seating arrangements, an outline of the curricular activity and, where available, a class time-table. A special grouping instrument was also completed giving detailed information about the grouping policy and its rationale. The teacher's questionnaire which was collected by the observers towards the end of the year reflected aspects of organizational and curricular strategies covered by both Barker-Lunn and Bennett but not dealt with in the summary sheets or the grouping instrument. Finally the observers were asked to write a descriptive account after each visit which recorded their general impressions of the classroom climate, the teaching methods and the relationships within the classroom. The use of these four sets of data enabled each teacher to be classified on each of the 19 dimensions used by Bennett for his teaching typology.

The main categories of the observation instrument, the Teacher Record, are shown in Table 2. Full details of the instrument can be found elsewhere (Galton *et al*, 1980). Its purpose was to record the various kinds of contact which the teacher engaged in with her pupils using a 25 second time-sampling unit. At each signal the observer noted down different aspects of these interactions. He first indicated the type of *conversation* or the nature of the *silent interaction* taking place. The silent interaction categories were included to show when the teacher was *gesturing, showing* by writing or demonstrating on the blackboard, *marking* pupils work in their presence, *waiting* for the class to settle, reading a *story* or listening to a pupil *reading* aloud. To deal with cases where the observer had difficulty in recording the activities two further categories, *not observed* and *not coded* were available. If no interaction was taking place then one of four categories under this heading was coded. These covered such events as visits from

Table 1. Instruments used in data collection (Autumn 1976 — Summer 1977)

Title	When completed	Focus
Pupil record (PR)	Each target pupil was observed once during each of the six observation sessions per term. Observations were made in the Autumn, Spring and Summer terms (1976–1977)	Pupil's activities and interactions with other pupils and adults
Teacher record (TR)	Each teacher was observed once during each of the six observation sessions per term. Observations were made in the Autumn, Spring and Summer terms (1976–1977)	Teacher questions and statements, silent interaction, no interaction and the audience, its composition and curricular activity
Session summary	This was completed at the end of each observation Therefore, six were collected each term (Autumn, Spring and Summer, 1976–1977)	Physical layout of the classroom, seating of all pupils; outline of curricular contents and methods used; apparatus, resources, etc. and incidents. Order and time of observations
Daily summary sheet (S2)	This was completed at the end of each day, therefore, three were collected each term (Autumn, Spring and Summer, 1976–1977)	Class time-table, and outline of organization to include all activities whether observed or not
Impressionistic account (S3)	This was completed for each class, once a term, at the end of the six observation sessions (Autumn term 1976, Spring term 1977)	Prose account of the impressions of the observer as regards the teacher, classroom climate, teaching methods, etc.
Grouping instrument (GI)	This was completed for each class in the Summer term 1977	Physical layout, grouping policy and rationale
Teacher's questionnaire (TQ)	This was completed for each class in the Summer term 1977	Classroom management/organization similar to Bennett's (1976) survey

other teachers or parents (*adult interaction*) and from pupils from other classes (*visiting pupil*), *not interacting* while silently monitoring or going *out of room* for some purpose or other. Finally the observer coded the type of the teacher *audience* (class, group or individual) its *composition* and certain features of the curricular *activity* of the child or children with whom the teacher was interacting.

A second instrument, the Pupil Record (Boydell, 1975) was also used in the study but does not concern us here. Teachers and pupils were alternatively observed, each teacher receiving twenty minutes observation time per session. There were two sessions a day and each class received a visit lasting three days each term throughout the year. The reliability of the

Table 2. The observation categories of the teacher record

CONVERSATION

	Questions	
	Task	
	Q1	Recalling facts
	Q2	Offering ideas, solutions (closed)
	Q3	Offering ideas, solutions (open)
	Task supervision	
	Q4	Referring to task supervision
	Routine	
	Q5	Referring to routine matter
	Statements	
	Task	
	S1	Of facts
	S2	Of ideas, problems
	Task supervision	
	S3	Telling child what to do
	S4	Praising work or effort
	S5	Feedback on work or effort
	Routine	
	S6	Providing information, directions
	S7	Providing feedback
	S8	Of critical control
	S9	Of small talk

SILENCE

Silent interaction
Gesturing
Showing
Marking
Waiting
Story
Reading
Not observed
Not coded
No interaction
Adult interaction
Visiting pupil
Not interacting
Out of room
Audience
Composition
Activity

---

instrument had been amply demonstrated previously (Boydell, 1974) but a further trial with team of observers in live classrooms gave average values on the main variables of 0·76 using the Scott (1955) coefficient. These figures were based on the individual coding of specific time units whereas in the study the total number of tallies was aggregated for each category in order to determine the teaching style. It is generally accepted that reliabilities of this order are satisfactory for this type of analysis. In some cases it also proved possible to join categories together during the

aggregation procedure thus increasing the overall reliability of the combination.

To identify teaching styles a cluster analysis was carried out using the
20 interaction variables (excluding the categories *not observed* and *not
listed*) and the two audience categories *class interaction* and *group interaction*.
The third audience category *individual interaction* was not included because
it was dependent on the levels of the other two. The 're-location' procedure
developed for the PMMD package (Youngman, 1975) was used which is
a modified version of Wishart's Clustan system of computer programmes
(Wishart, 1969) and this gave a stable four cluster solution. The analysis
was replicated on two further occasions, first, to check that using a different
initial random allocation made no difference to the result and, second,
to test the effect of excluding the two audience categories. This was done
because the audience variables are concerned more with the organizational
strategy rather than with teaching style and it was feared that the former
might exert a disproportionate influence and mask the variation in the
use of tactics by different teachers. However, even with the audience
categories omitted a similar solution to the one obtained in the fuller analysis
still emerged. This was of the utmost importance in showing that the interaction categories, indicative of tactical decisions, rather than organizational
strategies were the major source of differentiation between the clusters,
although as will be seen the two were closely related.

Characteristics of Teaching Styles

The main characteristics of the four cluster solution of the Teacher Record
data are given in Table 3. Their most obvious feature relates to the different
use made of the audience categories but, as has been pointed out, this
aspect of organizational strategy cannot be the major determinant of the
clusters since the solution remained stable even when the audience categories were omitted from the analysis. In terms of the total amount of
teacher – pupil interaction taking place, all four groups showed similar
patterns in that they were actively involved on more than three-quarters
of the occasions when observations were made. The manner in which this
attention was distributed varied considerably but it would be wrong simply
to describe teachers in cluster 1, for example, as 'individualized' and those
in cluster 2 as 'class orientated' since the variation between these groups
on the kinds of interactions which represent teaching tactics is highly
significant. It is this variation which can be used to provide descriptions
of each teaching style.

Style 1

This group accounted for 22.4 per cent of the sample and was characterized

Table 3. Cluster characteristics as percentage of total observations

		1 Individual monitors	2 Class enquirers	3 Group instructors	4 Style changer
Questions	Q1 Recalling facts	3.9	4.1	2.4	3.4
	Q2 Solution (closed)	1.1	3.3	2.0	2.4
	Q3 Solution (open)	0.3	1.0	0.9	0.6
	All task questions	5.3	8.4	5.3	6.4
	Q4 Task supervision	2.9	4.1	3.2	4.5
	Q5 Routine	1.3	2.2	1.5	2.0
	All other questions	4.2	6.3	4.7	6.5
Statements	S1 Of facts	5.6	8.0	11.9	6.0
	S2 Of ideas	2.1	4.2	1.0	2.6
	All task statements	7.7	12.2	12.9	8.6
Task supervision:	S3 Telling	15.8	11.2	11.6	11.8
	S4 Praising	1.0	1.3	0.6	1.1
	S5 Feedback	8.7	10.9	15.9	8.7
Routine:	S6 Information	5.6	7.0	6.7	6.8
	S7 Feedback	1.8	2.3	2.3	2.0
	S8 Critical control	2.0	1.5	2.4	2.6
	S9 Small talk	1.3	1.7	0.6	1.4
	All other statements	36.2	35.9	40.1	34.4
Silent interaction	Gesturing	1.8	0.9	3.7	1.8
	Showing	2.4	3.3	2.0	2.6
	Marking	16.4	5.7	7.4	9.4
	Waiting	1.7	1.6	2.1	2.0
	Story	0.6	1.8	1.0	0.7
	Reading	3.0	3.4	2.2	3.8
	All other interactions	25.9	16.7	18.4	20.3
Audience	Individual	66.9	42.5	52.3	55.3
	Group	5.5	5.8	17.7	6.3
	Class	6.9	31.2	11.4	14.6

by the low level of questioning and the high level of silent interaction. The teachers engaged in a large number of short-lived interactions which were usually concerned with telling pupils what to do (task supervision S3). The general impression gained, from a variety of accounts provided by the observers, was of pupils working mainly on individual tasks with teachers under a considerable amount of pressure. The observers describe some teachers moving rapidly from table to table but others sitting at their desks with pupils queuing up either for information or for some clarification of the instructions in the text-book or worksheet. The pupil – adult categories on the Pupil Record indicate that most of these interactions were brief. Some pupils wished to know how to spell a word, others wanted to know whether they should go on to the next exercise. Any attempt by the teacher at prolonged interaction with a pupil was usually prevented by the pressures resulting from the demands of the other pupils and from her concern to keep waiting time to a minimum.

Within such a complex organization the task of monitoring the pupils' work takes on a high priority. It is important not only to correct books but also to record progress so that where pupils are involved in planning their own time-tables regular checks can be carried out to see if each has fulfilled his quota. There was thus a very high level of interaction concerned with marking. Under the ground rules of the observation schedule, marking consists of the teacher giving feedback by writing corrections on pupil's work rather than by making oral comments. It is this particular characteristic which suggests that Style 1 should be labelled as *individual monitors*.

Style 2

This group comprised 15.5 per cent of the sample and was defined by the emphasis given to questioning, particularly questions relating to task work. The level of statements made was also relatively high which suggested, in keeping with the amount of class teaching, that much of the learning was 'teacher managed'. However, when examining the sub-categories of teacher talk it can be seen that much of the conversation related to the higher cognitive levels. Although the level of cognitive discourse in junior school classrooms appears, for the most part, to be concerned with the transmission of information, the teachers under Style 2 used a much higher proportion of both closed and open questions (Q2, Q3) and made more statements of ideas and problems (S2) than did the remaining groups.

The picture which came from the observers' impressionistic accounts was of teachers who introduced new topics to the whole class and then engaged in question and answer routines with individual pupils, reinforced by means of verbal feedback on their work. Because of this emphasis on problem solving, coupled with teacher control of these activities by means of class teaching, it seems apt to describe this group of teachers as engaging in *class directed enquiry*.

Style 3

This cluster consists of 12.1 per cent of the teachers and was in many ways the most interesting. The amount of group interaction was, on average, three times as high as for the rest of the sample. The decrease in time given over to individual attention allowed the teacher to engage in considerably more teacher directed interaction (questioning and stating) than, for example, teachers in Style 1. The main emphasis, however, was on making statements of fact rather than the presentation of ideas. This was coupled with a high level of verbal feedback and gesturing. Presumably, and the observer's descriptions tend to confirm this, these teachers preferred to structure the work of the group carefully before allowing them to engage in discussion among themselves. Hence there was an emphasis on giving information (S1) and, once the group began to interact, on returning to re-join the discussion and provide verbal feedback on the pupils' ideas and solutions to problems. Set against the general low level of cognitive questioning these teachers did nevertheless engage in above average amounts of open questioning. This suggests that they allowed the groups of pupils to come up with alternative answers to problems and did not always insist on their being the one correct answer. Such teachers appear to come closest in adopting the grouping strategy suggested by Plowden for coping with large sized classes. Although there was evidence for some less directed enquiry since these teachers also tended to ask more open questions the main emphasis must be placed on the information aspects of their teaching. Consequently this group might be thought of as *group instructors*.

Style 4

Fifty per cent of the sample came within this cluster. It appears to be a mixture of the other three since in the audience category, for example, these teachers had the second highest levels of individual, group and class interaction, even given that some of these differences are slight. They did ask the highest number of questions relating to task supervision (Q4), made more statements of critical control (S8) and heard more pupils read than did teachers in other styles but these features were not associated exclusively with one particular remaining cluster. Style 2, the *class directed enquirers*, also engaged in task supervision questions and reading while Style 1 teachers, the *individual monitors*, showed a similar need for an element of critical control.

Although overall there was considerable variation in the amount of higher order cognitive interactions between styles, when this was broken down between class and individual attention, then it appears that there is something about class teaching which is particularly conducive to such activity. For example, the individual monitors who have the lowest amount overall of this type of interaction nevertheless contrived to engage in 16.7 per cent of it when in conversation with the whole class. For the group instructors (Style 3) the corresponding figure is 19.5 per cent. Thus the use of certain types of tactics seems closely related to different organizational strategies and the impressionistic accounts for this group of teachers confirm that they all in one way or another make changes in their organization during the year. Some made *infrequent* changes shifting from a class to a more individualized approach as the year progressed. Others set up activity areas and the pupils *rotated* from one table to the next at regular intervals. The third sub-group carried out *frequent* changes which in many cases seemed unplanned, often in reaction to some undesired pupil behaviour. Thus one teacher, Miss S., tended to move swiftly to class activities at any time when the general level of 'busyness' dropped and the volume of noise rose to any marked degree. This additional evidence lends support to the description of the teachers in cluster 4 as *style changers* where the emphasis on certain sets of tactics varies according to the preferred pattern of organization at any time.

Organizational Strategies and Teaching Styles

These links between organizational strategy and teaching styles are interesting and in some ways surprising. The Plowden Report suggests the use of teaching methods which imply open-ended questioning tactics associated with pupil management of the learning environemtn using an integrated subject matter approach. The ORACLE study can find little evidence for this combination of tactics and strategy. At the other end of the scale those critics who argued that traditional standards have fallen because in the new informally organized classrooms teachers were taking to the extreme the belief that 'children should not be told anything but must find out for themselves' (Cox and Dyson, 1969), appear to have exaggerated their fears. As far as progressivism in its purest form is concerned it has not so much as failed as has yet to be tried.

Both Barker-Lunn and Bennett, however, also showed that the use of class teaching was strongly associated with certain groups in their respective typologies of teaching. Barker-Lunn's type 2 teachers, the more traditional, made more use of class teaching but they also believed in streaming, were less tolerant of noise and talking, showed less interest in the work of the slow child and had favourable attitudes to physical punishment (Barker-Lunn, 1970, pp. 52–53). In Bennett's (1976, p. 47) study the most extreme formal group were portrayed as follows:

> an extreme group in a number of respects. None favour an integrated approach. Subjects are taught separately by class teaching and individual work. None allow pupils choice of seating, and every teacher curbs movement and talk. These teachers are above average on assessment and procedures (weekly testing) and extrinsic motivation (awarding stars and grades) predominates.

If similarities do exist then the *class enquirers* (Style 2) who do most class teaching should exhibit the characteristics of Bennett's formal teachers while the *individual monitors* (Style 1) should have more in common with his informal group (type 1). The Bennett typology was based upon nineteen variables. For this comparison the five which described variations in the use of class, group or individual teaching were excluded. Data about the remaining fourteen variables was collected for ORACLE teachers in a variety of ways. The observers completed the teaching questionnaire, giving such information as whether there were weekly tests in mathematics and spelling, whether pupils were given a choice where to sit, whether the class were expected to work in silence and so on. From the observer records, the session and daily summary sheets (S1 and S2), it was possible to estimate the percentage of single subject and integrated subject teaching.

The results were then analyzed in exactly the same way as in Bennett's original research. For example, the data on single subject teaching were dichotomised to differentiate between teachers who were above and below the mean of this variable. The same procedure was used for integrated subject teaching. As with the Lancaster teachers, because aesthetic subjects were given so little time, some of the ORACLE sample were 'above average' on both 'single' and 'integrated' subject teaching.

The data are presented in Table 4. For comparison the figures for Bennett's formal and informal types are included. In general the differences between the *individual monitors* and the *class enquirers* were less marked than those between the teachers in the Lancaster study. Only on two of the variables, allowing *choice of seats* and *freedom of movement* was the trend almost as extreme. Seventy-five per cent of the *individual monitors* insisted on quiet. Forty-one and 50 per cent respectively gave weekly tests in arithmetic and spelling compared to 9 and 23 per cent of the informal teachers. Far fewer *class enquirers* gave homework, awarded marks or stars, and smacked pupils than did the formal teachers. On three of the key items, held by supporters of traditional methods to be essential components of 'good' teaching, the differences were completely eliminated or actually reversed. *Class enquirers* were equally likely to use the same balance of integrated and single subject teaching as the *individual monitors* and an equally large percentage were against seating by ability within the class. The *individual monitors* were more likely to discipline pupils by sending them out of the classroom. This latter finding conflicts with Barker-Lunn's claim that teachers who favoured less 'traditional' methods were likely to be more permissive (Barker-Lunn, 1970, p. 55).

Table 4. *Percentage of teachers in each teaching style who were above average on 'formal – informal' characteristics*

	Individual monitors	Class enquirers	Bennett informal	Bennett formal
Choice of seats	67	22	63	0
Seating by ability	25	22	14	50
Free movement	92	11	51	0
Quiet	75	89	31	100
Out of school visits	8	0	51	42
Homework	8	0	9	56
Marks	0	11	3	97
Stars	17	44	9	75
Arithmetic tests	41	78	9	81
Spelling tests	50	100	23	92
Children smacked	33	44	34	58
Sent from room	33	11	11	11
Single subjects	66	67	20	92
Integrated subjects	41	44	97	0

One further important finding from the Barker-Lunn study was that the teachers using the traditional approach (type 2) were less interested in the slow child. In this present study the two teachers who were most typical of the *class enquirers*, in that their use of the categories of the Teacher Record was closest to the means of the cluster profile, both told observers that they used class teaching to gain more time for dealing with the slow learners. In each case the observers commented that both classes were 'pleasant places to be in' where the teachers were observed to 'interact for lengthy periods with individual children who were experiencing difficulties with the work'.

Thus none of the ORACLE teaching styles can be identified with the extremes of the formal – informal dichotomy. This leads to an alternative suggestion as to why the formal group, who emphasised class teaching, were more successful. Possibly, as did the ORACLE class teachers, they engaged in more higher level cognitive interactions. Since the Lancaster study ignored these kinds of teaching variables when collecting data it is impossible to test out this hypothesis directly. Initial analysis of the ORACLE *product* data indicates that the *class directed enquiry* teachers were successful particularly in mathematics but less so with less able pupils than were a sub-group of the style changers who engaged in even higher levels of this type of intellectual transaction.

There is, however, support for other conclusions from the Bennett study. In particular, the use of individualized instruction at the expense of almost any other type of classroom organization is shown to create severe problems in that such teachers are so taken up with planning and running this complex learning environment that they have little time for engaging in any kind of direct teaching with their pupils. This leaves them with very difficult decisions as to which pupils to ignore and which to interact with. Some of the impressionistic accounts suggest that in classes where the teacher sits at the desk and silently marks books, the bright and slower pupils get extra attention: the bright ones because they finish work quickly and come out for a fresh task while the slower pupils, if they are disruptive, are called out by the teacher so that she can find out 'what they are doing'. It may be, therefore, that quieter average pupils who get on with their work lose out in this situation.

One alternative for overcoming these difficulties, where some class teaching is either impracticable or goes against the teacher's inclination, would be to make more use of group work. In the ORACLE study group work was taken to mean pupils working *cooperatively* on a *common task*. This differs from the more usual interpretation which in most cases means nothing more than pupils sitting at the same table engaged in their own separate tasks in a related subject area. In the absence of a common task the teacher has very few opportunities to talk with the group as a whole so that the amount of attention which each pupil can hope to receive must remain low. Considerably more detailed analysis needs to be carried out before the full effects of changing strategy in this way can be known. The ORACLE programme is a longitudinal study in which some teachers and their pupils will have been observed for three years so that the effect of changing teaching style can be investigated. Hopefully this will add a little to our knowledge and understanding of teaching. In reaching towards this understanding, the breakdown of the teaching process into strategy and tactics seems to provide a meaningful descriptive model. This should be of use, not only to the researcher, but also to those attempting to improve current practice in both the initial training and in-service fields.

References

ASHTON, P. *et al*, (1975) *The Aims of Primary Education: A Study of Teachers' Opinions* Schools Council Research Series, London, Macmillan Education.

BARKER-LUNN, L.J.C. (1970) *Streaming in the Primary School* Slough, NFER, pp. 26–27, 55, 58, 81.

BENNETT, N. (1976) *Teaching Style and Pupil Progress* London, Open Books.

BENNETT, N. (1978) 'Recent research on teaching: A dream, a belief, and a model' *British Journal of Educational Psychology* 48, pp. 127–147.

BOYDELL, D. (1974) 'Teacher-pupil contact in junior classrooms' *British Journal of Educational Psychology* 44, pp. 313–318.

BOYDELL, D. (1975) Pupil behaviour in junior classrooms, *British Journal of Educational Psychology* 45, pp. 122–129.

COX, C. and DYSON, A. (Eds) (1969) *Black Paper Two: The Crisis in Education* Critical Quarterly Society.

EGGLESTON, J.F., GALTON, M.J. and JONES, M.E. (1975) *A Science Teaching Observation Schedule* Schools Council Research Series, London, Macmillan Education.

EGGLESTON, J.F., GALTON, M.J. and JONES, M.E. (1976) *Processes and Products of Science Teaching* Schools Council Research Series, London, Macmillan Education.

GALTON, M., SIMON, B. and CROLL, P. (1980) *Inside the Primary Classroom* London, Routledge and Kegan Paul.

GALTON, M.J. (1978) *British Mirrors: A Collection of Classroom Observation Systems* School of Education, University of Leicester.

GRAY, J. and SATTERLY, D. (1976) 'A chapter of errors: Teaching styles and pupil progress in retrospect' *Educational Research* 19, pp. 45–56.

HARNISCHFEGER, A. and WILEY, D. (1975) 'Teaching/learning processes in elementary schools: A synoptic view' *Studies of Education Processes* No. 9, University of Chicago.

HARNISCHFEGER, A. and WILEY, D. (1978) 'Conceptual issues in models of school learning' *Journal of Curriculum Studies* 10, pp. 215–231.

SCOTT, W.A. (1955) 'Reliability of content analysis: The case of nominal coding' *Public Opinion Quarterly* 19, pp. 321–325.

SIMON, A. and BOYER, E.G. (Eds) (1970) *Mirrors for Behaviour II: An Anthology of Observation Instruments* Research for Better Schools Inc., Philadelphia.

SIMON, B. and GALTON, M.J. (1975) *Observational Research and Classroom Learning Evaluation* (ORACLE) – an SSRC Programme, University of Leicester.

STRASSER, B. (1967) 'A conceptual model of instruction' *Journal of Teacher Education* 18, pp. 63–74.

TABA, H. and ELZEY, F.F. (1964) 'Teaching strategies and thought processes' *Teacher College Record* 65, pp. 524–534.

WISHART, D. (1969) *Clustan 1A: User Manual* University of St Andrews Computing Laboratories, Fife, Scotland.

WRAGG, E.C. (1976) 'The Lancaster study: Its implications for teacher training' *British Journal of Teacher Education* 2, pp. 281–290.

WRAGG, E.C. (1978) 'A suitable case for imitation' *Times Educational Supplement*, 15 September, p. 18.

YOUNGMAN, M. (1975) *Programmed Methods for Multivariate Data* (PMMD), Version 4, University of Nottingham, School of Education, Nottingham.

Progressive Education: A Reformulation from Close Observations of Children

Stephen Rowland
Sherard Primary School

> To be the best scientific observers we must at once be the best providers for and the best teachers of those whom we wish to study.
>
> (Hawkins 1974, p. 45)

But can a classroom teacher scientifically observe the learning processes of the students he teaches? There are those who would argue that even if he had the opportunity to do so, in terms of experience of theoretical issues and resources available, his observations would lack the objectivity which is claimed to be an essential feature of scientific inquiry. Others would suggest that it is only measurable behaviours – whether performance in objective tests or the frequency of certain categories of interaction – that can count as valid material from which inferences can be drawn about the learning process itself.

There is not the space here to enter into the arguments about the nature of scientific inquiry that are raised by such objections. But the experience of our programme of research and inservice training suggests that a combination of teaching and research roles can provide insight into the learning process from material which is largely inaccessible to the objective observer of classroom life. We find that teaching and research can in practice be complementary activities as Hawkins suggests. For not only does the researcher gain a greater degree of access to the ebb and flow of the students' learning through the close and sustained contact of teaching and learning with them, but the teacher is enabled to direct his input into the students' learning more sensitively by conducting the rigorous description and analysis that are essential features of research. Thus we might state the corrollary of Hawkins' prescription: to be the best providers for and the best teachers we must at once be the best scientific observers of those whom we would teach.

We have attempted to combine the roles of teaching and research with pairs of teachers working together. One of the pair – the normal class teacher – tends to take on the major responsibility for managing the curriculum, while the visiting teacher/researcher is responsible for the research. But they share these tasks, the normal class teacher contributing to the gathering and analysis of material and the visiting teacher/researcher being fully involved in teaching alongside him. In practice, teaching and observation become largely indistinguishable activities. Daily fieldnotes which describe and analyze the students' work, together with samples of their writing, painting, models and so on, form the bulk of the research material.

First piloted in 1976, when Michael Armstrong came to work as teacher/ researcher alongside the author in his primary school classroom, the programme now involves four teachers seconded to work alongside teachers in primary and secondary schools in the Leicestershire Classroom Research Inservice Training Scheme. (The first, pilot, phase is described in Armstrong, 1980, the second phase in Rowland, 1980.) Also involved in the scheme are a further twenty-five teachers from a variety of schools who meet regularly to contribute material from their own classrooms and analyze it in groups. The work of this larger group not only provides a broader range of material from which developing theory may be corroborated, refuted or refined, but ensures that the issues upon which the research focuses, and the hypotheses which emerge, are both relevant and accessible to the classroom teacher. Since the teachers' contributions relate directly to their own classroom practice and serve to develop it, research and in-service training aspects become inseparable, with the teachers, in the final analysis, in control of both.

The broad aim of the research is to gain insight into the learning process and the quality of intellectual thought that is evidenced in the classroom. The descriptions, interpretations and evaluations which make up the research material take a form similar to that of the case study, with the work of individual students followed in detail. We do not aim to produce comprehensive generalizations, and our scope is very broad, but nevertheless a number of threads or issues have emerged to be of central significance. While these threads cannot yet be woven into a complete framework for understanding classroom learning, they do perhaps suggest the beginnings of such a framework.

There is not the space here to follow these threads in detail, but the research strategy and some of the implications for teaching may best be illustrated by reference to one of the issues that has emerged as being central to our findings. This concerns the nature of the relationship between teacher and student and the question of the student's autonomy within this relationship.

Researchers and educational commentators have often attempted to describe teaching styles in terms of the degree of autonomy which teachers permit and foster in their students. For example, the HMI report *Primary Education in England* (1978) conceived of the 'didactic' approach to teaching as one in which the organization of activities and the individual steps towards learning were clearly set out by the teacher, with the student following his lead. This approach was contrasted with the 'exploratory' approach in which 'the broad objectives of the work were discussed with the children but where they were then put in a position of finding their own solutions to the problems posed.' In practice, the report found, the individual teacher's overall style could be described in terms of a continuum between purely 'didactic' at one extreme and purely 'exploratory' at the other, with most teachers adopting an element of both approaches.

Our research suggests that this distinction (which may result from the observers' focus upon teachers and only the most readily accessible behaviour of their students) is unhelpful in describing the learning relationships between teacher and student. A more fundamental dimension to this relationship is not so much the degree to which the students are left to find their own solutions, but the extent to which they exert a control over their work, the nature of the teacher's collaboration in this, and the ways in which the student influences this collaboration. Our evidence suggests that where this controlling element on the part of the student is high, his activity is more likely to meet his intellectual needs and be appropriate to his level of experience (Rowland, 1979).

The nature of the control which the student may exercise might best be illustrated by examples of classroom activity as described and analyzed in research fieldnotes.

In this first example, Paula and Carol are working in an open plan primary school run on more or less informal lines. They are constructing a model camp site by building around frameworks of drinking straws jointed together with pipe-cleaners. Paula and Carol were both ten years old at the time and were two of a larger group of girls who would often work together.

Fieldnotes: 9 October (Monday)

On Firday Chris Harris (the normal class teacher) started off by talking to the class about work they might like to do connected to the theme 'School'. A poem was read and there was much discussion of the children's suggestions.

Carol and Paula wondered what it would be like if the school had not been built. What would the site of the school then have been used for? They suggested that it might be a campsite. Later they explained to me how there would be many tents where, on a fine night, children could come to sleep. Paula suggested that they would have to pay £1 a night to come and use the tents. She said there would also be a 'manager' who would live in the house alongside the camp site.

Carol and Paula had not been involved with some other children who had made various frameworks using drinking straws and pipe-cleaners the previous day. They had not seen the tent Jason had made using this technique, though they had seen one or two of the other structures. Paula's idea was that they could make tents by covering with tissue paper frameworks constructed out of drinking straws joined together with small pieces of pipe-cleaner.

By the time I came to watch them they had already made several tents. Some were based upon cubes, others upon long cuboids, others on square pyramids and there were various constructions of ridge rents (figure 1).

Figure 1.

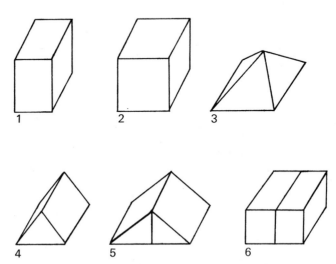

Each tent was covered with tissue paper, stuck down with glue, with entrances left open where required. They explained how tents like (1) were to be 'loos', the large tent like (2) was an 'entertainments tent' and the others were for sleeping. Another ridge tent they made but rejected saying that it was too large for their model. 'Look, it's even larger than the loos', Paula said. They felt that their ridage tents for sleeping in should be smaller than the 'loo' tents.

Inside the 'loo' tents Carol had constructed little W.C. bowls. For these she had used two different constructions (figure 2).

These frameworks were topped with tissue paper seats and accompanied by lavatory paper rolls made from pipe cleaners and tissue paper. Each tent bore the label 'Gents' or 'Ladies'.

Figure 2.

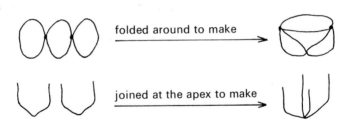

While Carol was experimenting with her seats, Paula was constructing 'The Manager's House'. This was to be a cuboid with a roof of trapezium cross section (figure 3).

Figure 3.

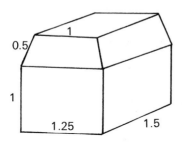

Numbers are lengths of members. Unit is one drinking straw.

Paula worked confidently at this, measuring up each member against another of corresponding length, before jointing it into the structure. When she had finished the framework, she stood it up on the table. It stood firmly enough but was a bit lopsided. She examined it and explained how this would be put right by shortening one of the roof gable members. She quickly cut a bit off this straw and, after reassembling, the house stood upright. I was surprised how well this repair job had worked, but pointed out to her that while the house stood quite upright and firmly, now one of the roof members was shorter than its corresponding members. Paula replied that she didn't think we needed to be that fussy and that, while it wasn't quite right, it would do. I agreed.

She then explained to me why the tents had been covered with tissue paper, whereas she was going to cover the house with sugar paper. Her explanation was along the lines that tents, being made of material were 'flimsy' whereas houses, being made of bricks, were 'stiff'. She was using an idea of scaling here: as canvas is to tissue paper, so brickwork is to sugar paper. This notion of scaling pervades much of the children's model making, not only with regard to length. It cropped up in a different form when we came to test the various tents for how well they would stand up to strong winds. Paula blew on the tents, a strong puff representing a gale, a light blow a gentler breeze.

Carol, having finished her 'loos', told me how their campsite should have an adventure playground. For this she would make a climbing frame like the one in the school playground. She went out on her own to examine this, but made no sketches. She soon returned and started to build. First she made a cubic framework and then a lattice on one of its faces as shown here (figure 4).

She explained to me: 'It's really a cube. You put two bits down like this (pointing to AC and BD) and then you cut out this bit (CD)'. She explained how this lattice on the front face was repeated in a vertical plane down from GH, EF and JK. It was also the same, she said, on the

Figure 4.

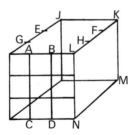

face LKMN and its opposite face. (I later inspected the climbing frame in the playground more closely and, except for one small detail, her representation of it is quite correct). It seemed extraordinary that she was able to analyze the structure in such detail and keep the information in her mind. Could she have done this before she had started working on the tent frameworks? I should guess that her work so far had given her some insight, increased her conception and perception of the geometry of frameworks. What had perhaps, earlier, been seen as a mass of horizontal and vertical bars, was now seen as a cube together with its sub-divisions and missing elements. While one cannot be certain, this seems the most plausible explanation for her considèrable insight and ability to remember the details of the structure. Just as, by representing our thoughts and feelings in words, we are more clearly to understand them, so by modelling, Carol increases her understanding of the spatial configurations which she represents. . . .

The following school day Paula and Carol continued to model the seats, lamp-posts, fountains, cash desk and till, telephone booth and other features of the campsite. The objects were then mounted on a piece of stiff cardboard (about 1m by 1.5m) and carefully arranged with pathways between the tents and so on.

The display is now very impressive. The light shines through the orange tissue paper of the restaurant tent onto the little tables (made of pipe-cleaners, plasticine and plastic lid) which are set out with minute silver paper knives and forks, candles and cardboard glasses. In the entertainments tent their favourite pop star (pipe-cleaners) performs into a microphone. Behind these tents were the 'Ladies' and 'Gents'. The climbing frame had been adapted so that it could have ropes hanging down from the central section. Near this is the telephone booth and, at the other end of the board, is the cluster of sleeping tents, paddling pool (a rectangle of silver card) and fountains. Lamp-posts stand amongst the tents.

Paula said that their model was 'Paradise'. But after discussing it amongst themselves they decided not to call it Paradise Camp Site. Laraine (who had now joined to help them) had said, 'It's going to be

Luxury here' and they finally decided to call it 'Mount Posh'. Thus the little sign in front of the model which says, 'Welcome to Mount Posh'. . . .

Now that all the individual items are assembled it looks not only charming but surprisingly realistic. Their attention to scale has been precise throughout. They have also used considerable ingenuity in overcoming difficulties as they arose. For example, the restaurant tables could not be supported by the thin straws alone, so each straw had been re-inforced by inserting a pipe-cleaner down its length. . . .

The level of teacher intervention throughout this work was minimal. The two original ideas – the technique of jointing drinking straws with pipe-cleaners and the School theme – had both been provided by teachers but in different contexts and on different days. Neither I nor Chris Harris had envisaged that they would be combined in this or any other way. Carol and Paula chose to respond to these two separate ideas by using them to construct what turned out to be their own fantasy world. Within such a world and the process of its construction I, as a teacher, played no significant part. While the girls were only too happy to talk to me about what they had done, my assistance (except in a few matters of material provisioning) was not required. This was not because the task they had set themselves was easy – on the contrary, it presented many considerable challenges – but because within their 'Paradise' they were the final arbiters upon whose judgements the value of the work depended. I was at best merely a sympathetic and interested outsider. This independence from my judgments was clearly demonstrated by Paula insisting that my criticism of her house was inappropriate: 'we needn't be that fussy'. From the delicacy and ingenuity of her constructions and her concern for such aspects as scale, it is clear that such a rejection of my tentative criticism was not merely a reflection of a lack of precision in her working style.

Their work was thus their own in the broadest sense. Their control over its purposes and methods was ultimate. When, at one point, we discussed the names of the various shapes they had made (cube, cuboid, prism, trapezium, etc.) they were fascinated to learn them as applied to their shapes, shapes which had now become part of their everyday and imaginary experience. During the process of their work they needed to conceive of geometrical abstractions. There is little doubt that their ability to do this developed in response to the needs of the present task. No one had designed the task in order to develop these specific skills. When I had introduced the technique of making jointed frameworks to some other children the previous day, I did have in mind that spatial ideas might emerge. But no one had suggested that Carol or Paula should use this technique and they had not been present when I demonstrated it.

Was this development just a matter of good luck? Clearly some play-like activities are more productive of significant learning than others. The work of Paula and Carol is not presented here as part of a claim that all play is educationally significant, or even that play should form a major part of the activity of a class of nine to eleven year olds but simply that some play, of which this was an example, clearly enables considerable learning to take place within a situation in which the children have complete control over their activity and in which the involvement of any adult is minimal. There may have been many types of learning associated with this particular activity, stemming from the social context and its imaginative and representational aspects, but attention is here drawn to the development of spatial awareness: how they learned the names of several geometric shapes, investigated certain of their properties and increased their understanding of three dimensional space.

The structure of this learning activity may be represented thus:

Schema 1

| Children select stimuli to which they respond | → | Children set task | → | They develop specific concepts/skills required by the task |

Such a schema may be contrasted with that which describes practical activities which are structured by the teacher. For then the teacher decides upon certain specific concepts or skills which he feels require development; a practical task is set such that the children encounter or practice these skills or concepts; the child performs the task and thus acquires the required learning. This may be represented:

Schema 2

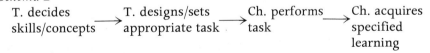

| T. decides skills/concepts | → | T. designs/sets appropriate task | → | Ch. performs task | → | Ch. acquires specified learning |

Schema 1 may be characterized as 'natural' learning, or learning which results from the children following 'the impulses inherent in childhood itself' (Piaget, 1969, p. 151). The links between the stages take place naturally and there is no question of the appropriateness of the skills/concepts to their activity. Nor is there any question of interpretation of the task or of its interest value. Once the sequence has begun it is limited only by the extent of the children's present experience and knowledge, but it serves to extend both.

On the other hand, an activity which follows scheme 2 may be limited by:

(a) The appropriateness of the decision to teach these specific concepts/skills to the stage of development, experience and interests of the child.

(b) The appropriateness of these concepts/skills in terms of the curriculum.

(c) The design of the task set: its suitability for furthering these particular skills/concepts.

(d) The possibility that the child will not interpret and internalize the nature of the task as the teacher intended.

This second schema is the basis for most curriculum design and much activity planning. Its success depends upon a high level of diagnosis of the individual children, knowledge of the subject matter and its relationship to the curriculum and to child development, ability to design or select appropriate tasks and to communicate them unambiguously. Attempts have been made to overcome these difficulties, or rather to bypass them, by programmed learning. But such techniques are appropriate only to skills and concepts which can be precisely defined and even then they tend not to stimulate their application to activities outside the structured course itself (that is, there is the problem of transference).

Schema 1 also has its problems. Learning cannot be left merely to the chance responses of the students to the environment. Even if children frequently do learn in this way there remains the problem not only of providing a stimulating environment but also of ensuring that they develop a comprehensive range of skills and knowledge. This requires the teacher to be more than merely a provisioner of the learning environment.

It is not suggested that classroom learning should follow the first 'play' schema rather than the second 'teacher-structured' one, but that, in his relationship with the child and his work, the teacher may exploit the child's natural tendency to learn, a tendency which is demonstrated in much of their play.

An essential feature of the 'play' schema, which is usually lacking in the 'teacher-structured' approach, is the degree of control which the student is able to exert over his activity. By 'control' is meant not only autonomy in the choice of the activity but also in respect of interpretations made in its course, its further development and overall objectives. Our observations suggest that where the student exercises control, his activities develop rationally in response to events as they arise while he bears in mind certain overall objectives. Thus the student's exercise of control involves a structuring to his activity. In the work of Carol and Paula, this structuring took place without significant intervention on the part of the teacher.

But clearly the teacher's contribution is often going to be more positive than in the example above. In his attempts to introduce the student to new areas of study, to provide opportunity for the development of particular skills or perhaps in order to stimulate enthusiasm, the teacher may take a more deliberate lead. In such cases, our evidence suggests that what is important is not so much whether the teacher adopts a 'didactic' approach (leading the student step by step through a process) or an 'exploratory' one (leaving him to find his own solutions having discussed the broad objectives) but rather the way in which he hands over a degree of control to the student. Once established, this control is not of an exclusive nature, indeed it may demand not only the teacher's collaboration but even his formal instruction (Rowland, 1981). Furthermore, through such exercise of control on the student's part, the teacher is able to gain insight into the nature of his understanding, increased awareness of the ways in which he interprets his learning environment and, thereby, to contribute to this environment in a more fruitful way.

But where the teacher takes this initiative in the student's activity, the handing over of control to him may present problems. A teacher who is over anxious to ensure that all areas of the curriculum are covered, that certain 'standards' are achieved, may feel that he cannot afford to do this; that it would leave too much to chance. The problem remains whether the teacher's enthusiasm results from such external pressures or from his own more personal values or interests. On many occasions have I entered the classroom with 'exciting ideas' to 'get the children going' and they soon take on my enthusiasm in the new work. But then, as the work proceeds, it becomes increasingly clear that the children have built up a dependency upon me. While they are keen to follow and act upon my ideas, they seem unable to conjure up any of their own. I become firmly established at the centre of the stage and cannot withdraw to the wings without the show collapsing. At the end of the experience we may all feel that it has been enjoyable but it has somehow got us nowhere. The question remains: 'and what next?'.

From this we should not conclude that the teacher should restrain his enthusiasm. Indeed, it should be infectious and inspire the kind of independent learning desired. The problem arises because of a failing in the relationship between the teacher, the learner and the subject matter. 'Adults and children, like adults with each other, can associate well only in worthy interests and pursuits, only through a community of subject matter which extends beyond the circle of their intimacy' (Hawkins, 1974, p. 49). As long as the subject matter is not seen as the possession of the teacher, as long as he is not seen by the students (or himself) as having sole access to it, then he will be able to be sensitive to the student's interpretations and reactions, to value these and to help the student to develop the activity according to them. Only then will the learner be able to regain control of the process of his own learning, while the teacher becomes, as Bruner puts it, 'part of the student's internal dialogue' (Bruner, 1966, p. 124). Later in the same book, he says, 'To isolate the major difficulty, then, I would say that while a body of knowledge is given life and direction by the conjectures and dilemmas that brought it into being and sustained its growth, pupils who are being taught often do not have a corresponding sense of conjecture and dilemma' (ibid., p. 159). It is the opportunity for such conjecture and dilemma that is the key to the student's retaining or gaining control over his activity. Our observations suggest that, when this opportunity is offered, children are indeed able to make the most of it and strive to do so, in order to control their work. As soon as a child says,

'I wonder what would happen if . . . .?' or 'How could this be so?' he has begun to define his problems, the essence of his control over the work.

This point concerning the problem of the teacher's handing over control to the student may be illustrated by a sequence of activity which involved David and Greg. I had been stimulated by some conversations with a mathematician, and my own reading, on aspects of the famous Fibonacci series. (This is a series of numbers which has many strange properties, some of which are not yet altogether understood.) From the outset of my introducing some of these ideas to David and Greg, I was only too aware that, while there seemed to be unlimited potential here for children to explore, it would not be easy for me to hand over control to them. Certain teachniques and approaches to constructing and analyzing the series needed to be followed if anything fruitful was to emerge. The problem seemed to be one of introducing such techniques in a way which did not then cast me in the role of the one who 'knows all the answers' and therefore force a dependence of the children upon me. In my enthusiasm for the investigations I also had to make a conscious effort to be receptive to what they thought about what we were doing and not to get carried away on my own path.

Fieldnotes: (12 October)

. . . I started working with David and Greg, two friends who are interested in numbers though they have no particularly striking skills in formal aspects of arithmetic.

I first explained the rule for forming a Fibonacci series. Starting with the terms 1, 1, each term is made by adding together the two previous terms:
$$1, 1, 2, 3, 5, 8, 13, 21, 34, 55, 89, \ldots$$
We made this series together and spent some time examining it, seeing how its terms grew. It soon became apparent to me that the arithmetic involved could be made much simpler by reducing each term to a single digit by adding the digits in its number (thus 13 becomes 4 and the 8th term would then be $8 + 4 \to 12 \to 3$). With Greg acting as scribe and David checking the calculations, they transformed the above Fibonacci Series into a Reduced Fibonacci Series:

1, 1, 2, 3, 5, 8, 4, 3, 7, 1, 8, 9, 8, 8, 7, 6, 4, 1, 5, 6, 2, 8, 1, 9, 1, 1, 2, 3.

When they got this far they realized that the last four terms were the same as the first four and that the series was repeating itself.

David and Greg clearly needed some help with analyzing this series. I suggested that we count the number of terms in the first cycle of the series, cut the series into two halves (12 terms in each half) and add together corresponding terms in each half. Like this:

```
   1  1  2  3  5  8  4  3  7  1  8  9      8  8  7  6  4  1  5  6  2  8  1  9
```

First   term in first half + First   term in second half = 1 + 8 9
Second term in first half + Second term in second half = 1 + 8 9
Third   term in first half + Third   term in second half = 2 + 7 9

and so on, with the sum of each pair being 9.

None of us could explain why this 9 repeated itself, but David and Greg were obviously excited by the discovery. It seemed to me better at this stage to help them to find more such patterns before attempting to untangle the reasons for them.

Greg then suggested that we make another series the same way but starting with 2, 2 instead of 1, 1. He did this, with David watching and checking his figures. Again, he found that the series repeated itself after 24 terms.

The rest of yesterday afternoon was spent constructing similar series starting with (3, 3); (4, 4) and so on up to (9, 9). I suggested recording these series in the form of a matrix. Greg worked at this slowly and accurately. David left all the calculating to Greg, preferring to concentrate on picking out the various patterns which emerged.

At the end of the day they both decided to take home large sheets of squared paper on which to continue the work. Greg was going to write up the results so far. David would try to make up a new series.

The next morning (this morning) David told me how he had 'got stuck.' In fact a small arithmetical error had thrown his series out. Greg had completed the matrix like this:

and so on

```
 [1  1] 2 3 5 8 4 3 7 1 8 9 [8 8] 7 6 4 1 5 6 2 8 1 9 [1 1] →
 [2  2] 4 6 1 7 8 6 5 2 7 9 [7 7] 5 3 8 2 1 3 4 7 2 9 [2 2] →
 [3  3] 6 9 6 6 3 9 3 3 6 9 [6 6] 3 9 3 3 6 9 6 6 3 9 [3 3] →
 [4  4] 8 3 2 5 7 3 1 4 5 9 [5 5] 1 6 7 4 2 6 8 5 4 9 [4 4] →
 [5  5] 1 6 7 4 2 6 8 5 4 9 [4 4] 8 3 2 5 7 3 1 4 5 9 [5 5] →
 [6  6] 3 9 3 3 6 9 6 6 3 9 [3 3] 6 9 6 6 3 9 3 3 6 9 [6 6] →
 [7  7] 5 3 8 2 1 3 4 7 2 9 [2 2] 4 6 1 7 8 6 5 2 7 9 [7 7] →
 [8  8] 7 6 4 1 5 6 2 8 1 9 [1 1] 2 3 5 8 4 3 7 1 8 9 [8 8] →
 [9  9] 9 9 9 9 9 9 9 9 9 9 [9 9] 9 9 9 9 9 9 9 9 9 9 [9 9] →
[10 10][1  1] 2 3 5 8 4 3 7 1 8 9 [8 8] 7 6 4 1 5 6 2 8 1 9 [1 1] →
```

and underneath had written:

'The top and bottom row of our pattern both have exactly the same numbers because: [10 10] 2 tens are wrong but [1 1] 'two' 'ones' are right because we are only using Single Figured numbers. You may be amazed to see a whole line of nines this is because 9 + 9 = 18 well 1 + 8 = 9 you see 18 is 10 + 8, and 10 + 8 = 18'

We had only talked briefly yesterday about the final 10, 10, → 1, 1, series. Note here that while Greg's style of writing is precise and logical, it is highly personal: 'You may be amazed to see . . . well . . . you see.' Though such comments are not part of the nature of a mathematical proof, here they appropriately demonstrate Greg's excitement and close identification with the ideas he expresses.

The 'boxed' numbers represent the pattern which David spotted yesterday. He also pointed out the column of third terms (that is, 2, 4, 6, 8, 1, 3, ...) explaining that this was really 'going up in twos, the 1 and 3 really meaning 10 and 12.' (They did not realize at this point that indeed every column is a 'times table,' reduced.) By now David, who had not done much in the way of calculating yesterday, decided to leave us so that he could work out for himself all the series we had made so far. I was surprised at his decision. I had expected him to avoid the hard work and only to get involved in the pattern spotting. But now he apparently realized that the activity had many possibilities and he would rather practise the appropriate technical skills before progressing further. So he went off without any of Greg's figures to do it all over again for himself. Only once or twice did he ask for my help after suspecting he had made a mistake because the patterns he had in mind were not coming out right.

So far Greg had been very much led by me in this work. He fully understood everything and worked out the calculations himself, but had not had any ideas of his own for further exploration. Hoping to encourage him to branch out more, I suggested that, if he wanted to make more series, he could either change the rule of construction (that is, replace the 'add two previous terms' rule of the Fibonacci Series by some other rule) or change the initial terms. He decided on the latter and, using the same rule, started another Reduced Fibonacci Series with (1, 2). He soon saw that his new series was merely the (1, 1) series displaced by one term (that is, 1, 2, 3, 5 ... instead of 1, 1, 2, 3). Pleased by this, he started again with (2, 3). Again he soon saw that this was the original (1, 1) series, but this time displaced by two terms (that is, 2, 3, 5, 8 ... instead of 1, 1, 2, 3, ...). His next series he started with (3, 4). This he completed until it began to repeat after 24 terms. Then the same starting with (4, 5) until this also repeated after 24 terms.

We then looked closely at our original matrix of series. I pointed out that the numbers (3, 4) appear adjacent to one another in the matrix as the 8th and 9th terms of the series beginning (7, 7). Greg noticed that his new (3, 4) series was merely a continuation from that point in the (7, 7) series. Similarly, we found that his new (4, 5) series was a continuation from the 10th and 11th terms of the (4, 4) series in our matrix.

We then saw that our original matrix contained every possible combination of two digits adjacent to one another and thus that any Reduced Fibonacci Series starting with any two digits could be found within that matrix.

By now we were treading on ground quite new to both of us. I had not envisaged all this. Greg was enthralled. He said, 'It contains everything. It must be magic!'

Greg then said he would change the construction rule. 'I am now going to add on certain numbers. I don't think you'll understand that'. (Even in this chat, he is concerned that his meaning may not be quite clear). He then showed me what he meant. It would be a straightforward arithmetical progression starting with 2 and adding 2 for each term, reducing to single digits in the usual way. Thus:

2, 4, 6, 8, 1, 3 . . .

And saw, with amazement, that this also occurred in the original matrix as the 3rd column. (He had forgotten that David had pointed out this feature yesterday).

He then made a similar progression in threes (3, 6, 9, 3 . . . .) and saw that this corresponded to the 4th column of the matrix. He then saw that any such arithmetical series (or 'table') was represented in the columns of the matrix.

Then Greg said, 'I'm going to think of something that might not be here,' (in the matrix). After some thought, he explained how he would make a series by adding the two previous terms and then adding 5 to this result. Thus after the two initial terms (5, 5) the third would not be 1 (5 + 5 → 10 → 1) but 6 (1 + 5 → 6). Each term would be similarly increased by 5 after adding the two previous terms. He soon had written:

5, 5, 6, 7, 9, 3, 8, 7, 2, 5, 3, 4, 3, 3, 2, 1, 8, 5, 9, 1, 6 . . .

and said, 'Come on. I want to see 5, 5 again'. Sure enough, the series repeated as he had expected after 24 terms:

. . . 3, 5, 4, (5, 5)

and, as Greg had intended, this series did not occur in his matrix.

Greg employed various strategies to further analyze this series, breaking it into halves, then quarters, adding corresponding terms and so on. This produced no further clear patterns. (Although had Greg used exactly the same strategy as I had used in analyzing our first Reduced Fibonacci Series he would have found a repeating number). But after various manipulations with the figures he ended up with four terms 8, 2, 4, 1. I pointed out to him the doubling relationship between these terms and Greg said, 'Yes, double it! That's given me an idea' and proceeded to explain how a new rule for construction could be: double previous term and reduce to single figure (that is, a geometric progression).

He went off to work on his own and soon returned to show me what he had done.

```
3 6  3 6 3  6
1 2  4 8 7  5         (1 2 4 8 7 5)
2 4  8 7 5  1         (2 4 8 7 5   )
4 8  7 5 1  2         (4 8 7 5     )
5 1  2 4 8  7 (5 1)   (Note 5 and 1 )
6 3 (6 3 6)           (Note 6 and 3 )
7 5  1 2 4  8 (7 5)
```

His words 'Note' refer to the displaced identity between series starting with 5 and 1 and between those starting with 3 and 6. The brackets suggest the repeating nature of the series. When we examined these series together we saw that every series except those starting with either (3), (6) or (9) is identical except displaced. Greg pointed out that the doubling series starting with (9) would simply be 9, 9, 9 . . . (that is, 9, 18, 36, 72 . . . → 9, 9, 9, 9 . . .). He then said the series starting with 10 would really be a series starting with 1.

He then said, 'If we were enormously clever we could triple them', that is, produce tripling geometric series.

He worked on his own while I watched. He completed this:

1	3	9	9	9	. . .
2	6	9	9		. . .
3	9A	9			. . .
4	3B	9			. . .
5	6	9			. . .
6	9	9			. . .
7	3	9			. . .
8	6	9			. . .
9	9	9			. . .

He saw that since $9 \times 3 = 27 \to 9$ and $27 \times 3 = 81 \to 9$, once 9 occurred in the series, it would simply continue to repeat itself.

When he had got as far as (A) he said, referring to the second *column* of the emerging matrix, 'Look, it's 3, 6, 9 again'. And at (B) 'We're just going to start again' (that is, the column will repeat itself).

Meanwhile David, working on his own, had completed the matrix of Reduced Fibonacci Series. It was near the end of the afternoon and he said, 'When I go home I'm going to make a new one'. He said he would start with (9, 9) and use the rule of adding the two previous terms and also 2 to this sum (that is, similar to Greg's invented series which David had watched him make). He said, 'This is going to be easy. It'll just be: 9 9 2 2 2 . . .' I asked him why. He said that since $9 + 9 \to 18$ and $18 + 2 \to 20 \to 2$ the next term would be 2 which would just repeat itself. Suspecting his reasoning here, I suggested he do it now. He was keen to, and soon saw that his hypothesis was wrong as the series started: 9, 9, 2, 4, 8 . . . He said, 'You've gotta make mistakes. It'll go back to 9, 9 anyway. I'll make it!' In spite of his mistake, he does not lack confidence and feels quite in control of the situation.

Sure enough, after 24 terms, David's series did start to repeat itself.

And so ended two days of arithmetic. David and Greg said they had enjoyed it very much. David had earlier shown some concern as to whether this would help them when they get to their secondary school next year. I said I thought it would. Thereupon they decided to spend three days a week doing 'this kind of maths'. 'We'd need a break sometimes', added Greg.

They did indeed go on to do much more work on this (though their decision to work on it three days a week was a little extravagant!) They went on to develop more series and explored ways of transforming them into straight line patterns.

No doubt much was gained by all three of us from this work. It certainly affected David and Greg's approach to arithmetic, now they saw numbers as 'beings' which had a certain mystique. This seems to be the underlying emotional response of the pure mathematician. The fact that the numbers did not count things did not mean that they were the meaningless abstractions which is often the case with 'sums'.

But throughout the first day of work, I was very much the performer and leader of the discoveries. While they did make their own series and spot patterns emerging, each development of the activity was initiated by myself. They were completely dependant upon me. This was demonstrated by the fact that the work Greg did at home after the first day was simply a repeat of what had been done with me. I do not mean to imply that it was therefore of no value, but that it demonstrates his inability, or disinclination, in spite of considerable enthusiasm, to take the work further on his own.

On the second day, David's decision to go off on his own and practise the technique of building series is a clear indication of his desire to make the work his own, to control it and to reduce his dependency upon me (and Greg) in making the necessary calculations.

The point at which Greg really began to exercise his control in the work is clearly seen. In the middle of the second day, after we had made Reduced Fibonacci Series starting with every possible combination of two figures, I noted, 'By now we were treading on ground quite new to *both* of us'. And then, only two lines later: 'Greg then said he would change the construction rule'. From this point onwards the nature of the series investigated branched out considerably, no longer following the Fibonacci rule of construction. Greg proceeded to initiate a sequence of investigations, inventions and hypotheses based upon a now heightened awareness of what a series is and some good approaches to discovering its pattern-making potential.

Is it really a coincidence that Greg started to take the initiative in his enquiries at the very point at which I also felt that I was treading on new ground? It seems that the freshness of the discoveries for me cast me in a truly collaborative role, rather than in a primarily leading one in which I possessed all the clues to the progress of the work. From this point the investigations took on a sense of spontaneity similar to that of an art as characterized by Dewey: 'The spontaneous in art is complete absorption in subject matter that is fresh, the freshness of which holds and sustains the emotion' (Dewey, 1934, p. 70).

Of course it would be unrealistic to suppose that each time we initiate an activity, or offer specific instruction or guidance, we can expect the student to make discoveries which are in every sense new to us. Usually we shall have trodden the ground before the student reaches it. But there is a strong sense in which as soon as he begins to tackle real problems, problems as he has constructed or interpreted them, then the learning that takes place and the knowledge which is gained is not merely a copy of the teacher's knowledge, but is a reconstruction of it. Such knowledge may view the same objective world and concern itself with the same facts, but will offer a perspective upon them which is individual and to that extent unique and new.

The two illustrations I have used relate to activities of a more or less mathematical nature. These were chosen because it appears that it is within the mathematics curriculum that children are most frequently denied the opportunity to exercise a controlling influence over their work. Many observations of children's writing, art and scientific investigations appear to confirm that learning is an active process of construction or reconstruction in which the student's control is of fundamental importance.

While this direction in our findings might be seen as reinforcing a 'progressive' rather than a 'traditional' approach to teaching, its implications go far beyond the questions of classroom organization and 'teaching style' that are normally seen as defining a 'progressive' approach. It suggests an epistemology which rejects the view that knowledge is absolute and objective, a commodity which can be possessed by the teacher and replicated in the student. On the other hand knowledge must have its roots in society: it is more than merely the description of the psychological state of the knower.

Such issues may seem to be highly philosophical considerations of little concern to the classroom teacher. But the analysis of students' work by an expanding group of teachers is leading us to consider such matters more seriously as a basis and rationale for our developing classroom practice.

The final objective of any educational research is to enable change to take place as a result of an increase in our understanding. An advantage of the research method reported here is that this change takes place in the process of the research. It is through his researching that the teacher is enabled to improve his teaching. The means and the ends of the research thus largely coincide.

References

ARMSTRONG, M. (1981) *Closely Observed Children* London Writers and Readers Publishing Corp.

BRUNER, J.S. (1966) *Toward a Theory of Instruction* Cambridge, Mass., Harvard University Press.

HER MAJESTY'S INSPECTORATE (1978) *Primary Education in England: A Survey by HM Inspectors of Schools* London, HMSO.

DEWEY, J. (1934) *Art as Experience* New York, Minton Balch.

HAWKINS, D. (1974) *The Informed Vision: Essays on Learning and Human Nature* New York, Agathon.

PIAGET, J. (1969) *Science of Education and the Psychology of the Child* Longman, London. p. 151.

ROWLAND, S.C.W. (1979) 'Ability matching: A critique' *Forum for the Discussion of New Trends in Education* 21(3), pp. 82–86.

ROWLAND, S.C.W. (1980) 'Enquiry into classroom learning' unpublished MED thesis, Leicester University.

ROWLAND, S.C.W. (1981) 'How to intervene: Clues from the work of a 10 year old' *Forum for the Discussion of New Trends in Education* 23(2), pp. 3–8.

6
Postscript:
The End of
Primary Schooling?

Introduction

The previous papers in this book have all been concerned with new directions which have recently begun to affect primary policy, research and practice and which seem likely to be even more influential in the 'eighties. This short last section takes a longer time perspective – into the first quarter of the twenty-first century. It is concerned with whether primary education will exist and in what form.

At least three different scenarios can be suggested. In the first and most unlikely scenario, primary education remains relatively undisturbed as the first stage in a three-stage system of education – primary, secondary and a more expanded further education stage, much as was envisaged in the 1944 Education Act. In the second scenario, primary education from three to thirteen is the only institutionalized and compulsory form of schooling: the school leaving age is lowered to thirteen after which a variety of post-primary educational provision is on offer with abundant and appropriately supported opportunities for would-be students to re-enter the educational system throughout life. In his book, *School and the Social Order* (London, Wiley, 1979) Frank Musgrove argues persuasively for such a system. His points about primary education are few but significant:

> the primary stage is vital and must be more highly developed; and it must be compulsory. It is vital because some abilities are never, or poorly, acquired if they are not learned by a particular age or at a specially critical period of growing up. The sequential nature of many aspects of human development – especially cognitive development – means that growth is in stages, and if an early stage is omitted, future growth is impaired. The six years before the age of ten must not be allowed to suffer from neglect.
>
> Life even in childhood is usually too simple to promote full mental development. Significant learning is unlikely to occur unless the environment is more complex and uncertain than 'normal'; and children may not seek out for themselves the possibly risky real-life situations which would stretch them. It is the job of the school to be more difficult than life. It is also its job to be more secure – to present problems in a controlled setting, without

the insecurities that real-life difficulties commonly entail.

To de-school the primary stage of education would be catastrophic: it would not equalize experience and opportunity; it would give advantage to upper-class children (who would probably be provided with an appropriate 'learning environment' anyway). It would widen the gap between the rich and the poor.'

(pp. 185–186)

Whilst not corresponding with Musgrove in every single detail, the editor's values and views are broadly congruent with the perspective he presents.

A third scenario, provided here in Tom Stonier's paper, involves a radical transformation of the educational system on a national and international scale consequent on the computer-based information revolution and a new post-industrial economy. Electronic information technologies replace the printed word as the primary repository of information; home-based education becomes increasingly important; cradle-to-grave education becomes the norm. Much of a child's education during the first decade of life takes place at home; the child plays in nurseries or play centres; primary schools cease to exist; primary teachers are replaced by television sets and 'surrogate grandparents'.

Each of the three scenarios assume that some form of primary *education* is necessary; two assume that it is even more necessary than in the past. But if Stonier's scenario approaches realization, a question mark is placed on the future of primary *schooling*. A book of readings published in 2001 may perhaps reinforce or remove that question mark.

Changes in Western Society: Educational Implications*

Tom Stonier
University of Bradford

Our Changing Society

Western society is experiencing a series of technological revolutions which is changing our societies and economies as profoundly as did the industrial revolution, and is possibly as basic as the neolithic revolution when hunter/gatherers became farmers.

The industrial revolution involved the invention of devices which extended the human musculature. The electronic revolution, in contrast, extended the human nervous system. The most profound, and of the greatest interest to educators, is the development of television and the computer. Television acts as an extension of our eyes and ears, transporting them across time and space. The computer is an extension of our brain.

Under the impact of the new technology, the technologically advanced sectors of global society have moved into a new era. It is not the purpose of this article to describe this new 'communicative era' in detail. Suffice it to say that every major cultural institution is being affected: religion, marriage, sex mores, the family, the city, the state, etc. Any one of these has implications for the educational institutions. However, this article will confine its attention to two aspects: 1. the emerging post-industrial economy and 2. the emerging information revolution.

The post-industrial economy. This term is not meant to imply that industry will no longer be an important component of the economy. Just as an industrial society needs a strong, though not dominant, agriculture, so a post-industrial society needs highly efficient manufacturing and primary industries (including agriculture). Manufacturing industry,

*From SCHULLER T. and MEGERRY J. (Eds), (1979) *Recurrent Education and Lifelong Learning* World Yearbook of Education, London, Kogan Page, pp. 31–44.

however, has been displaced by the knowledge industry both in terms of labour requirements and value output. The phenomenon is viewed with as much incredulity and lack of comprehension by most economists today as the shift from an agrarian to an industrial economy was viewed by the 'physiocrats' two centuries ago. The manipulation of information and the creation of knowledge are rapidly becoming the dominant form of economic activity.

Technology – the application of knowledge to solving human problems – is responsible for creating new resources and new wealth. It is crucial that educators understand that education, coupled with research and development, constitutes the most important form of investment a society can make. They must also understand that over the last two centuries the bulk of the labour force has shifted from farm operatives, to machine operatives, to information operatives. Among the last the shift has been from clerical, to managerial, to professional-technical, reflecting the need for increasingly sophisticated (educated) information operatives.

The information revolution. This is based on the emerging information machine technology. These information machines, usually referred to as computers because they were initially used for mathematical computations, have evolved at an almost incredible pace. The first non-mechanical computers were based on electronic valves. These were displaced by transistors, then integrated circuits, and now microprocessors. This latest step makes information machines so cheap that they will be coupled to most other forms of machinery. As such, microprocessors comprise a new 'meta-technology'.

A meta-technology is a technology which affects a large sector of existing technology. The classic example is the steam engine. Initially designed to pump water out of mines, it subsequently gave rise to a class of power machines which could be coupled to most other existing mechanical devices. The computer, initially designed to carry out mathematical calculations, will now be coupled to all forms of power machinery, creating 'intelligent' machines capable of 'learning' the operations currently carried out by their human machine operatives.

Industrial robots perform their tasks faster and more accurately, are able to work 365 days a year (limited only by the supply of electricity and normal wear and tear) and can be designed to carry out any and all routine manual or decision-making tasks.

Robots can be made to monitor and control their mechanical brethren, monitor an entire assembly line, test the final product, keep track of materials consumption, maintain optimum stocks of supplies, keep track of sales and orders and adjust production accordingly, devise optimum cashflow strategies, and communicate all relevant information to suppliers, customers, and top-line management. Early in the next century it will require no more than ten per cent of the labour force to provide us with all our material needs – food, textiles, furniture, appliances, housing, etc..

Educational Implications

The post-industrial economy is characterized by the following

1 It is primarily a service economy rather than a manufacturing one, with the knowledge industry predominating.
2 It is a credit-based economy characterized by a flow of credit information rather than cash transactions.
3 It is primarily trans-national rather than national.
4 Changes are taking place at an exponential rate rather than linearly.

A French report entitled 'L'Informatization de la Societé' (written in 1978 mainly by Simon Nora) points out that the cheap microprocessors, combined with satellite technology, broadcasting and telecommunications, will bring about such gains in productivity that the heavy industries and large corporations will decline and be replaced on the one hand by numerous small, but viable, entrepreneurial organizations, and, on the other, by non-profit organizations.

The main task of western governments in the late 1970s and early 1980s is to effect the orderly transfer to labour from employment in the manufacturing industries to employment in the knowledge industries. The most economic way to do this is to enter into a massive expansion of the education system. Such an expansion will do three things

1 Education, when done properly, is labour-intensive and will provide substantial employment.
2 An effective education system will encourage young people to remain in education, and attract older people back into it, thereby keeping a significant percentage of the potential workforce off the labour market.
3 An expanded and improved education system will produce a more versatile labour force of more skilled information operatives which, when coupled with research and development, will produce new knowledge, new technology, new industries, and in consequence new wealth.

Just as the British government is now collecting revenues from North Sea oil, so could an expanded technology generate income from wave-powered electricity, oil and other cheap chemicals from coal (after the oil runs out), single-cell protein for cattle feed, coastal fish farming, deep ocean minerals, etc. The importance of knowledge (organized information) as the critical input into modern primary and manufacturing industries has been discussed elsewhere. Suffice it to state here that an expansion of education, coupled with R and D, constitutes an investment in the future which, if made properly, will pay the government back many times over.

It becomes the major task of educators to understand the economic reasons for expanding education massively, to support such expansion, and to prepare for it. Education will eventually become the principal industry, but what sort of education do we want?

New objectives

If we are moving into a society in which most physical work is going to be done by robots – a society in which a mere fraction of the workforce can produce all our material wants and goods, then education for employment, although still a part, would become only one of the several objectives of the new education order. At least as important will be 'education for life', 'education for the world', 'education for self-development', 'education for pleasure'.

Education for employment. It is clear that society is going to need an increasingly versatile labour force, able to respond to the needs of a rapidly changing economy, and a rapidly changing society. Students of today are likely to undergo two or three careers in their lifetime. Some of the most important things we can teach are certain categories of organizational skills which allow individuals to develop entrepreneurial self-reliance to hunt skilfully for new areas of employment, or start up their own business.

Education for life. The primary emphasis of the new educational order must involve a shift in objective from making a living to learning how to live. There are two major aspects of learning how to face life in the twenty-first (or any other) century. The first involves understanding the world, the second involves understanding oneself.

Education for the world. It is not possible to understand the world if we do not understand the impact science and technology have on all aspects of society. Government, commerce and industry can no longer be run by *technological illiterates.* At the same time, we need to avoid training scientists, engineers and other specialists who do not understand the impact their efforts are making on the social system. That is, we can also no longer afford a society whose progress depends on technologists who are *humanistic illiterates.*

Understanding the world requires not only exposure to traditional disciplines – ranging from the natural sciences to the social sciences and the arts – which allow students to understand the natural and social world in which they live, but also a more global focus. We are all members of the human race living on an isolated planet, floating in a hostile space. We need education for environmental responsibility and, what is even more crucial now, education for developing harmonious relationships within and between societies. This means a playing down of ethnocentric and nationalistic values and an expansion of a more humanistic, anthropological approach. Young people must learn to enjoy and accept cultural diversity.

Apart from improving relationships within the immediate community, the major problem confronting this generation is to close the gap between the rich and poor nations of the world. If that cannot be accomplished within a reasonable period, it must presage international conflict. Improvement in third-world productivity will come, partly through the transfer of capital, but largely as a result of the transfer of information, leading to productive technology. Our students, as well as the educational establishment as a whole, must become increasingly involved. We need to expand the exchange of students and academic experts to provide practical solutions to problems confronting those parts of the world desperately struggling against poverty – a poverty not of their own making.

At the more individual level, we need to teach a whole series of skills on how to survive in this world. Most of these are either not taught at all or relegated to a minor position in the curriculum: how to deal with government bureaucrats, how to get the most out of interviews with physicians, how to be successful teenagers, how to be good lovers, how to be effective parents, how to grow old gracefully, how to face death. Most of the really important decisions made in life are not based on information acquired during formal education. Why not?

Even decisions central to education itself, such as which university to attend, or which career to pursue, are left largely to chance, or to last-minute advice from teachers who have no training for the task, and who are not compensated either for the task or the training. As for coping with the physical aspects of life – how to shop for food wisely, repair the plumbing, drive a car safely and maintain it mechanically (basic information necessary for survival in a technological society) – that is generally left out of the education of most. The author can only applaud the efforts of some educators to institute 'wRoughting' [A neologism for 'making with the hands' (as in 'wrought iron')] as the fourth R, to be coupled with Reading, wRiting and aRithmetic.

Education for self-development. It has always been the dream of educators to develop critical faculties so that students are able to understand concepts and develop them on their own. This should be expanded, however, not only to foster more creative imagination, but also artistic, physical and social skills. Particularly important among the latter are communicative and organizational skills. It is one of the sad features of the present education system that it gives the students very little chance to organize things themselves or to prepare for real-life situations. In the real world it is not only what you know that counts, but also how fast you can find out new things. Furthermore, the major activities of the real world involve interacting with *people*. Social development, by contrast with intellectual development, has always been part of the hidden curriculum. Such skills need to be fostered in a more conscious and systematic fashion.

Education for pleasure. First, we must educate for the constructive use of leisure time. Since the early nineteenth century the work week has been cut by half, and this trend will accelerate. Second, education itself must become a pleasurable activity. There has long been a hidden puritanical tradition in much of the curriculum which can be summed up by the attitude that 'it doesn't matter what you teach them so long as they don't like it.' The new attitude must involve the thought that if students are going to live in an information explosion and be happy, they must pick out of that mushrooming growth of new information what they consider interesting and enjoyable. Otherwise, the richness of the new information environment could lead to a sort of neurological indigestion – possibly leading to serious psychological disturbances.

There is another more vital aspect: in the future, obtaining and organizing information will become the dominant life activity for most people. What one enjoys learning most, one learns best. Enjoyment contributes substantially to the cost-effectiveness of time spent learning.

New technology and the new patterns of education

To a large extent, the changes in both objectives and approach will be a product of the new technology. The major impact will involve the displacement of printed information storage and retrieval systems by electronic ones. This will result in an almost unbelievable increase in the quantity of information available to the average home. These features coupled to an accelerating information explosion will lead to a cradle-to-grave education system with less emphasis on the existing centralized, institutional form of education and a development of home-based education, at one end, with an expansion of community-based education at the other.

Electronic education. The use of radio and television for information communication, reorganization and storage, and the use of computers for information processing and storage and retrieval, represent new technological developments as important as the invention of the printing press. Education television at the pre-school and primary school level has come far in the last two decades. In the USA the Children's Television Workshop's *Sesame Street* and *The Electric Company* have built up an impressive record of research and practical experience. In Britain the experience has moved well beyond the experimental to the routine, not only with the government-sponsored programmes of the BBC, but also with independent broadcasting, such as Thames Television. The increasing sophistication of TV aimed at children reflects the increasing sophistication of adult 'entertainment' including such programmes as *Panorama, Horizon, The World About Us*, etc. whose educational value cannot be overestimated. Nor should educators underestimate the value of historical drama, travel, and other documentaries. The experience and utility of formal courses involving television, such as those put on by the Open University, will be greatly expanded as cable television comes on line allowing for simultaneous broadcasts via telephone or other cable links, and as home video-recording systems, for example, the Post Office's Prestel, BBC's Ceefax, etc, that colourful box in our living room will become an information screen displacing telephone directories, travel agents, estate agents, encyclopedias, and even our daily newspaper.

The use of computer-assisted learning is also developing rapidly. It is most easily adapted to, and most needed in, teaching mathematical skills at all levels. An example of the extensive use of computer-assisted mathematics instruction is found in the system developed in northern Ontario: the project began in the late 1960s under the sponsorship of the Ontario Institute for Studies in Education and a number of community colleges, particularly Seneca College in Toronto. Tens of thousands of students have gone through the programme since then with some of the following advantages emerging: students complete a course in roughly one-third of the time required for a standard course, with teacher intervention involving less than ten per cent of the time. The cost per student is approximately one-third. Most students like it: student drop-outs in remedial maths were reduced by eighty per cent and one girl commented: 'It's the first maths teacher that never yelled at me.'

The advantages of computer-assisted teaching are several: a computer can give individual attention which the average teacher in the classroom situation cannot hope to give. Computers have infinite patience, never put down a student, and rely on positive reinforcement. They can monitor a student's progress more accurately than any other means so far devised, and are getting cheaper all the time. The main resistance will come from the educators themselves who do not understand the new technology and are frightened by it. Such educators, in their ignorance, disparage TV and the computer, and create a generation gap between themselves and the electronic teaching professionals on the one hand, and their students on the other.

Home-based education for the young. The major shift in technology, then, is the emergence of the electronic home-based education capability using the television screen and the new communications systems which allow a tie-in via telephone, air waves, or local cable television to the local education authorities, a second tie-in to national and international computer network systems and, finally, a tie-in to the global library archives. As these networks expand, the home television set will have available to it information which vastly exceeds the largest city library and which makes owning a mere encyclopedia seem as primitive as owning a Victorian slate to scratch on. There is a second, enormously important feature about this new technology: in addition to being a much greater source of information, television also provides a form which is more easily assimilated. Our brain was designed to cope most efficiently with visual images, the major sensory input of primates. The development of language in our proto-human ancestors involved the evolution of a translating mechanism which could translate visual images into abstract sound patterns. Reading involves a 'second order' visual abstraction of audible abstractions of visual images. Although it may be true that we cannot do much abstract thinking without words, as far as memory storage is concerned, it is much more efficient to use visual images.

Thus traditional reading, writing and arithmetic – the sciences, geography, history, etc – can all be learned either by playing 'games' with a home computer, by playing 'games' with friends (on the computer), or by looking at live programmes, films or video-tapes which deal with geographical, anthropological, historical, etc subjects. Coupling computer-based learning to educational TV in the home means that tailor-made, child-oriented education will be able to replace the much less adaptable, mass classroom-based education currently foisted on all children in western countries save those whose parents have the financial resources to afford individual tutoring.

Finally, we must add to the home-based education system one other ingredient. It is not enough to provide highly sophisticated and advanced electronic teaching devices. There must be a human touch. That touch should be provided by the western world's most under-used resource: its mature citizens. There is reason to believe that the human species evolved post-reproductive females (an anomaly according to classical evolutionary theory) in order to facilitate the transfer of information across the generations. That is to say, grandmothers were humanity's first information storage and retrieval system. (This is not to exclude grandfathers, although in the old days they were probably killed hunting giraffes.) Using older people to provide the cultural heritage and the personal touch would be of enormous benefit to both the young and the old. Each mature person could be assigned to a group of two or three children for a period of perhaps ten or more years. Parents moving from one locality to another might consider leaving their children in the care of the surrogate grandparent in order not to interrupt their education. This may become perfectly feasible as travel becomes increasingly more efficient and cheap.

The upshot of evolving such a system is that young children as they begin to learn to speak – the most important thing they must ever learn in their lives – become progressively immersed in an information environment which is enormously rich and pleasurable. They will learn most traditional skills on their own or within small groups of neighbourhood children. The efficiency, flexibility and depth of learning will be considerable.

School-based education. During the first decade of a child's life, most of its learning will involve education in its own or a neighbour's home. However, children need to play with other children to facilitate their own emotional growth and to acquire social skills. Such play may take place in 'nurseries', as is the practice today, or it may involve play centres in a neighbour's home (rented by the government). Periods of play alternating with home-based learning also provide rest periods for the grandparent.

As the children grow older, groups of friends will go to school to avail themselves of facilities such as gymnasium, sports, laboratory, dramatics, etc, while at the same time beginning to interact with large peer groups.

However, school experiences should not be structured strictly in terms of age groups, except where that is appropriate (for example, certain kinds of team sports). Learning how to handle laboratory equipment, learning how to swim or how to play chess, may best be handled by mixing ages. The idea of peer teaching will be discussed later on.

One of the primary functions of the traditional school is that of an institutional device for educating for community interaction. School is also a place (and stage) where one begins to encourage the children to develop organizational skills and to prepare them to assimilate a more systematic body of information. That is, the schools can now begin to consolidate a child's information base in a more formal, uniform way – at least where it is necessary to have such uniformity. As discussed later, in general, the new objective of education will not be to educate for uniformity, but rather for versatility and diversity. Nevertheless, it may be necessary to achieve a common data base, and to socialize the children into certain accepted group values.

Community service for teenagers. As the children approach their teens, a profound shift in interests occurs. Partly as a consequence of shifting hormonal patterns, the interests begin to shift to members of the opposite sex and to an enlarging awareness of the community in which they live. Part of the emerging interests relate to the desire to enter the adult world and share some of its responsibility and be accorded some of its status. In the western world university education is sometimes interspersed with work experiences. There is no reason why that principle should not be enlarged at the university level and brought down to the teenage period. Teenagers are not only eager to accept certain job responsibilities, but very much look forward to the financial rewards which give them a measure of independence. In a way, teenagers constitute an ideal underclass: all the mucky jobs in our society tend to be done now by ethnic minorities who stand very little chance of moving beyong those jobs. It usually takes them several generations to move up. In the process they are subjected to serious deprivation (often denigration) in holding down those jobs.

Consider, on the other hand, having teenagers do all the nasty jobs which society still needs. It is understood that this is part of their service to humanity and it is understood that as they grow up, they move into the better jobs. The use of a teenage labour force should also be coupled, perhaps somewhat later, with a period of 'community service' – a form of national service which is not militarily oriented, although it may be appropriate to exercise a fair amount of discipline. Certain units, for example, might be used for land reclamation, community work and work overseas. Some youngsters might stay on for further training for a career in the police, fire, ambulance corps, coastguard, etc which will continue to be an important career sector. Others may become involved in digging irrigation ditches in the Sahel, or planting trees in the denuded tundras in order to improve global productivity. The emphasis should be on global, rather than national, service. In other instances, the work would be done in the local community. The main objective of such a programme would be to break the school routine, to mature the students by introducing attitudes of discipline, group integration, and community service. Provision should be made for students who for reasons of conscience or talent would be excused from such service. In general, however, young people are ideally suited to become involved in service activity which would become their cultural passport to adulthood.

Community-based education. Following the teenage schooling and the community service phase, students would advance into higher education. They might do so only after a period of several years of paid employment or, alternatively, after a substantial period of leisure. Higher education will be a mix of traditional university, coupled to electronic data media, based at home or in a similar environment. Much of the university education of the future will involve students moving around from one institution to another. This trend is developing in the USA, where the credit system allows students to spend one or two years at one institution then shift to finish off at another institution, perhaps even to go through three or four. This makes for a much better education because, first, moving among communities is in itself an education and, second, different institutions have different strengths and weaknesses which can be exploited by a mobile student force. Increasingly, as higher education becomes mixed with appropriate work experiences and with practical applications outside the university classroom, the majority of the population will attain by their mid-thirties perhaps twenty years of schooling. A very substantial minority will have gone on to the equivalent of doctorate degrees.

Information recycling. This process has already begun, as witnessed by the marked rise in adult and further education. In many instances it is spearheaded by middle-calss housewives who have time on their hands. It also increasingly involves people who for reasons of finance, social background, or some other lack of opportunity were unable to move into higher education earlier in life. Many universities in North America and an increasing number in the UK are starting to cater for mature, part-time and extramural students. An increasing number of commercial and industrial companies are also sending their employees and managers on to courses or are organizing series of in-house seminars.

Among the most exciting of experiments in western education is the UK's Open University. The use of electronic facilities in the student's own home represents one of the major patterns for future community-based education. One should not, however, overlook one of the most popular aspects of the Open University courses, which is the gathering of students at some particular place during the summer.

A different paradigm in community education is offered by the New School for Social Research in New York City, where the vast bulk of its student body involves adults taking evening courses. The importance of the New School is not only that it acts as an intellectual centre, but it also acts as a centre facilitating social intercourse. Adult education is an important facilitator of personal interactions.

Lastly, with the continued expansion of global transportation systems, organized travel will become as much a part of the educational scene as will the traditional classroom. Moving groups of people to different sites to satisfy different kinds of interest will be a major new industry coupling education with tourism.

New attitudes and approaches

Exploring knowledge. The traditional authoritarian approach which provided immutable 'facts' served industrial society well. It provided not only the 'facts' necessary for operating in a simpler society, it also provided the socialization for national, industrial conformity. However, the authoritarian approach will be negated by the need for a more versatile, self-reliant population. Furthermore, the practice of information recycling will make apparent the relativistic nature of much knowledge. Another reason for shifting from a central authoritarian to an exploratory mode is to exploit the student's own interests. Interest is probably the most important single correlate of the efficiency of information transfer.

The expanding information environment will make it increasingly difficult for teachers to keep up with new developments. At the same time it will allow students to become 'experts' at a much earlier age. As a result of the decentralization and democratization of education, there will be increasing reliance on peer teaching (that is, students teaching students), and teaching across age groups – at times in reverse (that is, students teaching teachers). The common effort of exploring new knowledge can be extremely rewarding, and is probably very much more efficient as a method of effective learning than the traditional hierarchical one-way approach which is the basis of contemporary education.

Interdisciplinarity. Knowledge may be defined as organized information. In the past two centuries a whole host of new disciplines have proliferated. These tend to organize knowledge in what might be called a vertical fashion. What is desperately needed now is the emergence of professional generalists (in contrast to professional specialists) capable of organizing knowledge along horizontal lines. Such integrators of knowledge are still few and far between in present educational circles. Professionalism is associated with specialization, and attracts a degree of snobbish appeal (bred by ignorance about the nature of knowledge). The difference between a professional and a lay person is that the professional is able to understand relationships which escape the lay person. It is as professionally challenging and difficult to establish relationships *across* disciplines as it is to establish them *within* specialisms. In fact, the case could be made that it is more difficult and therefore requires a higher degree of professionalism to be a generalist.

297

Interdisciplinary courses are beginning to appear in a number of western universities. Vital to interdisciplinary courses is the recognition that either they are oriented toward a broad problem, for example, the attainment of peace, or they are created on a very broad knowledge base, such as the interaction of science, technology and society. The Science and Society course at the University of Bradford illustrates a number of the points considered above. For example, the first year, although highly structured, does not develop knowledge along disciplinary lines. Instead students learn about major technologies such as energy, materials, food and medicine. In the process they obtain and assimilate information from traditional disciplines such as physics, chemistry, engineering and biology. In addition they are also introduced to economic, historical and sociological aspects. Another feature of the course is that, because the students coming into it have a very varied academic background, increasing efforts have been made to allow the students to learn on their own by means of computer-assisted or audio-visual assisted materials, coupled to peer teaching. That is, students whose background is strong in one subject teach those who are weak in it. The peer teaching is greatly strengthened by having both the traditional literary and the more modern electronic information back-ups, for example, lecture notes, textbooks, tape-slide sequences, video-taped lectures, and programmed computers.

The world is going to need specialists – doctors, engineers, architects, lawyers. However, in the future society will increasingly require professional *generalists* able to integrate the mass of new and rapidly expanding information. It is much easier (when it is done properly) to convert a generalist into a specialist than the other way around. A specialist, in spite of the popular myth to the contrary, can experience enormous difficulties in shifting from a paradigm appropriate to one area, to another in a second area. This is not true for a generalist who has been rigorously trained.

Use of information. Again it must be emphasized that the authoritarian mode of handing down information, using the carrot of academic rewards, and the stick of economic and physical deprivations, will be displaced by a greater reliance on self-motivation. If the education system is properly structured, it is the student who perceives the need for information and searches for it. Among the most important skills to be taught is the technique for obtaining information, organizing, and applying it. This skill of acquiring 'meta-information', that is, information about information, is greatly facilitated by engaging students in project work, either by themselves or with colleagues. Such projects should be designed, wherever possible, to be productive, that is, to solve real problems, rather than merely to be sterile repetition of previous student exercises. This will shift the educational process from passive to active learning and will be greatly facilitated by the availability of electronically based information which bypasses the intellectual limitations of individual teachers.

The Science and Society course already referred to may serve as an example. Students are required to engage in a variety of activities during the first two years designed to help acquire communication and organizational skills. These involve, in addition to the more traditional essays and class reports, etc, team projects, class debates, simulated public hearings, simulation games, and audio-visual reports. The use of projects in the second and fourth year is designed to help students acquire meta-information, that is, how one goes about obtaining, applying, and storing information. Projects also allow the students to develop a specialist base in accordance with their own interests. In addition, the projects (which comprise a third of their formal university time) generate new information. Such new information becomes a part of the learning experience, not only for the students but for the staff as well. Furthermore, in the earlier more formative years of the course, the evolution of the course involved a very significant input from the students themselves. Such innovations and modifications were always subjected to rigorous examination by staff.

Future orientation. The only way to learn to live with rapid change is to be educated for it. As Alvin Toffler has pointed out in *Future Shock* the only insurance against future shock is to educate for the *changing* future. Increasingly we must teach students the techniques of forecasting, and where we teach about the past it is to help us understand the future. History can no longer be used merely as a series of facts relating to some sort of a time context. History must become an important tool for testing social theories and the realities of the world in which we live. Just as evolutionary theory allowed biologists to predict the existence of creatures never seen (and subsequently discovered), so must historical analysis allow us to predict certain features of society, including how to move into a future shaped by human needs and desires.

A systematic examination of the future is slowly beginning at several universities. The core of the fourth year of the Science and Society course at Bradford University is centred on future studies. Postgraduate programmes are emerging such as the one at Houston (Clear Lake City) in Texas. Such courses explore methods of forecasting, future scenarios, and how one distinguishes between likely and unlikely scenarios. Equally important is the effort to include normative as well as objective analyses.

It will not do to continue a morbid preoccupation with the past . . . with the inequities which have manifested themselves throughout human society – slavery, famine, torture, war, economic injustice . . . what is more important now is to create the conditions for moving into a new social order in which the material wants of society are easily satisfied with almost no physical effort on our part, and where the major economic and needs. This, then, is the challenge to education: to understand what is now happening to our society, and to respond to it imaginatively and, most important, effectively.

T. Stonier

References

ADVISORY COUNCIL FOR APPLIED RESEARCH AND DEVELOPMENT (ACARD) (1978) *The Application of Semiconductor Technology* Cabinet Office, London, HMSO.

GOSLING, W. (1978) *Microcircuits, Society and Education* London, Council for Educational Technology for the United Kingdom, Occasional Paper 8.

HOOPER, R. (1977) *The National Development Programme in Computer Assisted Learning: Final Report of the Director* London, Council for Educational Technology.

MCHALE, J. (1976) *The Changing Information Environment* Boulder, Col., Westview Press.

STONIER, T. (1976) 'The Natural History of Humanity: Past, Present and Future' Inaugural Lecture, University of Bradford: Bradford, UK.

STONIER, T. (1978) 'The social impact of the information technology' *Eurocomp 78* Proceedings of the European Computing Congress, Uxbridge, UK. Online Conferences Ltd.

Contributors

Robin Alexander is Lecturer in Education at the University of Leeds.

Eric Briault was until recently Visiting Professorial Fellow at the University of Sussex.

Joan Blyth was until recently Senior Lecturer in History, The City of Liverpool College of Higher Education.

Elizabeth Engel is research officer at the National Foundation for Educational Research.

Maurice Galton is Senior Lecturer in Education at the University of Leicester.

Roy Garland is Lecturer in Education at the University of Exeter.

Harry Gray is Principal Lecturer in Education Management at Huddersfield Polytechnic.

Wynne Harlen is Senior Research Fellow at Chelsea College, University of London.

Jack Kerr is Emeritus Professor of Education at the University of Leicester.

Ronald King is Reader in Education at the University of Exeter.

Barry MacDonald is Reader in Educational Evaluation at the University of East Anglia.

David Oliver is Headteacher of Evesham Church of England First School.

Stephen Rowland is a teacher at Sherard Primary School, Melton Mowbray.

Colin Richards is Lecturer in Education at the University of Leicester.

Tom Stonier is Professor in the School of Science and Society, University of Bradford.

Joan Tamburrini is Principal Lecturer in Education, Roehampton Institute of Higher Education.

John White is Reader in Education at the University of London Institute of Education.

Author Index

Subject Index

Subject Index